ROUTLEDGE LIBRARY EDITIONS:
MANAGEMENT

Volume 46

TEACHING MANAGEMENT

TEACHING MANAGEMENT
A Practical Handbook with Special Reference to the Case Study Method

HARRY NEWMAN AND D. M. SIDNEY

LONDON AND NEW YORK

First published in 1955 by Routledge & Kegan Paul Ltd

This edition first published in 2018
by Routledge
2 Park Square, Milton Park, Abingdon, Oxon OX14 4RN

and by Routledge
711 Third Avenue, New York, NY 10017

Routledge is an imprint of the Taylor & Francis Group, an informa business

© 1955 Harry Newman and D. M. Sidney

All rights reserved. No part of this book may be reprinted or reproduced or utilised in any form or by any electronic, mechanical, or other means, now known or hereafter invented, including photocopying and recording, or in any information storage or retrieval system, without permission in writing from the publishers.

Trademark notice: Product or corporate names may be trademarks or registered trademarks, and are used only for identification and explanation without intent to infringe.

British Library Cataloguing in Publication Data
A catalogue record for this book is available from the British Library

ISBN: 978-1-138-55938-7 (Set)
ISBN: 978-1-351-05538-3 (Set) (ebk)
ISBN: 978-1-138-48295-1 (Volume 46) (hbk)
ISBN: 978-1-351-05634-2 (Volume 46) (ebk)

Publisher's Note
The publisher has gone to great lengths to ensure the quality of this reprint but points out that some imperfections in the original copies may be apparent.

Disclaimer
The publisher has made every effort to trace copyright holders and would welcome correspondence from those they have been unable to trace.

TEACHING MANAGEMENT

*A Practical Handbook
with Special Reference to the Case Study Method*

HARRY NEWMAN
BA, IA(Harvard), M.LITT(Cantab)
and
D. M. SIDNEY
BA(Oxon)

LONDON
ROUTLEDGE & KEGAN PAUL LTD

First published in 1955 by
Routledge & Kegan Paul Ltd
68/74 Carter Lane, London, E.C.4
Printed in Great Britain by
The Millbrook Press Ltd Southampton

HN to Norman C. Rimmer
DMS to EAS

FOREWORD
by Lt Col L. F. Urwick

THIRTY-FIVE years ago the late H. A. L. Fisher, at that time Minister of Education, appointed a committee under the Chairmanship of the late Sir Henry Newbolt to consider *'The Teaching of English in England'*. The committee included many names famous in the world of teaching and its administration. It examined over a hundred witnesses drawn from leaders in the theory and practice of education in the following proportions:—

Eminent officials with a lifetime's experience of the public administration of educational effort	13%
Representatives of the various national voluntary associations concerned with teaching and its results	33%
Individuals engaged in teaching	46%
Individuals engaged in administering education expressing their personal views	8%

Among the principal conclusions at which the committee arrived was the following:—

'The English are a nation with a genius for practical life, and the chief criticism directed, whether by parents or pupils, against our present system is a practical one; it amounts, when coherently stated, to a charge that our education has for a long time past been too remote from life. We have come to the conclusion that this charge is supported by the evidence.'[1]

and

'It must be realised that education is not the same thing as information, nor does it deal with human knowledge as divided into so-called subjects. It is not the storing of compartments in

---

[1] *'The Teaching of English in England'*, London, H.M. Stationery Office, 1921, reprinted 1941, p. 7 and passim.

FOREWORD

the mind, but the development and training of faculties already existing. It proceeds not by the presentation of lifeless facts, but by teaching the student to follow the different lines on which life may be explored and proficiency in living may be obtained. It is, in a word, guidance in the acquiring of experience.'[1]

Moreover, it is 'guidance in the acquiring of experience', not primarily for livelihood but for life. As the committee pointed out, the idea that the student should learn only that which he is going to do is 'the educational "lie in the soul", whether it comes from the selfishness of those who wish to employ or the shortsightedness of those who wish for employment'[1]. But it is paralleled by the equally dangerous delusion that education makes a man too good for manual labour. Both derive from the idea that education should be 'exclusively an affair of vocation'.[1]

In the middle of the twentieth century a major, if undetermined, proportion of those who achieve a higher education will earn their livelihood in modern business, principally in some activity involving the supervision of the work of others. A quarter of a millenium of the material results of the industrial revolution has produced a society fundamentally different from that of preceding handicraft ages. Man gains his bread not by the individual exercise of some isolated skill, but by participation in progressively larger systems of human co-operation. These systems are, to a degree not always appreciated, dominated by the postulates of a mechanised economy. They are systems designed to use mechanical appliances, not as tools, a mere adjunct to individual labour, but as a complete substitute for human physical effort. And a substitute for collective physical effort demands imperatively for its effective use that men should work collectively in accordance with the laws underlying its structure.

---

[1] *'The Teaching of English in England'*, London, H.M. Stationery Office, 1921, reprinted 1941, p. 7 and passim.

FOREWORD

The machines are based on the physical sciences. And they therefore postulate for their use extreme accuracy. A modern factory is itself, if it is effective, a single highly-geared machine. It is much more important that the general design should be appropriate and that the work of the individual should dovetail with precision into the overall plan than that he should himself be particularly skilled. To conduct such a factory successfully so as to secure the optimum productivity from the combination of materials, equipment and human labour involved demands a refinement and intricacy of social discipline which are something quite unprecedented in human history.

The body of knowledge and practice bearing on this art of conducting business undertakings is of comparatively recent origin. It is usually described as Management or Scientific Management. Before the beginning of this century it was virtually unheard of. But it has since made tremendous strides in the United States of America where there are close on 700 educational institutions with the right of granting university degrees in business management or the kindred subject of administrative engineering. In the USA in 1951 there were 380,000 students at university level 'majoring' in these fields.

In Gt. Britain, with its more conservative and established society, the adaptability necessary to meet this situation in terms of educational facilities has been lacking. Those engaged professionally in teaching at the universities, particularly the older universities of Oxford and Cambridge which largely set the tone of the national educational life, have felt that this new field of knowledge was too new and too unorganized to be regarded as a serious vehicle for education. This attitude has been reinforced by relics of the mediaeval contempt for trade based on the religious prejudice against usury. This developed into the unpleasant social snobbery characteristic of the nineteenth century. 'The best

FOREWORD

people', the gentry, did not go into business: as an occupation it was felt to be somewhat derogatory. Those who did so, instead of entering one of the professions, were felt to have admitted that they were somewhat too interested in 'mere money-making' and, accordingly, to have lost caste. Even to-day a brilliant student at either of the older universities who announces that he is going into ordinary competitive business is regarded as somewhat unusual. If he announces that he is going into the 'family business' that is different: it is assumed that within a comparatively brief period he is assured of a directorship by inheritance. He will be protected, for all but a few years, from the socially questionable occupation of participating personally in the rough and tumble of the mills and the markets.

The jealousy of established faculties is also a factor which tends to exclude new fields of knowledge from recognition in a university environment. And, since most universities are governed oligarchically by a council composed of the heads of existing faculties, it has considerable latitude for enforcing procrastination. The attitude of existing faculties is usually strongly biassed in favour of devoting limited resources to their own enthusiasms.

Of course, university professors do not admit these elements in their climate of opinion, even to themselves. They are convinced that their refusal to organise any form of education adapted to the requirements of those students who are contemplating a business career is founded solely on their determination to preserve the purity of the educational process, to defend it from a destructive vocationalism. But, their attitude often comes dangerously close to the other fallacy emphasised by the Newbolt Committee, the idea that education makes a man too good for business.

The argument from vocationalism is gravely weakened by the readiness with which even the older universities in Gt. Britain have extended special educational facilities and the

FOREWORD

opportunity of securing a degree to those contemplating almost any other calling but business. Engineering, veterinary work, forestry, agriculture and so on are provided for. The writer recently interviewed a candidate for a business position who, after five years as a naval officer in World War II, had gone to Cambridge where he had secured a degree in Estate Management. A question as to why he had chosen this particular field of study if he was contemplating a business career elicited this answer: —

'I examined the various courses offered at Cambridge and came to the conclusion that Estate Management came closest to enabling me to acquire some of the knowledge I should require in business and at the same time to secure a degree. It included some economics, law and accounting.'

Some years previously another candidate, also from Cambridge, said that he had taken the first part of the Economics Tripos and the second part of the Psychological Tripos, securing a 'first' in both. When asked why he had made this unusual shift in the middle of his academic career, he replied, 'I examined the second part of the Economics Tripos and came to the conclusion that it "hadn't got its feet on the ground"; it was all right for someone who wanted to be a professional economist, but no earthly use to a man contemplating a practical business career'.

To a further question as to how his college authorities had viewed such a change of subject by a student who was obviously likely to secure academic honours in the second part of the Economics Tripos, he replied 'They didn't like it. But I was in no way dependent on them financially. I told them that if I couldn't get the kind of education I wanted, I should go down'. To-day a very much higher proportion of students are dependent on the university authorities financially or are in receipt of government grants which can be removed if they are not amenable.

The older universities are often supported in this oppo-

FOREWORD

sition to providing any form of education in 'management', or, for those contemplating a business career, by eminent business men themselves. Having attained positions of responsibility and distinction in competitive business without any formal intellectual preparation for their tasks, they are inclined to doubt whether anyone else could benefit by such education or indeed whether there is any element in the art of managing people in business which can be conveyed by formal instruction. They ascribe their own success exclusively to inherent qualities: 'leaders are born, not made'.

The Federation of British Industries, only ten years ago, was distinctly 'cagey' about the possibility of teaching the subject of management. 'It is becoming increasingly clear', they wrote, 'that there is a science of management and of business administration which it may be possible to teach academically and which should certainly be studied practically.'[1] In the following year a Committee appointed by the Cambridge University Appointments Board which included a number of chairmen of important businesses issued a report containing the sentence: 'It is, of course, not suggested that it would be desirable to supply in Cambridge anything in the nature of a commercial course.'[2]

This attitude of academic superiority to vocational studies is not unknown in the United States. A recent authoritative report refers to it in secondary education. . . . 'The powerful, widespread and very unhappy distinction of atmosphere and general standing between academic and vocational courses'. But, the report continues, 'It is a strange state of affairs in an industrial democracy when those very subjects are held in disrepute which are at the heart of the national

---

[1] *'Education and Industry'*, Report of the Education Committee of the Federation of British Industries, May 1944, Para. 38.

[2] *'University Education and Business'*, Cambridge University Press, 1945, p. 23.

FOREWORD

economy and those students by implication condemned who will become its operators.'[1]

It is certainly a strange state of affairs that in Gt. Britain, which has boasted in the past that she was 'the workshop of the world', the two senior universities should still consider the art of conducting a workshop unworthy of their attention. Nor can they escape their share of responsibility for the fact that the boast is now no longer tenable.

As a consequence, the task of instructing younger men in the art of management has, in Gt. Britain, been thrown back upon the technical colleges ... usually in the form of part-time evening courses for students already engaged in business during the day. And as there are some grounds for thinking that the teaching of management subjects to men with some practical experience may well prove a more economical, effective and generally desirable method than attempts to teach them to those with no business background, the fact that Gt. Britain has not followed the American pattern may have advantages in the long run.

The art of teaching adult groups is, however, in some ways, much more exacting than that of teaching undergraduate students. There are usually a greater variety of intellectual levels: the groups are less homogeneous mentally. There is almost invariably a greater variety of experience and outlook. Students are sacrificing scanty leisure in order to learn something which they hope will be useful to them. They demand more of their teachers and are less inclined to tolerate instruction which is deficient in sympathy or in the arts of communication. They are aware immediately if the instructor is merely conveying information culled from books and unfertilised by practical acquaintance with the problems he discusses with them.

---

[1] *'General Education in a Free Society'*, Report of the Harvard Committee, Cambridge, Mass., Harvard University Press, 1950, p. 29.

FOREWORD

This book written by two men with special experience of teaching management subjects under both British and American conditions is therefore particularly welcome at the present juncture. Its simple statement of methods which they have found successful, and those which they have found less successful, in this type of teaching cannot fail to be of the greatest help to both teachers and students of management. The space and attention they have devoted to the 'case method' are particularly valuable. The method is something much more than the use of illustrative examples. It is a means of stimulating students to take an active part in the learning process, of particular value with adults who may feel some resentment at finding themselves compelled to go back to school. I recommend it strongly to all who are interested in education for business management.

In particular it should prove invaluable to the hundreds of practical business men who, without previous professional experience as teachers, have devoted some portion of their leisure to part-time instruction in technical colleges. British business owes a debt to them which it can never repay. Without them there would be no management education at all. The remuneration offered has often been so small as scarcely to meet their out-of-pocket expenses, and never sufficient to offer much attraction to men at their salary level.

Yet, they have come forward, year after year, to take courses and to assist the exiguous full-time staffs in countless ways. They have done it, partly for love of the game, because they were interested in management, partly because of that long tradition of voluntary public service which is one of the glories of this country. Perhaps, most of all, they have done it, because of an unconscious recognition of the fact that experience of teaching was making them better managers.

There is a cynical proverb in this country 'Those who can't do, teach'. As far as management is concerned it

FOREWORD

would be nearer the truth if it were reversed. 'Those who can't teach, can't do'. Accepting Sir Charles Renold's definition 'Management is getting things done through people', it is obvious that the manager can only get more done either through more people or through teaching his existing people to do more, more easily. In the words of a Professor at the Harvard Business School—'Coaching is a way of administration: it is administration'.[1]

Possibly a clearer recognition of this essential link between the two callings may presently persuade our older universities to abandon their attitude of superiority to management. It is most desirable in the national interest that they should do so, because the absence of any Chair or recognised faculty in the subject at Oxford or Cambridge is discouraging to brilliant younger men who may be considering an academic career in the subject. A young man has to be very convinced of his vocation for a particular field of study if, in choosing it, he is aware that he is sacrificing any prospect of attaining the greater prizes of academic life. Gt. Britain is desperately short of qualified professional teachers in management of the highest intellectual quality. As compared with the United States there are virtually none. This national handicap will persist so long as the older universities maintain their present attitude.

It is also in their own best interest to make a change. Despite handicaps and prejudices, the need for study of the subject becomes more and more clearly recognised every year. The universities are increasingly dependent on public funds to supplement their endowments. And while the most scrupulous care has been taken hitherto to prevent this fact from encroaching on their academic independence, a politically conscious democracy is not likely to tolerate permanently

---

[1] Myles L. Mace *'The Growth and Development of Executives'*, Boston, Graduate School of Business Administration, Harvard University, 1950, p. 112.

FOREWORD

institutions which ignore the health of the economy on which it depends. In refusing to devote attention and resources to management, Oxford and Cambridge are exaggerating the central criticism of the Newbolt Report. They are making our education more, instead of less, 'remote from life'.

Particularly because it is such a valuable corrective to this tendency—in the teaching methods and attitudes it describes as well as in the larger issue of demonstrating that management is a teachable subject—that I recommend that book to *all* engaged in the teaching process, whatever their subject.

EDITOR'S INTRODUCTION

SINCE the end of World War II most impressive strides have been made not only in rationalising the activities of the various professional bodies interested in management but also in developing a nationwide framework for management studies. What would normally require at least a generation to achieve in the evolution of a new academic discipline, has been compressed into less than a decade.

It is too easy to overlook what *has* been done, regardless of the extent of the achievement, and to concentrate instead on what has *not* been done. This book starts from the premise that remarkable progress has been made in a very short time and that much of the credit belongs to the management teachers and training officers who have selflessly devoted themselves to their task.

However it would be contrary to the spirit of scientific enquiry and management methods to avoid a realistic assessment of management education today with its shortcomings as well as its opportunities of improvement.

The main stream of what is called management education today is the result of the confluence of two established streams of education. One stream is training for commerce which dates back to the early part of the last century, when courses were organised in an attempt to keep pace with the expanding needs of business for clerks, accountants and junior executives. The other is training for and by professional institutes, which originated at the turn of the last century. Unfortunately, the educational programme which thus evolved to meet the new and ever-increasing demands from industry and commerce for well trained managers does not always appear to be sufficiently related to the on-the-job requirements of the modern manager. This book is part of the

EDITOR'S INTRODUCTION

search for new and more effective methods of management education. It attempts to analyse some of the problems and to suggest some practical and constructive solutions.

Some may say that the title of the book is misleading since so much of the text deals with participation methods. It is true that the authors have placed more emphasis on the case study than on other teaching techniques, but this stems from a firm belief that management subjects, particularly where they involve human relations problems, can best be taught by example rather than by precept, by active participation rather than by passive absorption.

Because they feel it is one of the most eloquent statements on this subject, the authors have reproduced in Appendix B a letter from Lt Col Urwick to the Dean of the Harvard Graduate School of Business Administration, in which he reviews the merits of the case study method and its educational implications.

However, they are not advocating American solutions to management education problems, not only because circumstances and requirements are different here, but also because the most successful systems and methods can evolve only from existing teaching techniques and traditions. After all, Harvard has by no means found the final solution and at this moment may be in a transitional state which can ultimately lead to a student body composed exclusively of men and women who have had several years' experience in business.

Nor are the authors suggesting that the case method is a panacea. They present it, at the least as a useful teaching aid; at the most as an attitude of mind on the part of students and teachers alike.

Finally, they are not attempting to provide teachers and training officers with a how-to-do-it manual for tool and technical subjects. The book is designed to do nothing more than to provide other teachers with the opportunity to

EDITOR'S INTRODUCTION

follow the same process as did the authors in thinking and working through some of the basic problems of management education. If the book can also help readers to analyse the relative merits of the various teaching techniques in relation not only to syllabus, classroom and the individual student, but, even more important, to the application of what is learned to the student's everyday job, the authors will consider their efforts amply rewarded.

H.N.

ACKNOWLEDGMENTS

The authors would like to acknowledge the useful criticism and helpful suggestions which they have received from the following:

> Paul Alston Esq
> J. O. Blair-Cunynghame Esq
> Richard Blythe Esq
> David H. Bramley Esq
> Dr A. M. Brown
> Roy S. Butler Esq
> Dr Peter Castle
> Charles Eastman Esq
> Joseph A. Hunt Esq
> Graham Hutton Esq
> Norman C. Rimmer Esq
> Dr Arthur Roberts
> Jerome F. Scott Esq

The authors owe special thanks to their wives, Mary Newman and Elizabeth Sidney, not only for their forbearance but also for their active help at all stages in the preparation of this book.

CONTENTS

Foreword by Lt Col L. F. Urwick   page   v

Editor's Introduction   xv

Acknowledgments   xviii

Part I   THE ENDS AND MEANS OF MANAGEMENT EDUCATION

I Introduction   3
The problems of teaching—the environmental audit—the personal audit—attitudes towards management education—the approach to teaching—qualities required in the teacher.

II The Students and the Syllabus   15
Advance information about the class—analysis of a class list—biographical information about students—students' individual differences—considerations in planning the syllabus—reading lists and homework assignments—interpreting the syllabus—an example of interpretation.

III The First Class   45
The classroom—personal introductions—presenting the course—reading and note-taking—props for self confidence.

IV The Lecture   54
Planning the lecture—basic considerations—aids to teaching—visual aids—the blackboard—the easel—the magnetic blackboard—diagrams and charts—use of colour—use of films and filmstrips—use of other aids.

CONTENTS

V Participation Methods 74
The discussion group—directed discussion—planning the discussion—plans for a session—the chairman's part—non-directive discussion—the teacher's role—modifying attitudes—similarities of method—summary.

VI Role Playing 95
Problems in role playing and their solution—variations in role playing—other situations for role playing—plays and playlets—committee work—the trainer's part.

Part II THE CASE STUDY APPROACH TO MANAGEMENT EDUCATION

Introduction to Part II 114

VII What is a case study? 117
Brief illustrations—the success story—the limited objective case—human relations and technical problem cases—technical cases—a combined human relations and technical case—descriptive cases—different uses for different cases—the case for case studies—limitations of case studies—the balance drawn.

VIII Writing a case study 161
The original version—the first draft and final alterations—some pitfalls—no focal point—subjectivity—insufficient detailed information—other inadequacies—common sense rules for case writers.

CONTENTS

IX Running a case study session 183
The case—the teacher's notes—the discussion—lessons in retrospect—group variations—conclusions to be drawn—the role of the teacher—visual aids—how the teacher plays his part—providing the situation—starting the discussion clarifying views—seeking evidence—fresh leads—summarising.

X Case study in the course 214
The teacher's syllabus—case discussion—report writing—one student's report—another student's report—role playing and speaking—assignments.

Part III MEASURING THE RESULTS OF MANAGEMENT EDUCATION

Introduction to Part III 246

XI Reception and assimilation 247
The academic tradition—validity of the system—comparing students' answers—one teacher's analysis—further answers—the teacher's comments—alternative methods of examination—less conventional examinations—self evaluation for the teacher—challenge and mission.

Appendix A Sources of Visual Aids 271

Appendix B Letter from Leader, Education for Management Anglo-American Productivity Team, to Dean, Harvard Graduate School of Business Administration 272

Index xxiii

PART I
THE ENDS AND MEANS OF MANAGEMENT EDUCATION

CHAPTER ONE

INTRODUCTION

IN 1930 J. A. Bowie, then Director of the Faculty of Technology of Manchester University, wrote:
'No observer in close touch with modern industry can fail to be struck by the difference between the way in which the average manager approaches the solution of the technical problems that arise in his business, and the way in which he tackles labour problems. For the former he recognises that thorough analysis and patient investigation are essential, but, in regard to the latter, he more usually reacts emotionally, and not rationally. The scientific spirit seems to leave such men when they pass from technical to human problems... The critical, self-examining attitude is essential to sound business judgment. The manager has continually to guard against hasty generalisation, undue susceptibility to emotional bias, the influence of impulse and prejudice, and other enemies of impartial thinking. To cultivate in the student the suspended judgment, the detached and impartial attitude, the careful weighing of possibilities are important tasks of the business school and its staff. It should always be the aim, wherever possible, to delve for reasons, causes, and principles rather than confine instruction to the mere communication of information.'[1]

Many people, both inside and outside industry, occupied or interested in management education have long accepted this assessment of the teacher's task. This book discusses

---

[1] Page 54, *Education for Business Management*, J. A. Bowie, Oxford University Press 1930.

some of the ways they have devised for carrying out the task which is as difficult as it is vital.

In a country with the oldest industrial system in the world, the burden of habit and tradition is heavy and cannot be removed easily. The teacher nevertheless must be sure that he develops in his students an awareness of the implications of the problems he discusses, a new questioning attitude to custom, and a habit of looking critically not only at past behaviour but also at the new theories he himself may advocate. Unless he does this, the teacher cannot feel that he has contributed to the solution of current management problems nor justify his own activities.

The Problems of Teaching

While most teachers are aware of the social importance of their job, some rather more intimate self analysis yet remains to be done. Teachers of management are, on the whole, poorly rewarded financially; they must often work in the face of some opposition or at least of indifference. In these circumstances, insight into some of his own problems and into those with which he must contend outside teaching itself, is essential if the teacher is going to be free to devote most of his energies to the main educational task.

The Environmental Audit

The first of his difficulties is that teaching in industry or in educational institutions, if well done, is a very time consuming activity. Making a lesson plan for every class, gauging the amount of the period which can be devoted to each part of the material, deciding on visual aids, preparing them, planning points for general discussions, deciding on questions to be asked, and so on, can take at least twice as much time as the class itself. When this preparatory work is being done for the first time it takes even longer. For the part time instructor with other commitments the burden is

INTRODUCTION

much heavier. He must try to fit his preparation into spare moments. If he takes his responsibilities seriously he will find himself devoting most of his leisure time to marking homework, or criticising students' reading notes. In fact, the part-time teacher must be prepared to compromise with his own ideal standards of instruction and to face the frustrations this may involve.

Secondly comes the financial reward. In an American reference book, called *The Writer's Market*, the introductory section attempts to state the reasons why journalists write. The chapter has the title 'For What?', and the first paragraph reads 'For money'. The second paragraph reads 'Old Sam Johnson said any man who wrote and did not write for money was a plain damn fool. No better literary advice has yet been given'. The management teacher and training officer could never convincingly claim a similar motive. Few training officers, even in the most prosperous and enlightened companies, earn £2,000. The situation is comparable for the management teacher.

The high quality expected of management students might explain why teachers are attracted to the profession, but the evidence is to the contrary. The management teacher is faced with an extremely varied body of students differing radically in age, background, education, job, responsibility, technical or other specialist knowledge, as well as in aim, and often there is very little he can do about it. The Ministry of Education imposes qualifications of age only and states that students for the Intermediate Certificate of Management must have reached an educational standard 'which in the opinion of the college authorities will enable them to profit by the course' before they can be admitted. This allows, perhaps rightly, for quite a wide variation in standards. In this respect the training officer enjoys a considerable advantage over his colleague in the technical college because he can at least depend on a more homogeneous group of trainees, generally with the same job experience and at least with a common company background.

The Personal Audit

What, then, prompts a person to adopt this profession? Every management teacher and training officer should ask himself this question, because in the answer will lie an important clue to his own attitudes and their effect on his teaching ability and on his students. It is futile to attempt to classify the infinite variety of responses which would be given to such a question but a few examples will illustrate the significance of a teacher's motives, and the importance of some self knowledge to anyone working in this field.

One elderly teacher in a technical college, for instance, seems to have come into this work from a variety of motives. He is able but lacks the academic qualifications which would gain him university work. A technical college has offered him a form of academic life and the security of established conditions of employment. He is a self denying man who needs to feel that he serves the community in his work, but also he dislikes the strain of a competitive life. Although in many ways an effective teacher he has become frightened of innovations which he might not be able to master and which might therefore jeopardise his position and status. He rejects, violently and emotionally, any new teaching methods or visual aids. He cannot pass on his skills to other members of his department, or discuss objectively their different teaching methods. He has thus limited his ability to adjust to the changing needs of management education and to the more varied make up of his classes.

The next example is that of a personnel and training officer in a large company. Faced with the prospect of a successful career as a university tutor in economics he decided instead to train for personnel management. Instead of dealing with abstractions he wanted to deal with people and

INTRODUCTION

he was attracted to industry because it was a challenge and because he realised its enormous importance in shaping his life and those of millions of his countrymen. With different opportunities of careers ahead of them either within industry or outside many trainers and teachers have made a similar decision for similar reasons. Like him they have a lively interest in the problems of people and are seeking to promote attitudes which will lead to that willing co-operation and co-ordination on which business ultimately depends. Like him they attempt to establish close personal relationships with students, to integrate the group and to modify intolerance and prejudice.

Two teachers completely wedded to the academic approach provide further examples. Both believe only in the lecture method and in as extensive a use of abstractions, general principles and theory as possible. Both of them encourage students to take comprehensive notes and to record verbatim the numerous definitions and rules which they dictate. They both prepare reading lists of books far beyond the students' level of understanding and set very theoretical questions in examination papers. Some knowledge of their background suggests why it is difficult for these teachers to abandon this method of teaching. One is from a foreign country where he earned several technical degrees. He has not been able to find a suitable university post and entered management education. He is out to make certain that his students appreciate that they are being taught by a man well qualified to be a university professor. The second teacher is from a working class family. He has worked on the factory floor and gained his knowledge through WEA lectures and university extension courses. He went into management education keenly conscious that he had no university degree. As a result, he makes every possible effort to adopt what he considers to be an academic approach and his teaching methods are indistinguishable from those of his foreign counterpart.

In each of these cases, some insight into their own motives might enable these teachers to assess the needs of the situation objectively and not in terms of their personality problems. This is an essential first step, because so much of the frequently expressed frustration stems from within and not from without.

Attitudes Towards Management Education

Once this personal audit has been made, it becomes possible to consider external difficulties and to see them in their proper perspective. They do not have to be exaggerated to assume serious proportions.

In the first place there is the attitude of management to training, whether it is within the firm or conducted in the evenings at nearby technical colleges. Many companies, particularly the smaller ones, do not take their management (as opposed to technical) training seriously enough. Only recently has top management begun to realise the importance of executive development schemes, of refresher training courses for senior executives, and of additional training programmes for promising members of middle management. If there is a trade recession, and economy measures have to be introduced, the training department may often be one of the first victims. This suggests that, lip service notwithstanding, many top executives still consider management training to be an unnecessary frill. The implications are important. Industry, although it is subsidising management education more than ever before, puts little pressure on the universities to introduce management training at any level. Business executives are not yet readily attracted into teaching, and management teachers are comparatively seldom accepted for part time consultancy. This, of course, rules out that close liaison between industry and education which is so essential for a two way flow of ideas

INTRODUCTION

and experience. It also means that certificates, personnel card entries, and diplomas are not valued sufficiently highly, and that the rewards are not great enough to make it worthwhile for many people to devote their spare time to training for management.

Management education has not yet achieved full recognition in the universities, although progress has been made in breaking down the artificial barriers which exist between commerce and industry and the professions. A student at Cambridge, for example, was talking to his tutor about the need for some form of post-graduate training as a preparation for business, which he proposed to make his career. The tutor was not very enthusiastic. The student asked him for his reasons and pointed out, in support of his suggestion, that the University offered a degree in Agriculture. The tutor paused for a moment and then said 'Ah, but people go into agriculture to *lose* money'. The unwillingness to accept management studies as an academic discipline probably stems partly from the comparative inadequacy of the conclusions from research into subjects like group dynamics, the social and political structure within industry and the problems related to its growth, organisation and size. It also stems almost certainly from the traditional academic aversion to teaching subjects which are vocational rather than educational. Unfortunately this unwillingness tends only to exacerbate the problem because teachers often strive to give the subject a consciously academic flavour, which divorces it even further from practical aims and applications.

There are other and more obvious difficulties. The lack of funds for adequate training facilities and staff, the inevitably overworked secretariat inside industry and in outside educational institutions are both constant sources of irritation and frustration to the teacher. He may have to do without visual aids, or advance class lists, or adequate reference libraries, or suitable classrooms, or case material from industry. He may find himself burdened with more administrative work than he would normally wish to do. Furthermore, he may even find that some of the students are neither really interested in learning something they can apply in their jobs nor in broadening their outlook in preparation for the assumption of higher management responsibilities. They may want nothing more than the paper qualification.

It is no good letting the sense of frustration grow in proportion to the number of external irritants and obstacles. What is important is that the teacher should recognise that these are facts in the present day teaching situation so that he can make an accurate assessment of their effect on his instruction and on the way his students will receive it.

Once the teacher or training officer adopts this attitude he is in a position to take constructive action. First, he can try to persuade industry and its top management that training *is* important. He can turn a deaf ear to the views of 'academics' and feel satisfied in doing the job which is immediately required and on which our economic future depends. He can devote his energies to making up for the lack of facilities and funds by his own efforts, perhaps in improvising visual aids, in preparing his own class list analyses, or in collecting his own case studies.

With this enlightened outlook and with effective instruction he should be able to convert even the paper qualification sceptics to a proper appreciation of the real value of his courses.

Some of the difficulties which originate in attitudes towards management training in this country have been outlined. They have been described sufficiently perhaps to show the personal qualities required of the teacher who is to surmount them successfully. Other qualities which he

INTRODUCTION

will need are related to the subject he has to teach and the type of student he will find in his classes.

The Approach to Teaching

Management is not a subject like engineering or physics, and to teach management is to teach a constant social process and not a comparatively static system of facts. It is true, of course, that management has its own system of facts —otherwise it could not be taught at all. The basic information on which it depends, however, is either highly specific or highly abstract. The skill in management lies in the application of general principles to particular situations, and in the choice of the appropriate principles to be applied. It may be argued that the same could be said of physics or engineering—but the difference is that the laws which apply in these subjects can usually be tested again and again in similar circumstances. In management, as in psychology, sociology and economics, which are some of its constituents, there is seldom, if indeed ever, the possibility of such rigid experimental control.

The study of management is sufficiently advanced for some predictions to be made, but these are at a different level of abstraction from those made in physics. In management the *kind* of behaviour that is likely to result from certain actions in certain situations can often be predicted. The *exact* behaviour, however, can very seldom be predicted, for the variables are too many and too complex. Whether or not management can ever become an exact discipline, it is certain that in the present day the teacher must attempt to teach not so much the science of management as an objective approach to its problems.

This approach must be taught to classes ranging from young people with very little experience of industry to mature managers who will probably have had more practical experience than the teacher. In the first case, with the young and inexperienced, the instructor's problem is to present theories of management in such a way that their practical implications and importance become apparent. This can probably best be done by quoting many examples. The teacher's problem with the older group is to make sure that its members recognise how the theories he puts forward relate to the practical experience they have had. This is the more difficult job, especially if the students are not very intelligent and are set in their ways.

Qualities Required in the Teacher

To carry out these tasks successfully some special qualities of mind and character are required.

The usual list of qualities which are useful in teaching generally are, of course, useful in teaching management as well. Enthusiasm, sympathy, confidence, tact, sincerity, a sense of humour—all the attitudes and behaviour generally conveyed by these words are helpful. However, teachers who lack even the majority of these qualities can satisfy a class and be successful in their teaching if they have three essentials.

First must come a good brain, or high intelligence. Without this the teacher cannot cope with the complexity of his subject, nor illustrate difficult concepts and general principles with clear, understandable and unmistakable examples. More important still, he cannot relate to general principles the examples his class will produce, nor co-ordinate the experiences volunteered by its various members and formulate them into abstract concepts.

Second, and related, is a good understanding of the subject. Ideally the teacher should have wide theoretical knowledge of the subject, together with extensive practical experience. Next best, perhaps, is theoretical knowledge, enlivened with detailed examples from reading, from experiences supplied by practising managers, and from

INTRODUCTION

observations on visits to factories and offices. The teacher of theory who has no examples, no experiences to quote, and who has never been inside a factory or office, had best set about repairing this omission. Meanwhile he may be of some help to his class if he presents general principles with some humility and directs the discussion based on them. Such a teacher can rarely help young and inexperienced students, and he should not be allowed to attempt it. The practical man who is incapable of thinking in abstract terms also has serious drawbacks. His teaching will be anecdotal and will seldom help students to gain insight into management problems.

The third essential in a teacher is more difficult to define. It is a compound of a scientific attitude and humility: a sincere recognition that no one person can know all about the process he is describing. It is a teacher's recognition both of the limitations of his knowledge and of the fact that his class may often include people who have more practical information and experience than he has. When teaching managers (those who are practising while he is in some way preaching) the teacher must always be prepared to listen and learn. Inevitably, good knowledge of a management subject implies that the teacher knows his own and the subject's limitations. This does not mean that the teacher must be deferential to the point of diffidence. If he is putting forward sound theories he will have confidence in them, because his knowledge should include the practical evidence on which the theories are based. Nevertheless, when students produce examples which seem to invalidate a theory he must be prepared to examine them without prejudice. If such analysis fails to discount the examples he must be genuinely prepared to think again.

The teacher of management, in a firm or technical college, who has this scientific humility and who honestly, critically and constructively examines the information he imparts, will do much to encourage similar attitudes in those he is teaching. If he does this he will at least have the immense personal satisfaction of knowing that a most important job is being done and done well.

CHAPTER TWO

THE STUDENTS AND THE SYLLABUS

On the card issued to those who have completed the job instruction sessions of the Training Within Industry programme is the maxim 'If the worker hasn't learnt, the instructor hasn't taught'. While this is a useful and salutary reminder to teachers of their responsibility in the learning process, it does not tell the whole story. Even the best of teachers cannot teach unless students want to learn; and students want to learn only in so far as they recognise gaps in their knowledge and feel the need to fill them.

This has somewhat obvious but nevertheless important implications for the management teacher. In the first place it stresses the need to find out as much as possible about the students and their intentions. Secondly it stresses the importance of arranging or adapting the syllabus for them so that it meets as many of their requirements as possible. Thirdly it stresses the necessity of choosing teaching methods which make use of the information students already have and which keep alive their interest for learning more. These methods are fully discussed in later chapters.

In one way the management teacher at a technical college is more fortunate than his counterpart in industry. The students who attend evening classes have usually made the effort of their own accord. They have recognised the gap and, however dimly or unrealistically they have perceived it, they have at least taken the trouble to do something about it. The trainer in industry can have no such assurance. He often has to begin, as the instructors in Training Within

Industry sessions begin, by making apparent some of the deficiencies which his training course is designed to make good. Since some, at least, of his students are likely to think that their presence on a training course is a criticism of their ability, he has often to lean over backwards in his efforts to restore their *amour propre*. He conducts 'conferences' and 'development groups' which sound convincing and satisfy the most status conscious of his class. He will be sensible, too, if he uses teaching methods which play down his part as trainer. While he may not have been aware of it in making such arrangements, he has gone part of the way in following up the three implications with which this chapter began.

Advance Information about the Class

In most respects but this, however, the training officer is better off than the technical college teacher. In the first place, he has the advantage that his class usually has a homogeneity of job interests, industrial background, and, most important, levels of responsibility and authority. These factors in common frequently mean that, if he handles the situation well, his group will be integrated more easily, its initial diffidence will be more quickly overcome, and discussions will be of greater immediate relevance.

Furthermore, it is normally a simple matter for the training officer to get information from records in the personnel department which will give him useful guidance. Age, education, previous training records, work and progress reports, can all play a helpful part in a preliminary assessment of the group. They can indicate the speed at which the syllabus can be covered. They can suggest groupings for stimulating controversy and vigorous discussion, e.g. the 'old hands' versus the new, the disciplinarians versus the democrats, the skilled technicians versus the self trained craftsmen. Such information, although useful in planning, should be considered only as a temporary expedient during the first few meetings of the group. After that, personal observation and additional data from the students themselves will form the foundation for directing the speed and course of instruction.

The technical college teacher may have much greater difficulty in getting details about his class. Naturally, on courses lasting for several months or a year, it is possible for him to get to know a class of students, to sort out the bright from the slow, the talkative from the shy, and to teach accordingly. With shorter courses there is not time for these facts to emerge quickly enough to be of use to the teacher. It is, therefore, particularly important for him to find out as much as possible about his students before his class first meets. It is obviously sensible if this information can be obtained in a co-ordinated way by the departmental head in the ordinary process of enrolment. The teacher might well expect to know at least each student's name, age, position and, perhaps, something about his company.

Analysis of a Class List

A fair number of assumptions can be based on this information. One instructor, for example, was asked to give a series of special lectures on an aspect of management studies not included in the regular syllabus. The classes were to be held once a week on Monday evenings from 6.30 to 8.30.

He requested the class list, which he received about a fortnight before the beginning of the course. He was dismayed at the unwieldy size of the class, but decided that he would have to group the students as carefully as possible to overcome this difficulty. The list was as follows

ENDS AND MEANS OF MANAGEMENT EDUCATION

CLASS LIST OF TECHNICAL COLLEGE MANAGEMENT COURSE

Name	Age	Position	Type of Company
X......	28	Superintendent	Clock manufacturers
......	33	Foreman	Electric light bulb manufacturers
....(Indian)	24	Technical officer	Electrical research station
......	38	Sales service rep	Vacuum cleaner manufacturers
......(Mrs)	37	Production manageress	Decorative plastic manufacturers
......	42	Trimming dept manager	Dress manufacturers
......	35	Plant draughtsman	Aeroplane engine manufacturers
......	27	Section superintendent	Electric light bulb manufacturers
......	38	Chief time study engineer	Clock manufacturers
......	25	Foreman	Motor car accessories manufacturers
......	39	Works manager	Refrigerator manufacturers
......	47	Office supervisor	Public utility
......	23	Asst employment officer	Motor car accessories manufacturers
......	27	Chief draughtsman	Rotoprint agency
......	33	Toolmaker	Duplicating machine manufacturers
......	32	Chargehand inspector	Motor car accessories manufacturers

THE STUDENTS AND THE SYLLABUS

Name	Age	Position	Type of Company
. . . . . .	40	Commercial manager	Clock manufacturers
. . . . . .	43	Works super-intendent	Carburettor manufacturers
. . . . . .	36	Chief tool designer	Beauty shop machinery manufacturers
. . . . . .	27	Asst production engineer	Light engineering works
. . . . . .	24	Receptionist	Car hire agency
. . . . . .	33	Chief inspector	Bell manufacturers
. . . . . .	38	Managing director	Engineering consultants
. . . . . .	42	Chief clerk sales and service	Public utility
. . . . . .	25	Chargehand	Motor car accessories manufacturers
. . . . . .	30	Time study engineer	Refrigerator manufacturers
. . . . . .	32	General manager	Manufacturing chemists
. . . . . .	34	Planning engineer	Carburettor manufacturers
. . . . . .	37	Asst works manager	Signalling equipment manufacturers
. . . . . .	28	Production planning engineer	Accounting machine manufacturers
. . . . . .	33	Researcher	Electrical equipment manufacturers
. . . . . .	37	Production planning supervisor	Water heater manufacturers

ENDS AND MEANS OF MANAGEMENT EDUCATION

Name	Age	Position	Type of Company
......	22	Trainee circuit manager	Oil distributors
......	34	Factory superintendent	Electric light bulb manufacturers
....(Indian)	24	Asst engineer	Cable manufacturers
......	29	Production engineer	Motor manufacturers
......	36	Deputy machine shop superintendent	Vacuum cleaner manufacturers
......	33	Asst to commercial manager	Clock manufacturers
......	34	Production control manager	Refrigerator manufacturers
......	27	Asst to planning engineer	Carburettor manufacturers
......	38	Superintendent	Electric light bulb manufacturers
......	36	General manager's staff	Refrigerator manufacturers
......	30	Transport dept accountant	Public utility
......	58	Retired managing director and management teacher	
......	35	Sales rep	Vacuum cleaner manufacturers
......	40	Supervisor	Motor car accessories manufacturers

Added to this list was the information that nine of the students had attended a similar course before. The instructor began with an analysis of the facts. He found out that fourteen were below 30 years of age; seven were 40 or over and the remaining twenty-five in their 30s. He established that the level of responsibility had a close correlation with age, especially in the 40-bracket. Next he discovered that thirty-two out of the forty-six were connected with production in some form, generally light engineering, and that five came from a motor car accessories works and four from a clock factory. He also noted that:

(a) all levels of management were represented, ranging from nine with extensive responsibility to two chargehands and eight overhead staff with no subordinates;

(b) there were wide differences in education and social status within the group;

(c) the two Indians, the woman and the management teacher might require special attention.

This analysis made the teacher realise that he would have to keep his lecturing to a minimum and arrange for maximum participation by the class, not only because some of the students had attended a similar course before, but also because there were so many with specialist knowledge. For example, the thirty-two members of the class whose jobs were connected with production would be bored while he explained in simple terms how a factory was organised. He decided to set up a panel of experts who would be seated in a separate part of the classroom. They would be called on to provide technical information on production, to illustrate the lecture from their own experience and to answer technical questions, especially those indicating the differences between light and heavy engineering. Depending on further information, which he planned to get at the first meeting, the teacher thought that he might adopt a similar 'panel of experts' formula for his other specialised lectures on organisation and sales management.

With such a mixed group and with two hours at his

disposal for each meeting, the teacher decided to divide the first fifty minutes among a lecture, question periods, brief discussions, and where relevant, the use of the 'panels'. After a ten minute break, he would then run a case study session, since this method offered the best opportunity for drawing on the extremely varied experience of the group.

His preliminary analysis suggested certain other possibilities which he might want to exploit. He could, for example, deliberately make use of the variations in skill and experience in the class. He might use the younger and older age groups for bringing out the differences in attitudes stemming from variations in age and responsibility. He might also get members of the group to illustrate the pressures and misunderstandings which exist between foremen and higher levels of management, between overhead personnel and productive workers.

The list also provided useful guidance on class seating arrangements. The two groups from the clock factory and motor car accessories works would have to be scattered through the class to encourage integration of the group as a whole.

The two Indians might conceivably have difficulty with the language and so would have to be seated close to the lecturer (not, however, on the classic imperialist assumption that understanding is improved by speaking louder to those who do not know English).

Finally, the class list showed that he might have two special problems: one woman in a class of forty-five, and a management teacher.

In the case of the woman, he felt he must not only avoid making her the butt of humour himself, but he must also prevent this tendency developing in the class, at least until friendly and informal relationships were established. In the management teacher he felt he had a potential critic whom he must quickly convert to an ally. He decided to handle the problem by calling on the management teacher for his advice and views on various subjects, and establishing his special status in the group as early as possible.

Biographical Information About Students

Although a class list is helpful for preliminary planning, the really important details must come from the students themselves. It is a simple matter at the first meeting of a course to get such information. The very process of asking for it shows the students that they will receive individual attention and thus tends to inspire confidence in the teacher's ability.

Information from the members of the group can be used to supplement the conclusions drawn from the analysis of the advance list. Whereas this analysis can indicate general problems arising from the composition of the class and can also lead to plans for their solution, students' biographies can form the basis for the programme of instruction by providing insight into attitudes and backgrounds.

The problem here for the technical college teacher and the tutor of a residential educational centre differs once again from that of the training officer in industry. The first two, because they are normally dealing with very heterogeneous groups, are in much greater need of this information. It can shorten the time the group will take to be integrated and can heighten the effect of the teaching techniques employed, if only because they will be used with an adequate understanding of the capacity and psychology of those at whom they are directed.

Procedure for collecting data is simple. The teacher can list on the blackboard the headings for the details he is seeking and ask the students to write them down and hand them in. Unless standard sized sheets have been provided for this purpose the teacher will find himself not only with the requested biographies but also with a filing problem. The ideal way of coping with the problem is to use duplicated or printed forms specially designed to fit in with the other records which will have to be kept during the course. These need not be complicated. Some teachers have found it quite satisfactory, for instance, to prepare a special quarto loose leaf notebook for each course. They place the official college attendance and grading forms at the front, followed by a section for each student arranged in alphabetical order. These individual sections are composed of a biographical sheet, monthly progress reports, note-taking and outside assignment grading sheets and an annual assessment form.

THE STUDENTS AND THE SYLLABUS

STUDENT'S BIOGRAPHY

Confidential

Name .... Age ....

Address ....

Married/Single   No. of Children ....
(cross out one not applicable)

Name of Company or other Employer ....

Title of Job ....

Description of Duties (including number and type of subordinates) ....
....

Previous Education ....
....

Technical Qualifications ....
....

Previous Business Experience ....
....

Hobbies and Interests ....
....

Aims in Business Career ....
....
....

Reasons for taking this Course.......................
....

PROGRESS REPORT—(Monthly)

Date	Student's Name		
		Marks	Comments
	Class Discussion		
	Note-Taking on Outside Reading		
	Note-Taking on Class Work		
	Homework Assignments		
	Written or Oral Reports		
	Attitude (reflected by attendance, questions, general interest)		

The headings for the biographical forms deserve particular attention. If a teacher can learn something about the student's educational background and professional training, his business responsibilities and status, and, most important, his reasons for taking the course, the effort will have been well rewarded.

One teacher uses a biographical form which has the following headings: Name, Address, Age, Previous Education, Hobbies and Interests, Professional Training and Qualifications, Job Title, Job Description (including number and type

ANNUAL ASSESSMENT FORM

Student's Name			
Course Work	Marks	out of Possible	Comments
Final Examination		70	
Class Discussion		15	
Homework & Note-Taking		15	
Total		100	Rank in Class ...... out of ......
Personal Assessment (covering critical ability, grasp of factual knowledge, attitude to work, social skills, improvement during Course)			

Report sent to Student's Employer   Date........

of subordinates), Aims in Business Career, Reasons for Taking This Course. He reports that he gets better and more informative results by explaining fully why he wants biographical details and by assuring students that the information they provide will be treated as confidential.

A second teacher asks his students to write biographical

details and motives on separate forms. He announces his intention to circulate the biographies among members of the class, so that they can become acquainted with one another more quickly. Another teacher, running a first year course in Management Studies concluded that the motives coupled with the job descriptions gave him considerable insight into his students at the start of the course. He also observed at the end of the academic year that those students with motives most closely associated with their own jobs made the best records. One departmental superintendent in a food manufacturing firm had written at the first meeting 'I have held my present job for nine months. I hope to rise into a senior position of management in my firm and hope that the course will help me in this aim'. Another, a management trainee in the tobacco industry, wrote 'My object in taking this course is to give me an initial picture of business administration, which I can develop and draw upon to enable me to reach my immediate executive ambition. The incidental discipline that night school imposes, together with the opportunities given for expression and argument will help me, I hope, to be a more active member in my various social and political activities'.

Students more concerned with form than content showed less satisfactory results. This approach was best illustrated by the students who listed the acquisition of the certificate or diploma as their object in taking the course, or by the student who wrote 'I want to be able to converse more intelligently with my business associates'.

Students' Individual Differences

Apart from attitudes and motives, which the teacher can consciously attempt to reshape during the course once he has recognised them, there are many other useful pointers to be deduced from the biographical forms. Job descriptions can give the teacher a useful idea of students' special interests and skills, in addition to indicating the type of problems with which students are likely to be acquainted. This knowledge can often prove most helpful in the successful direction of a group discussion or a case study session.

Even to the training officer in industry, who knows much more about his students from personnel records, a biographical sketch can be extremely useful. This is particularly true in very large companies where the problem can be as complex and difficult as that facing the technical college teacher. In one large company, for example, which runs courses for foremen and middle management, the trainee is asked to write a brief description of his career in the firm and to point out those personal qualities which he thinks could be improved by further training. He is then asked to explain how he feels the proposed course fits his particular training needs. Once again the answers are treated as confidential. This technique has provided training officers with most helpful background on the students' attitudes, motives, capacity, and analytical ability.

Some form of record of this sort is an invaluable guide to the main needs of a class. In addition, the records inform the teacher of individual differences and difficulties for which he must allow if he wishes to make each student an effective member of the group. In a north country technical college class, for example, there was a German refugee who was the head of an administrative department in a textile firm. From his comments in class it became clear that he had a highly critical attitude towards his own colleagues. The teacher encouraged the student to write a description of his own department, the problems he had encountered, and how he had tackled them, and a detailed account of the personalities involved. With the student's permission he then let the class ask questions and discuss the points raised by his case study. The discussion revealed to the student his bias in writing the case. He had unconsciously distorted some of the facts in his own favour and had been unreasonable in his assessment of the people in his department. At the time he reacted violently against the conclusions reached by the class, but before the end of the course the teacher discovered that this psychological wedge had opened the student's mind to a greater self understanding. His judgments of his colleagues, as he admitted to the teacher privately, became more reasonable and balanced with the result that relationships improved as did the student's job efficiency.

Such individual therapy is not always practicable as it is time consuming and demands a considerable psychological skill and insight on the part of the teacher. There is also the danger of the student's employer becoming antagonistic to management teaching if he feels that he and his firm are being held up to a group of students for criticism even though the final result may be to improve the performance of one of his employees.

Another example comes from industry. A training officer in a firm making metal castings was introducing the Job Relations section of the Training Within Industry programme to a group of foremen. It was based on an analytical approach to human relations problems. There were twelve in the group, ranging in age from twenty-six to fifty-seven. The oldest member had been with the firm since he was fourteen and had eventually been promoted to foreman pattern maker with four men under him. However, he had been unable to adjust to the changing needs of his job, particularly where paperwork and administration were required. The foundry foreman and others found it easier to by-pass him in the course of day to day problems. His frustration resulting from this situation and his feeling of inadequacy led to a very belligerent and unco-operative attitude towards the course. He scoffed at the Training Within Industry methods of dealing with human relations problems and said that no one could teach him how to handle men after his forty-three years of experience. The training officer, who had taken the trouble to look into the foreman pattern maker's background, let the other members of the group argue the matter out with him. At the end of the course he admitted that his views had been considerably altered. The training officer subsequently arranged a series of follow up interviews to see how he was progressing in applying what he had learned.

In sum, the importance of accurate and detailed record keeping for any teacher of management inside or outside industry can hardly be over emphasised. This is particularly true if the teacher feels that encouraging critical ability, awareness of human problems, co-operation within the group, and greater tolerance and objectivity are all at least as important as getting students to acquire facts and figures. Record keeping admittedly imposes another time consuming burden on the already overworked teacher, but it means that he will be in a position to gauge the real merits of the students and to give them guidance and encouragement accordingly.

Considerations in Planning the Syllabus

Interest in the subject is a prerequisite of learning, and the teacher who studies the needs, motives and capacities of his students has taken the first step towards engaging their interest. Other conditions which encourage learning should be borne in mind when planning a course.

Although children can be made to learn a great deal unquestioningly by rote, adults do not naturally learn this way, and make much better progress if they can see a general plan in what they are doing and a reason for spending time on any one aspect. However potentially interested they are in a subject, few people are roused by abstract discussion or consideration of detailed aspects which they can relate neither to a main theme nor to a practical problem. For these reasons a course should be planned to begin with a general introduction of the whole subject, and to allow at intervals for the recapitulation of material covered and for the relation of special problems to the main theme. Sub-sections and particular lectures should be planned in the same way. The plans for a lecture, as for a course, should be outlined to students in advance so that they are not left to work out for themselves why any session has taken a particular turning.

People learn by repetition, and a judicious variation on themes already covered will not bore a class, but help it. This point, which should be remembered in planning the details of a syllabus, is illustrated by the following example.

A teacher planning a year's course on Personnel Administration decided to break down his material into sections covering the main practical functions of a personnel department.

Instead of including the less tangible aspects of personnel work under such headings as 'maintenance of morale', 'standards of supervision', and 'constructive attitudes within the company and towards trade unions', he covered these crucial subjects in his introductory talk and again at the beginning of each new section of the course. When he came to the final subject, joint consultation, he was able to draw on all the factual data and the human relations aspects previously covered and integrate them realistically. This is an approach which can be followed profitably not only in the main plan of the course, but in each section and each lecture. The most successful lecturers are not those who say the most, but those who appreciate that three or four important points may be as much as a class can absorb in an evening. They are not afraid to stick to these points and present them again and again in different ways and with different examples.

Finally, people generally remember the beginning and end of a talk or discussion better than the middle. At the beginning their attention is fresh, while the change of activity at the end seems to allow their last impressions to sink into their minds. This fact can be exploited in a number of ways in designing a syllabus. It is another reason for summarising main aspects at the beginning and end of each course, each section of a course, and each lecture. It is a reason for breaking up formal lectures by brief discussions, for punctuating discussions at intervals with brief summaries before the group turns to another point, for using the blackboard and other visual aids to summarise and recapitulate, and for allowing students a break before they turn to new material.

Within the framework of his teaching schedule the teacher should plan individual lectures (using the same sets of rules to encourage understanding, learning and participation), and should work out, at least in general outline, his requirements in teaching aids, the amounts of time he will devote to discussion and special projects, and what he will ask his students to read and to undertake in homework. These problems are discussed in detail in subsequent chapters. It need only be pointed out here that once again advance planning is essential if the teacher is to make his own aids, or if he wishes to be sure of the use of equipment shared with other members of a training department.

Reading Lists and Homework Assignments

The teacher should, of course, compile a reading list for every course he runs, and he should try to make sure that students read at least what he considers an essential minimum. Students who make the effort to read as well as to attend classes find their whole understanding of a subject enriched, and their learning made easier. They can contribute to discussions and argue usefully even on subjects of which they may have limited practical experience.

The teacher can anticipate some of the excuses or complaints which students may make about reading. Many will say they have no time to read. One way to meet this objection is to select the essential material in a book and assign perhaps the two or three most important chapters. A teacher should be sufficiently familiar with any basic text to say 'Well, see if you can read pages 100-120 and the two sections on Resistance to Change in Industry'. Another way is to include reading in a homework assignment, and to set a question which requires a summary of a particular text or chapter. When there is time in a course or session the teacher may allot twenty to thirty minutes to private reading before opening a discussion. Just because it is generally the more interested and advanced students who will read, the difficult problem is to get most students started on a text. Thereafter they may continue of their own accord.

Another common complaint is that texts are not obtainable or are out of the library. The teacher can help here in the way he designs his reading list. If he knows a basic textbook which will be useful throughout the course, he can probably ask the librarian to stock a number of copies, and he can recommend his students to buy a personal copy. For reading on special aspects of the course he should try to offer a number of alternatives, so that students do not all queue for the same text. Some teachers are able to maintain a course library, with texts reserved for the course and for the students currently attending it. A course library has a number of advantages. It can usually be kept in good condition and, especially if the teacher is himself responsible for issuing books, a check can be kept on which texts are being read and which students are reading.

As a general rule a teacher should not recommend any text which he has not studied himself. Every teacher is under some obligation to keep himself familiar with new books and articles coming out on his subject. He should be ready to answer student's questions on whether an author is worth reading or how the views expressed in some new paper fit in with the general opinion.

Homework serves the same purpose as reading in

encouraging learning and developing the critical faculty. However poor his execution, the student who writes a paper has had to think about his subject and has had to order his thoughts to get them down in writing. Once again the teacher should do all he can to encourage students to complete the homework he sets.

Students who are taking a diploma or certificate in management are generally required to complete a certain number of pieces of homework and to reach a certain percentage of marks before they can sit for the examination. This condition does make it much easier for the teacher to persuade students to do homework, but as any experienced management teacher knows, the fact of the rule certainly does not mean that the required amounts of homework are automatically returned on time by every student. Where there is no rule of this sort it is often very difficult indeed to persuade a busy part time student that he should spend any of his scanty leisure in writing essays, though many teachers report that students expect to be given a solid assignment.

At least the teacher who urges his students to do homework cannot be accused of any ulterior motive. Correcting papers is a time consuming occupation and one on which the conscientious teacher must spend a great deal of thought and energy. The teacher who struggles to persuade unwilling students to do some homework is struggling purely in the interests of learning. It is well worth trying to devise a plan for homework which will fit in with the interests of different class members. Some students will answer whatever question is set, because they must in order to qualify for their examination. Others are prepared to spend time on a subject which relates to their job, or which interests them. A teacher might introduce the question of homework by saying:

'In this session we are going to cover the following... You are expected to prepare at least three papers during the session and I am now going to give you a list of subjects to choose from. When you have decided which interests you most, you can plan your reading accordingly. If anyone would like to write on some other topic within the same general field, will he please come and discuss it with me at the end of the class?'

Some students prefer to make a thorough study of one subject in a long paper, rather than prepare three or four short essays. The teacher should be ready to accept this alternative and mark the longer paper accordingly. Students who are not preparing for an examination will seldom do a set piece of homework, and the teacher who believes that written work of this sort is an indispensable aid to learning (a belief he might reasonably hold, at least for a number of subjects) had better reserve part of his teaching sessions for the students to carry out written assignments. However, many students will do some kind of work outside the class on a subject which interests them. The student who collects figures for a graph or submits an organisation chart of his department to a discussion group is probably getting at least as much benefit from his homework as the student who writes set essays. Project work, which involves collecting material outside class hours, may achieve the same end. In a training course run by a firm of management consultants, for example, work study, production methods, design and market research are all taught by the project method. Students are given the machinery and raw material for the manufacture of lamp shades, but they must evolve the design-production procedures and marketing arrangements. Projects like this have the advantage of giving the student a greater sense of obligation to his group and thus obtaining from him his most conscientious efforts.

Marking is a problem which is likely to concern only those students taking an examination. They are usually anxious to know how they will fare and should gain some idea from the marks they receive over the year. However, it is not always necessary or useful to set homework and demand answers throughout the year of the sort required in the examination. A teacher may encourage his students to learn course subjects thoroughly by writing detailed papers on them for the first two terms, and not until shortly before the examination give them questions to be answered briefly in the twenty to thirty minutes they will be expected to spend on each question in the examination. Or he may give assignments that are not related to the final examination, such as those described in Chapter Ten. Where students are not taking an examination, marking, which is likely to suggest the schoolroom, may be alien to the whole atmosphere of the course. Papers written by these students should be read carefully and criticised as fully as time permits in order to draw students' attention to omissions or to encourage them to question doubtful conclusions.

Interpreting the Syllabus

This consideration of the problems connected with the preparation of the syllabus is designed to show that the best results are achieved when general considerations are related to the differences of personality and intelligence among the members of any student group.

To turn to particular examples, an adult residential college running a series of foremen's courses has found one way to meet this requirement. It produces a course outline, for the use both of students and tutors, in the form of a combination notebook-textbook. The book is in a loose leaf format, with six to eight pages of tests introducing brief notes on such subjects as Management and Supervision, the Human Factor in Industry, Industrial Relations, Communications. These notes are printed on the left hand side of the page (see sample page overleaf) and trainees are asked to fill in their own supplementary notes both on the course and later when back on the job.

ENDS AND MEANS OF MANAGEMENT EDUCATION

From Supervisory Management Notebook[1]

5 Changes in techniques of production, both in processes and in types of equipment
  (a) what changes of this kind have you seen in your own industry during your working life?
6 Changes in market conditions, and in the range of commodities offered to the customer
  (a) have the products changed in your industry?
  (b) if so, what effects has that had on consumers' demands?
  (c) on the structure of the industry?

FOR DISCUSSION

1 Is this process of change in its infancy or near completion?
2 What newer developments seem likely to affect the structure of your own industry?
3 What changes do you foresee in the shape and character of British industry as a whole in, say, the next fifty years?

SECTION IV C

INDUSTRIAL PRODUCTIVITY

KEY TO INCREASED PRODUCTIVITY

1 Greater output for a given expenditure of time and effort

[1] N. C. Rimmer (Ed) Newman Neame Ltd 1952.

THE STUDENTS AND THE SYLLABUS

An Example of Interpretation

With a longer course of study the problem is rather more complicated. The teacher must first examine the syllabus carefully and decide the emphasis he will need to give to the various parts of the subject. He must also make certain that his personal interpretation of the subject does not conflict with the examination requirements. To take a specific example, The Nature of Management is a required introductory subject for Part I of the joint Ministry of Education-British Institute of Management course on Management Studies. It is described in the official outline syllabus as follows:

THE NATURE OF MANAGEMENT

Management. The art of directing human activities. Application of scientific method to management. Inductive thinking. The importance of standards. Responsibilities of management to different social groups. Training for management. Relative values of theory and experience. Progression from grade to grade. Selection of staff. Specifications and tests. Adjusting the theory to the individual.

Organisation. The principal functions and their co-ordination.

Distribution. Types for different products. Study of markets. Price determination. Publicity. Service. Warehousing. Transportation.

Development. Production. Materials and methods. Research. Designing for production. Organisation of design department and flow of work. Inspection.

Control. Financial management. Capital and income. Analysis of expenses. Costing. Estimating. Incentive methods.

Personnel. Selection. Placement. Training. Transfers. Promotions. Retirements. Health. Welfare. Safety.

Production. Organisation and inter-relationship of the sections concerned with planning, estimating, rate fixing, tool design and manufacture, manufacturing, progress, wages, costing, works engineering, labour bureau, welfare and canteens. Routes of essential documents through the organisation and of work through the shops.

Purchasing. Buying and inspection of materials, etc. Storage. Records.

Some Modern Developments. Social purpose in industry. The status of the individual. Significance of the working group. Some unsolved problems.

So much for the syllabus. The following are typical of the questions which students have to answer at the end of the year.

1 'In managing any corporate enterprise one must analyse exactly what there is to do, then plan or synthesise the best procedure. This analysis and planning have then to be followed by organising the work entailed, securing the co-operation and interest of all and finally safeguarding the welfare of the enterprise.'

Use this statement to show, with the aid of appropriate examples, that management is the art of directing human activities based on the reasoning processes associated with a science.

2 (a) Explain and discuss Taylor's plan of organisation known as 'functional foremanship'.

(b) Of what significance is it that Taylor apparently recognised the existence of only one kind of authority?

3 What selling methods are available to (a) a speciality food manufacturer: (b) a concrete mixer manufacturer: (c) a

THE STUDENTS AND THE SYLLABUS

manufacturer of high grade furniture: (d) a producer of women's highly styled gloves or hats.

In all cases give reasons for your answer.

4 Some reasons for providing adequate inspection facilities in industry are—to detect sub-standard goods and to investigate and fix responsibility for failures.

(a) Discuss the relative importance of these objectives by reference to any commodity of your choice.

(b) Mention four further purposes of inspection and support your statements by suitable illustration.

5 'All the expenses incurred during a period should be charged to the costs of goods produced during that period.'

State and substantiate your opinions concerning the foregoing contention.

6 Prepare a detailed outline of the objectives, functions and methods in personnel administration.

7 Attempt *either* (a) *or* (b)

(a) Draw a chart showing the inter-relationship of the sections concerned with planning, estimating, rate fixing, tool design and manufacture, manufacturing, progress, wages, costing and works engineering.

Justify your chart structure.

(b) Describe with the aid of a flow chart the route of a manufacturing order through any company of your choice. Comment critically on the procedure.

8 (a) By reference to any raw materials used in your industry, discuss some of the problems involved in devising specifications for the guidance of the purchasing officer.

(b) Briefly discuss the 'perpetual inventory' or 'maxima and minima' method of stock control. Under what conditions is it likely to prove satisfactory?

9 Write an essay of not less than 300 words on one of the following:

(a) The status of the individual in industry.

(b) Group problems (eg conditions of employment, pensions

scheme, wage differentials, etc) in modern industry and business.

(c) The social purposes of industry.

The instructor who has to teach this course for the first time may well feel it a considerable responsibility to expand this outline into material which will equip his students to pass their examination, and which can be usefully related to most managerial jobs and comfortably covered in the number of hours of class work he has at his disposal. This last problem particularly afflicts inexperienced teachers. A few have difficulty in filling in the time (a fault which may spring simply from insufficient knowledge of the subject, but which is sometimes caused by ignorance of the limitations of students' knowledge and a fear of taking them over familiar ground). Probably more have difficulty in reducing their material sufficiently: it seems to them impossible to do justice to some aspect of a subject in the three or four teaching hours which are all they can allow for it. These are the teachers who plan highly concentrated lectures and cram information into their students to satisfy their own intellectual integrity, often at the expense of a class's interest and nearly always at the expense of proper discussion and assimilation of important points.

A rough guide for inexperienced teachers is to plan never to spend more than half the total syllabus time in set lecturing (say a maximum of forty-five minutes in a session of one and a half hours), and where possible to restrict the lecture to a third of the time only. This means that the lecture can cover only those few points which the teacher considers essential to the understanding of the subject. All other material is kept for informal presentation in the discussions which will be encouraged during or after his talk. He makes the same preparations if he plans to teach entirely through guided discussion. He gets clear in his own mind the few

THE STUDENTS AND THE SYLLABUS

essential points which must be discussed and understood. The many other aspects which he may consider interesting, useful and illuminating are noted, but introduced only if required by the class.

One instructor, asked to teach The Nature of Management for the first time, studied the outline syllabus and the papers which had been set in the previous years, and prepared his own detailed syllabus along the following lines:

PURPOSE
1 To give the student a bird's eye view of the various parts of a business;
2 To familiarise him with the terminology, applications and nature of the specialised aspects of business operation;
3 To emphasise the inter-dependence of these specialised functions;
4 To explain the roles of the manager and of management in business;
5 To make the student aware of the importance of the human relations or personality factor in technical matters as well as in management practice and organisational structure;
6 To begin the development of the critical constructive approach and situational thinking.

METHODS
1 Short lectures and directed discussion of relevant problems and topics;
2 Limited objective case studies;
3 Talks by three visiting businessmen;
4 Projects outside the classroom;
5 Directed homework and outside reading;
6 The syllabus will be covered by relating the subject matter to the setting up of a fictitious company by the class. After the introductory meeting, the students will be shown three electric plugs of the same size, but manufactured in different ways. This will pose the basic problem about the product to be produced and will in turn lead to the following subjects:

SYLLABUS
Finance. This will begin with the problem of raising the capital

to launch the firm and will at a later stage cover financial control.

Market Research. Preliminary market research will be the starting point on this subject.

Business Law, Purchasing, Factory Layout, Production, Engineering, Work Study, Accounting, Sales, Distribution, Office Organisation, Personnel, Research and Development will all be dealt with as they naturally occur in the process of organising and developing the hypothetical company, department by department.

Management. On the basis of information collected from their spare time projects, such as week-end market research on consumer preferences in electric plugs, the students will themselves discuss management problems as if they were a board of directors. They will also discuss problems from a middle management viewpoint in their capacity as department heads (selected in accordance with their day time work).

Human Relations Problems. Apart from pointing out special human relations problems which might arise at various stages of the development of the student's own company, the teacher will be using film strip or other limited objective case studies.

Admittedly, many teachers, perhaps the majority, follow the syllabus closely, and try by the traditional lecture method to cover the various subjects listed.

Either approach might prepare the student equally well for the final examinations, but the results both in terms of the type of examination answer and the actual relevance to the daytime job would vary widely, as will be seen in Chapter Eleven.

CHAPTER THREE

THE FIRST CLASS

Because of his penchant for striped suits and his habit of pacing back and forth on the rostrum, a certain university lecturer has become known affectionately as 'the Caged Tiger', a nickname which he considers a term of endearment and special recognition well worth preserving from one generation to the next. At his first lecture each year he takes special pains to pace during his introductory remarks and just before the end of the hour he makes his students gasp with fright by wandering backwards absent-mindedly until he seems to be in serious danger of falling from the rostrum. He never falls, but the audience does, annually.

He has recognised the importance of the teacher's first impact on the group. Although one may disagree with the method this particular teacher has chosen, the problem of the first meeting deserves special attention.

Experienced teachers and training officers agree that it is unrealistic to expect more from the first meeting than
1 to introduce oneself
2 to meet members of the class
3 to learn something about them
4 to explain the scope and aims of the course
5 to describe the teaching techniques that will be employed
6 to distribute and comment on the reading list
7 to give instructions on note taking
8 to answer students' questions
9 to fill in administrative forms, if necessary, and explain the regulations
10 to arouse the students' enthusiasm for what is to follow.

In many respects, meeting his class for the first time is, for a teacher, like a first night performance for an actor or a solo recital for a virtuoso. The teacher or training officer is on trial and the students have that same reassuring feeling of security as a panel of critics waiting for the curtain to rise or the artist to appear on the stage. Many teachers consciously ignore this heightened emotional situation and plod through the meeting in a tired dreary way intended to impress on the students that the course is not glamour, histrionics or sugar coated pills, but good solid learning for those prepared to put their backs into it. The opportunity for making contact with the students is thus lost and potential enthusiasm perhaps permanently damped.

The Classroom

Like the actor's or the virtuoso's the management teacher's performance will depend on the amount of time and trouble he has taken in preparing for it. Unlike them, however, he is required not only to perform but to do his own stage managing. In the 'good old days' the hardness of the chairs, the coldness of the room and the bleakness of the general surroundings were considered by many to be the most efficient ways of making students thoughtful and of keeping them awake. They were successful, for students pondered a great deal about their discomfort and not about what was being said. Few teachers are yet fortunate enough to have classrooms which compare in attractiveness and comfort with good modern offices. Instead of rooms with pale coloured walls finished in a matt surface which reflects light without glare, they often find themselves in dreary and dirty Victorian caverns. Instead of fresh and cheerful if somewhat unoriginal creams and yellows, they discover heavy imitation panelling and chocolate brown paintwork.

Many teachers will be able to do little in the way of major alterations, but most will be able to do something. They can

THE FIRST CLASS

make certain that there is adequate ventilation at all times. If students are allowed to smoke, teachers can ensure that there are enough ash trays to go round. They can check that the blackboard is visible and that its messages will not be obscured by dazzle when the lights are switched on. Now that good cheap prints are available, and several schemes for lending pictures are in operation, no classroom need be without some form of decoration on its walls. It is not even outrageous to expect some floor covering or to suggest curtains of inexpensive but well designed cotton which are within the means of most colleges or training departments today. These improved working conditions have been dismissed as frills unsuited to students who come from factories and warehouses. In fact, however, they are often surpassed in the students' own offices or factories.

Whatever the decoration of the classroom, its size and arrangement matter most. Where the teacher has a choice it is obviously more appropriate to have a group of ten students in a small room than in a lecture room built for thirty or more. Informal methods are hampered by formal rows of chairs. A small discussion group of about eight to ten people is best arranged with the chairs in an oval or a circle

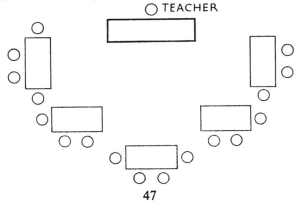

or with students sitting round a large table if they need to make notes. The teacher should not be specially indicated by having a chair twice as comfortable or half as large again as those used by the students. In a larger class, the teacher can help students to feel more like participating members of a group by arranging the room as shown on previous page.

The usual arrangement with the teacher out in front alone faced by rows of students is by no means always suitable. It has all the trappings of a classroom situation and inhibits easy discussion. Ideally all members of the group should be able to see and speak directly to each other without having to turn around in their seats.

If he has done his best to provide reasonable working conditions for himself and his class, the teacher can go ahead with an easy conscience, and his students with comfortable bodies. (It is probably superfluous to remind management teachers of the importance of breaks and canteen facilities. Every course should be arranged so that students do not sit for more than two hours at most, without a chance to move around and get a cup of tea and something to eat. Important for all courses, this becomes doubly important for evening classes, to which many students come straight from work and at which they are frequently tired and hungry.)

Personal Introductions

The first thing a student would like to know is who his teacher is and what his qualifications are. The simplest solution to the problem of opening the session is for the teacher to introduce himself, to welcome the students to the course, and to tell them why he is qualified and interested to teach them the particular subject he is taking.

After this, many teachers have found it effective to ask members of the class to introduce themselves, giving names

THE FIRST CLASS

and brief descriptions of what they do. Depending on the size of the group, thirty seconds to two minutes per person is adequate for this purpose. Here it is often helpful to pass out lapel identification tags or, better still, name cards which can be placed in front of the students and can be easily read by the teacher until he has familiarised himself with the names.

Although the sequence will vary according to circumstances, biographical forms (described in Chapter Two) can be circulated immediately after the introductions. If the teacher has time to prepare an enlarged version of the form as a visual aid, he can refer to each of the headings and explain exactly what information he wants and the form in which he wants it. Alternatively, a list of headings on the blackboard is almost as effective.

Presenting the Course

At some stage in the first meeting it is essential for the teacher to outline the syllabus for the course and to tell the students what they can hope to get from it. For example, when a firm was giving its departmental managers a refresher course in principles and practice of management, the training officer explained that it was part of a development programme to prepare promising executives for top management jobs. Two directors came along to say the same thing, with the result that the natural antipathy of active executives to a 'return to the schoolroom' was overcome.

At an opening meeting for a group of first year students in Management Studies at a technical college, the teacher who was mentioned in the previous chapter was faced with the problem of explaining what they would learn in The Nature of Management. The syllabus listed Management, Organisation, Distribution, Development, Control, Personnel, Production, Purchasing and Some Modern Developments. His task was to explain these technical terms in words which were understandable to the group and to relate this one subject to the five year course. He began by producing a drawing of a bird in flight which he attached to the top of the blackboard. He then drew the obvious analogy of the bird's eye view and produced a simple visual aid showing the various aspects of management, manufacture and distribution.

A training officer introducing a course in work study, with special reference to time and motion study methods and work measurement, devoted most of his first meeting to getting the foremen to air their objections and prejudices on the subject. He listed these largely irrational comments and kept them on view at subsequent meetings and checked off each one as the students agreed that it was not really valid. At the end of the course he produced the completely discarded list and said 'You may have wondered originally what the scope and objects of this course were. Here, gentlemen, was your syllabus—and you prepared it and completed it yourselves'.

Other solutions have been found equally effective. One teacher gave his students a detailed set of notes covering the points to which his colleagues normally devoted the first hour. He then spent the remainder of the time telling his class stories and jokes illustrating his approach to the course.

Another enterprising and more ingenious teacher, always nervous at the prospect of new faces, played a tape recording of a post mortem discussion with his previous class about the shortcomings of the course. He then used the recording as a basis for explaining what he proposed to do to satisfy the objections of the previous class and to introduce improvements based on its experience. He ended the hour by asking students to adopt the same self critical and questioning attitude in their approach to the course.

There are no rigid rules about the method of explaining

the course and the techniques to be used. What is important is that students should see the relevance of what they are going to learn, and understand how it relates both to their jobs and to other subjects. They should feel that the teaching techniques will be both interesting and stimulating.

Reading and Note Taking

At the first session the teacher should certainly devote some time to the question of reading and note taking. His students will expect him to tell them about the amount of reading they will have to do. However there is no excuse for wasting a valuable quarter of an hour dictating the titles of books to be read. If he is properly prepared the teacher will already have compiled and duplicated a list of recommended books, and may perhaps have included a few comments on each.

There are two opposing points of view on the question of note taking during lectures. Some teachers ask students to put away pens and pencils before the lecture begins; they feel that lectures should be used only to interpret reading, to relate theory to on-the-job practice and to discuss controversial issues. A majority thinks that students cannot be trusted to learn technical information on their own initiative and that the teacher's function is to convey factual knowledge. Both these generalisations may be useful in different circumstances. Usually some procedure between the two will seem best suited to the subject and the students. One statement most would accept is that some guidance on note taking is essential. Participation and critical thinking can be developed even in taking notes, and some teachers make a practice of instructing their students to leave half of each notebook page blank so that later they can fill in their comments on the information they have recorded.

After the first eight weeks of a course, one teacher at a technical college asked his students to submit their notes to him. They were surprised by his request. He was astonished by what he saw. He had assigned one of the standard introductory books on management. The notes ranged from a practically verbatim copy of the text, meticulously typed on foolscap sheets, to telegraphic phrases, abbreviations and catchwords, scribbled on scrap paper, which could not possibly have made sense to the writer two hours after he had written them down.

This teacher was so appalled at the extraordinarily low standard of note taking that he adjusted his schedule in order that he might be able to devote a special period to the subject. His recommendations were as follows:
1 buy a loose leaf notebook with plenty of room so that you can keep one notebook for each subject
2 leave a three inch margin on the left of the page for notes which represent afterthoughts on the subject or which list cross references
3 use outline or brief sentence forms in such a way that there is a logical progression of thought and major points stand out
4 introduce a second colour to emphasise important facts and ideas
5 leave one or two blank pages after each set of notes on a book for additional comments later on in the course.

Time must be left in the planning of the first class for students' questions, for filling out administrative forms and for explaining regulations which will affect the students during the course. This initial meeting should not be conceived *in vacuo,* however. It is very much an introduction to further meetings and therefore the thread of continuity must be established with a small reading assignment and an announcement of what will be covered at the next session.

The basic aim of the first class has not yet been discussed. It is the crucial but intangible factor of establishing contact —getting 'on net'—with members of the group. There is no

THE FIRST CLASS

simple formula for establishing this relationship. One can do everything logically and efficiently and the sympathetic spark may still not be kindled.

Props for Self Confidence

Many an old timer has admitted in private that he still feels nervous about the first session with a new group of students. One of these experienced teachers has devised what he considers a foolproof system for putting everyone, especially himself, at ease. If the chairs in the room are in rows, he first suggests to the students that they should be arranged less formally in a semicircle. He then introduces himself and tells the class briefly about his background and special interests and gets each member of the class in turn to do the same. He says a few words about the course, gives them some encouraging statistics about how many of the previous classes have passed the course, and finally makes a plea that they forget about examinations and concentrate on learning how to apply what they learn to their daytime jobs.

Another teacher runs his first class every year like a committee meeting. He acts as chairman and passes out previously prepared agenda with such headings as 'Purpose of the Course', 'Home Assignments', 'Outside Reading', 'Examination Requirements', and so on.

While there is no formula for establishing *rapport*, the teacher can at least avoid major pitfalls by following some such procedure as that outlined at the beginning of this chapter. First impressions are important and merit attention and careful preparation. If the group gets off to a successful start it can mean that a perhaps disproportionately large part of the teaching struggle is already won.

CHAPTER FOUR
THE LECTURE

THE lecture is still the basic teaching technique in the great majority of technical colleges and training departments. It is an effective way of ensuring that everyone in a group receives the same information at the same time. It is a comparatively simple method of conveying facts to groups who need basic information—for example, executives learning the elements of accounting, or newly promoted foremen learning company organisation—and of presenting ideas to a very large group which may meet only a few times.

Even in these circumstances, however, the formal full length lecture is now employed much less often than the short lecture combined with discussion and demonstration. This technique is the one that often seems the most satisfactory to the management teacher who feels he must convey some standard instruction to his students, and who yet wishes to keep their interest and persuade them of the usefulness of the material. Like all other techniques, however, it can encourage or discourage learning according to how it is developed.

Some of the principles of successful lecturing are demonstrated by the salesman who persuades a customer to buy some article in which he was originally only vaguely interested.

The good lecturer is something of a salesman, certainly to the extent that a salesman who knows his job defines and strengthens his customers' needs. A customer, who had been thinking for some time that he would like to buy a writing case, recently went into a leather goods shop. The customer was not sure just what sort of case he wanted, nor the price he was prepared to pay. Having decided that he would probably know when he saw it, he walked aimlessly around the department store. Then the salesman spoke to him; the salesman seemed confident and said he understood what the customer needed. He began to define these needs, in fact, and increased the customer's desire for a case. He produced a writing case and displayed it, briefly indicating its usefulness and its relevance for the customer's purpose. He opened it and showed its contents, giving examples of the use of each article. He let the customer handle each article himself. The salesman answered some questions, and then quickly replaced each article in the case, closed it and once more briefly commented on its merits. By this time the customer really wanted the case. He bought it and started using it immediately, and now cannot think how he ever did without it.

Sales techniques have unfortunate connotations, and the analogy must not be pressed too far. There are some important lessons to be learned from this example nevertheless. The salesman stimulated a rather vague interest, the kind of interest that draws many students to start a course. He showed the complete article and indicated its usefulness and then demonstrated how each of its separate parts was related to the overall function of the article. He allowed his customer to ask questions and to experiment. He recapitulated the selling points, and once more drew attention to the general merits of the complete case. He impressed the customer throughout by his competence and sincerity. In this small instance he showed great skill in sustaining or increasing motivation, presenting information in an orderly and relevant way, and behaving in an appropriate manner so as to give confidence. In all these respects, he can serve as a model for the management lecturer.

Planning the Lecture

One training officer was recently required to lecture to a group of middle management in his company on selection methods. His talk was part of a general training course for these managers, intended to give them a wider picture of the company's work and the services of the specialist departments. The training officer knew some members of the course, but others had come from different units of the company. Unfortunately, the personnel department had not recently been required to make any important selections for the departments represented on the course; so the trainer had to abandon the idea of developing a discussion on those lines. One member of the course, however, had attended a group selection board before joining the company. The training officer eventually decided to give a short lecture and to encourage discussion by giving a good many examples, asking the group to help in certain parts of the talk.

His first aim, he recognised, had to be to gain and hold interest in the subject. Few managers in the company needed convincing that finding suitable personnel was a problem, and one which vitally affected the running of their departments. However, some at least of the group were probably sceptical of the value of modern selection methods, others were ignorant of them, and a few probably dismissed the idea of careful selection in a situation where there were often too few men for the jobs and—as they saw it—all but the totally and obviously unfit must be accepted.

The training officer also suspected that, besides certain attitudes towards selection methods, the group held similar views about the general work of the personnel department. Some managers appeared to use the personnel department as a dumping ground for all minor grievances among employees. Others regarded the personnel department as an encroachment on their own domains—they tended to be hostile, for instance, about any personnel forms they were required to complete.

Taking these views into account, the trainer planned his lecture as follows:

THE LECTURE

Introduction
What is the use of selection methods?

1 The range of the problem. Brief commentary on the number of vacancies in different departments and grades. Point out that careful selection has always seemed warranted for certain grades. Is it warranted for others?
2 Specific example: a discussion of labour turnover in one department. Before the personnel department was in operation labour turnover was high amongst all operatives. Over the last few years the department has built a growing core of operatives who stay put. One explanation may be the new selection methods employed.

NOTE Prepare two large charts of labour turnover figures for this department to pin up on magnetic blackboard.

3 These new methods, however, could not have succeeded without the interest and co-operation of the departmental manager concerned. Brief commentary on his co-operation, leading to remarks on the relationship the personnel department needs to have with line staff before it can be useful to them.

Part I
What are the modern methods of selection?

Analogy: Suppose you are installing new plant. You determine function, load, cost, etc, and then obtain estimates and evaluate them. Modern selection methods work on similar general principles: analysis, specification, evaluation.

NOTE Write these three headings along top of blackboard.

Evaluation of people is something every manager attempts and some are very skilled at it. Failures are generally due to:
1 Poor specification;
2 Personal bias.

Modern methods try to cope with these two problems. This talk will outline first, problems of analysis and specification, and then the main methods of evaluation which try to counteract personal bias. Under this heading will come the forms we use and why, and the method of interviewing and why. These are the basic methods of selection and enough to concentrate on.

(The training officer expected that his talk so far would take seven to ten minutes. He hoped in this time to have fostered interest in his subject by emphasising its practical value and to have countered some opposition by indicating the personnel department's proper relationship to the line. He had now introduced the few general principles he felt necessary in his talk, but had tried to prevent their sounding purely abstract by giving examples and by presenting some visual material. He had also outlined the rest of his talk so that the course could recognise and follow a broad plan in what he was saying.)

Part II
The preliminaries—analysis and specification.

Detailed job analysis differs only in degree from the general description of the job in his section that any foreman can give. Comment on why this degree is important.

NOTE Ask each member of the group to write down a description of a job—for example that of the commissionaire at company head offices.

A problem is to find headings which cover the main items in a job analysis and are equally useful in drafting a job specification. One set of headings is the Seven Point Plan suggested by the National Institute of Industrial Psychology. Discuss.

NOTE Write these seven headings on the board under 'Analysis'. Ask the group to itemise their job descriptions under these headings; write up a summary of their ideas and add any sections omitted.

It should now be simple to decide on the sort of man we want for commissionaire. The ideal man seldom appears, so we need to know the limits of tolerance.

NOTE Write across the board, under the main heading 'Specification', three sub-headings: 'Essential', 'Desirable', 'Undesirable'. Ask the group to itemise their specifications and complete the sections as before.

THE LECTURE

Explain that this is the principle of analysis and specification, and mention some techniques of detailed job analysis. Remind them that poor specification is a common fault in selection and cause of failure.

NOTE Under section on 'Analysis' and 'Specification' chalk up '= accurate specification'.

Part III
Evaluation.

Now that we know what to look for, the possibilities have to be sifted. The net is cast as wide as possible.

Higher technical appointments mean advertising, sorting letters received, sending off application forms.

Unskilled jobs mean cajoling the employment exchange, inspecting those who come to the gate, helping them to fill in a form.

Here are the forms this company uses.

NOTE Have a supply of forms for higher and unskilled jobs and give each member of the course a copy of both.

Point out the main items in their design. Discuss why they are designed like this.

(The training officer now expects to have been lecturing for thirty to thirty-five minutes. As he has broken up the time with demonstrations and practical work he feels justified in continuing longer than would be advisable in straight lecturing. He is deliberately giving only the broadest outline of his subject, leaving aside details of, for instance, job analysis and recruitment to be picked up by the group if they wish in discussion. If the discussion develops in that direction he means to encourage the member of the group who has attended a group selection board to describe his experiences. He explains all the visual material because he knows that the simplest forms and diagrams are often misunderstood even by intelligent groups. He also describes the purpose of the form because in this company the departmental managers concerned have a final say in selection.

The personnel department sends them the candidate's application form, and later the candidate, to be interviewed. The training officer means to ensure that members of this course, at least, can get the best value from the document.)

Let's suppose a candidate comes to your office.

NOTE Draw a large pin man under 'Evaluation'.

Suppose he's your ideal of a company commissionaire. What's he going to look like?

NOTE Encourage the group to describe the ideal candidate's appearance and manner. Complete the drawing with appropriate labels. Ask for the worst possible commissionaire and draw an alternative design.

Point out that both these figures show personal bias. Relate to 'Specification' and discuss dangers of bias, with examples.
Discuss problems of interviewing without bias.
1 What to look for. Show the relevance of some aspects of the candidate's history, with examples.
2 How to look for it. Mention one or two mistakes on the part of the interviewer which prejudice an interview.

So, by working to a system, by recognising personal bias, by studying facts rather than impressions, we hope to overcome the other source of failure in selection.

NOTE Complete 'evaluation' by writing '= check on personal bias' at the bottom of this section.

Part IV
Summary.

Run over the main phases and point out how they attempt to improve on earlier methods.

(The training officer felt this lecture plan would ensure that the main aspects of selection were covered. He knew that a great deal had been left out. He had still not mentioned, for instance, psychological tests. But he also knew that a group's capacity to grasp new information is strictly limited. He was determined not to lecture for more than

THE LECTURE

forty-five minutes, and left all other information to be introduced as required in discussion. He made sure that the essentials, as he saw them, were repeated two or three times in the lecture he designed.)

Having completed his lecture the training officer decided he would start a discussion with a short demonstration. He obtained a tape recording of an interview with a candidate who was rejected by the personnel department, and also the candidate's application form which he had duplicated with only personal details (name and address) altered. He decided to give each member of the group a copy of the form. When everyone had studied it he would play them the recorded interview, and ask them if they agreed with the personnel department's decision not to take the man, and to give their reasons.

Basic considerations

Many variations could be made on this training officer's plan, but to be useful they would have to be guided by the same considerations which formed the basis of his approach.

1 Much more time must be spent outside the classroom preparing material and analysing the students' needs, than will ever be spent in giving the lecture itself.
2 Where much has to be said the subject must be ruthlessly pruned to its essentials, and the lecture broken up so that students never listen to a single voice for more than twenty minutes.
3 Wherever possible, alternative sensory stimuli must be introduced. Another sound—from the students' own voices, from the tape recorder—will stimulate interest. A diagram, or a scribble on the blackboard, will mean that the same information enters through eye as well as ear.
4 The plan of the lecture must be given at the outset, referred to in transit, repeated when the lecturer comes to a stop. Important items reach the students several times, in

this way avoiding any confusion with less essential parts of the lecture.
5 The plan of the lecture must be clearly established before the class begins. This particular training officer used his plan to decide exactly what teaching aids he would need and he prepared them well beforehand. For some teachers this may mean booking special equipment (such as the tape recorder); for others designing charts; for others at least the accurate marking of texts from which they mean to quote.

Aids to Teaching

So much fuss has been made about visual and auditory aids that two impressions have been created:
1 that a teacher cannot be effective unless he makes extensive use of them;
2 that, if he decides to use teaching aids, he is certain to incur considerable expense.

Neither is true. It is quite possible to give a highly successful lecture or run an effective discussion group without a single teaching aid. It is also possible to plan the most elaborate use of teaching aids without spending more than a few shillings.

A selective list of sources for visual and auditory aids is appended to this book. The points which follow are intended to serve as a simple commonsense guide to the benefits and shortcomings of the most frequently used aids.

Visual Aids

Visual aids are accessories to management training which can be used or abused like any other teaching method. At least, they can provide a fresh approach to a subject. Well designed diagrams shown at the appropriate time may strikingly illustrate a point in a talk, and sharpen the attention and quicken the imagination even of a class which already seems absorbed in the subject.

THE LECTURE

A message written on the board, a recording or an illustrative graph can serve to repeat information in a new form which has the added interest of novelty or variety. Coming to the brain a second time, the idea has that much more chance of staying there.

A large chart on the wall may help a class to follow the intricacies of a talk on production or organisation, without the students being overcome in a struggle to relate detailed information to a general pattern. Here the visual aid helps to show the purpose and relevance of different items.

Any visual aid can constitute a pause for rest and assimilation. Its presentation and demonstration will take time, and the breaks involved can be introduced skilfully to give a class the opportunity to consider and absorb a difficult problem, before going on to something new.

The Blackboard

The teacher whose department is poorly equipped with aids, and who lacks funds to buy them, need not despair at this list. All these potentials can be realised by a skilful instructor with no more than a blackboard to help him. But if he is to rely on a blackboard, some basic practical problems should be borne in mind. Probably every teacher has been embarrassed at some time by a blackboard that was too small or wobbly or difficult to see. A blackboard on an easel almost certainly suffers from the first two faults—it cannot in the nature of things be very large, and it often leads a life of its own, walking several paces backwards whenever it is to be written on.

To be most serviceable, blackboards should be fixed to the wall, and may usefully extend the whole of one end of the classroom; they should be at a height which can be seen from every seat, and reached without discomfort by most teachers.

Once these requirements are met, only four rules are

essential for effective use of a blackboard. The first is to use it often and without too much respect. Even experienced teachers tend to write on the board slowly and reverently and far too little.

The second is to write legibly. Teachers whose ordinary hand can be read by members of a class will also be legible on the blackboard. Teachers whose ordinary hand is hardly legible to their relatives should stick to capital letters.

Rule number three is to write quickly. The class watches the teacher write and it is part of the process of providing them with new stimuli that they should do so. But a slow crawl across the board may dull attention and develop a general feeling of lethargy or of irritation. Writing quickly on a blackboard is a skill which comes to everyone with practice.

The fourth rule is never to use abbreviations which can be misunderstood. Speed must come from the movements of the hand and not from the shortening of words. This is particularly important when writing proper names or references, but abbreviations of even ordinary words increase the difficulty of reading. It is probably irritation at this that has caused students to criticise a teacher as 'too lazy' or 'too slapdash' even to put things up on the board properly.

A blackboard can be used in various ways. Writing on the board may be employed to provide a definite break in the class work, to reiterate previous material, to present it in a new (sensory) way. The teacher may say 'I'll just summarise as far as we've got', and deliberately turn to the board and devote himself to writing on it. Whatever he has to put up, he should not make any comments until he has finished. A class can watch writing on the board with interest for up to two or three minutes, but it is generally unwise to go on longer than this without pausing and discussing the material. All material on a board should finally be read aloud to the class, to drive home the message yet again, and

THE LECTURE

to ensure that any misreading or misunderstanding of words is brought to light and amended.

The blackboard may also be used simply to jot down significant points in a lecture or discussion. Explaining the rudiments of accountancy a teacher may say 'Now let us be clear about this. Credit goes in the right hand column and debit in the left. You can remember because credit has an R in it'. As he speaks he chalks up the two words:

    Debit   Credit

Thus extra stimulus is provided as the talk goes on.

There are occasions when the teacher's own elementary designs and scribbles on the board will gain and hold attention better than a finished diagram painstakingly prepared beforehand. A simple drawing can have something of the effect of a cartoon, emphasising major issues. A teacher could open a course on Communications by writing on the board 'Communication between any two people involves not only the senses and the intellect, but introduces problems of attitudes'.

Alternatively, the teacher could briefly discuss some complexities of communication and then say 'It's like this', and draw on the board:

One teacher, uncertain of his own artistic ability but convinced of the need for a diagram to illustrate the logical development of his argument, solved the problem by drawing the diagram on the board in pencil with the aid of a ruler before the class assembled. He then traced the relevant parts with his chalk as he came to the appropriate points in his lecture. Even those who steadfastly refuse to draw diagrams can enliven their written messages with (judicious) underlining, asterisks and by circling words in colour. This can usefully be done when reading out the material to the class. Yellow and orange are often more effective than red, which is difficult to see except in good light. Most classrooms are supplied with a box of these coloured chalks in addition to the usual white.

When one aspect of a subject or when one diagram is completed and thoroughly discussed, the board should be cleaned before another theme is started. This is not only to ensure that different materials are not muddled and confused: the act of cleaning will itself emphasise to students that an item is covered, and will prepare them to attend to a new subject.

The great asset of a blackboard is its adaptability. The teacher's use of the board is closely and immediately related to the work of the class. The diagrams and notes he chalks up can be modified to suit the class, and the teacher who has mastered this medium need never feel that his most elaborate preparation is wasted, or that he cannot provide a visual aid to almost any aspect of a lecture or discussion.

The value of a blackboard, however, is also its limitation. It is not suitable for the presentation of complex and detailed diagrams, or for material such as graphs and charts which may be valueless if they are inaccurate. Visual aids of this sort need not be elaborate but they require careful preparation, and a suitable place to display them in the classroom.

The Easel

An easel, which is nearly valueless as a support for a blackboard, may here come into its own. Effective display boards for smaller diagrams or for unmounted material may be made of soft wood or cork—or any material to which paper designs can be easily fixed by drawing pins. The board may be fixed to the wall beside the blackboard or propped on the easel. Where even a little money is available, however, it might be usefully spent on a magnetic blackboard, which combines blackboard and display.

The Magnetic Blackboard

A common type of magnetic blackboard consists of a pair of steel sheets, each the size of an easel blackboard (say 2ft 6in by 2ft) and mounted on shallow wooden frames. The two frames are hinged together so that they close to form a shallow case; the steel sheets are painted with blackboard paint. Prepared diagrams can be attached to these surfaces with magnetic pins very quickly and with no risk of damage, and the display can be changed or elaborated, as the class desires, with chalk-written additions.

An example of the use of the magnetic board has been given earlier in this chapter. A further description of its use in a specific class discussion is given in Chapter Ten.

Of all the aids so far devised, the magnetic blackboard has the greatest flexibility and widest range of uses. For example, if the teacher wishes to describe the growth of an organisation he can place the appropriate labels on the board as he names each department. Subsequently, if he wishes someone from the class to show how he would like the organisation revised, the teacher can ask the student to come up to the board and rearrange the cards. This saves considerable time by removing the need for erasing and rewriting. The board is equally valuable for exercises in evaluation. For instance, in the previous example of the qualities required in a commissionaire, it would have been a simple matter to place three cards (Essential, Desirable, Undesirable) across the top of the board. Then, as the class suggested qualities, the teacher could have rapidly printed them on cards and placed each under the appropriate heading. As the discussion proceeded the cards could have been switched from one category to another, either by the teacher or by a member of the class.

Reference has just been made to visualising as you go. For a group discussion, where the points to be emphasised cannot be planned in advance but must emerge as discussion develops, this system is invaluable, particularly when used with the magnetic board. Two or three colours can be used. Secondly, it is easier for the teacher to print on paper or card than to write on the blackboard. Thirdly, both print and drawings stand out better against a white card background. Finally, they can be mounted and removed from the magnetic board with far greater ease than is required to perform similar operations on the blackboard. The necessary equipment is simple and inexpensive:

1 a roll of white card or heavy paper;
2 three felt tip pens;
3 a bottle each of green, red and black (or any other colour) ink;
4 a small box for holding them and a ruler.

The paper or card can be cut to a suitable size in advance, so that the teacher has only to pick his colour or colours, decide on the copy or drawing, and complete the aid while the class continues discussion.

Diagrams and Charts

Diagrams and charts which are bought ready made generally conform to the rules of good visual presentation. The management teacher is unlikely to find ready made material for all his purposes, however, and may have little money to spend on what is available. Once again, some practical considerations will help him to buy or prepare his material more effectively. He must be sure that all his display is large enough to be clearly visible to everyone in the class. He must keep his material clean, since a display loses a great deal of its effect if it is allowed to become dingy and soiled. This means ensuring that material is carefully stored between classes, and protected (for example by mounting on cardboard and enclosing in a cellophane envelope) if it is to be handled.

Use of Colour

Colour should be used in diagrams, for it is a cheap and highly effective way of attracting attention. One study showed that magazine advertisements using colour were remembered by about three times as many readers as black and white advertisements. One colour, added to a black and white design, was enough to produce this effect; adding more colours did not greatly increase the precentage of readers who remembered the advertisement.

In preparing his own material the teacher must follow the rules of good design and deal with one subject only in each diagram. It is not possible usefully to combine, for instance, information on numbers attending a training course over a period of years (one problem) with information on the time devoted to different aspects of that training syllabus (a separate problem). Time spent defining exactly what is to go into a diagram is always well spent.

A rule now followed in most professionally prepared diagrams is that of keeping to a fixed symbol to represent a particular object or a particular number of objects. For example, a diagram might be designed to show that the number of clerical workers in a company had trebled in three years. One way of drawing this would be:

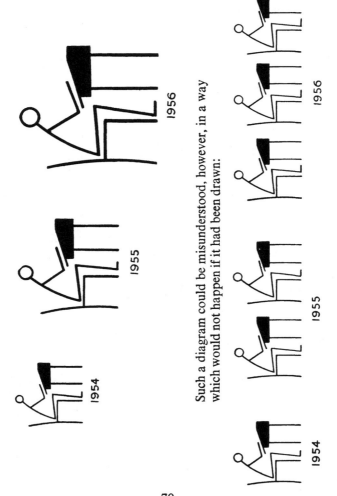

Such a diagram could be misunderstood, however, in a way which would not happen if it had been drawn:

THE LECTURE

Some management subjects (for example, work study and motion study) have many symbols which are generally accepted and recognised. Any symbols already in current use should be used in preference to those of the teacher's own invention. Teachers who prepare a good deal of visual material in subjects not traditionally expressed visually tend to build up a vocabulary of symbols with which their classes become familiar.

Use of Films and Filmstrips

Although some teachers work with no more than a blackboard, an increasing number of management teachers, in industry at least, can hope to use more elaborate aids, such as films or filmstrips, at least occasionally during a course. Filmstrips are the more popular because they are easy to present and are cheaper than films. They are generally used to introduce a class to a problem situation, and in this way they constitute a variation on the case study method described later.

Films have a special value in the presentation of technical subjects. A film of motion study, for example, may convey information on space, layout, size and weight of materials, and techniques of measuring movement much more succinctly and completely than could be done in a series of lectures or classroom demonstrations. Or a film may convey an idea of a process or of the work of a department much more vividly than even a skilful talk could do, especially to people who have little knowledge of the particular firm or industry. It is possible to film a process from angles that would not be seen by a person being taken round for demonstration, or to show, through the use of a slow motion camera, movements and procedures in more detail than the eye could catch. Many firms use films to good effect on their induction courses for new employees, for publicising a safety programme, for prestige and public relations, sales training, time and motion study, technical training, and for general education. (See Appendix A for a list of sources.)

Some films not originally intended for training purposes at all can be usefully employed to illustrate a subject. Many training institutes have used the film of the Tennessee Valley project to illustrate aspects of organisation and managerial control. Some films made for commercial showing are valuable for training. *The Chance of a Life Time,* a film in which workers take over control of a small country works, and so learn both the limitations and the capabilities of their own management, is one example of this type of film, and one that is available for private showing.

Films and filmstrips are fairly sure to be a popular feature of any training programme. The simplest of them tells a story, and all are acceptable because film is associated with entertainment and leisure activities. The teacher can be fairly assured that any films he shows will gain and hold attention. Whether they do more than this, however, will depend on his skill and initiative in relating the problems shown to the principles of management he wishes to demonstrate. Just because films have leisure associations it is sometimes difficult to persuade a class that they are intended to be the basis for thought and discussion. However, if the films are as effective as General Electric's *The Inner Man Steps Out,* which describes human relations problems in supervision, then this problem will not arise.

Use of Other Aids

Though there are fewer auditory than visual aids to training, they have considerable scope. Some of the uses of tape and wire recorders are discussed in later chapters. The most easily obtainable is a gramophone, and some teachers use it effectively to illustrate class work. However, unless the teacher has a recording machine with which to make his own records he must use his imagination, knowledge and

THE LECTURE

ingenuity to discover the material he needs from records on the commercial market. Talks on safety or working conditions in relation to noise may well be illustrated from records. One successful course on communication opened with a general discussion of difficulties of understanding others with examples from industry, politics, private life and contemporary art forms—the latter including records of modern atonal music.

At all times the teacher should ask himself exactly what he wishes to illustrate and why he believes a visual or auditory aid would help. He should remember the total pattern of his lecture. He should think out an aid which is single purposed and unambiguous, and yet which does not do violence to its context. He should ask himself which form of presentation—graph, table, diagram, chart, record or film—is likely to be most effective. Careful preliminary thinking on these lines reduces the work of preparing aids and may well reduce outlay on materials.

CHAPTER FIVE

PARTICIPATION METHODS

THE methods used in teaching greatly affect the interest and enthusiasm of the student. It may be possible to convey some information from the teacher's brain to the student's in a series of bald announcements; but useful learning begins only when the student's mind is stimulated —when he thinks and questions and argues. The student who participates in class work in this way is learning and applying information to his own problems—and the wise management teacher therefore uses all his skill to encourage participation in his classes.

Of course, any teaching method may produce participation. A brilliant and provocative lecture may rouse a group to furious discussion which will continue long after the class is finished. But some methods are much more difficult than others, and the teacher who relies on formal lecturing, for instance, has probably chosen the most difficult method of all for encouraging participation.

Participation is best encouraged by informal methods of teaching, such as the guided discussion and group analysis of a problem, and demonstrations prepared and presented by students, rather than by lectures or teacher's explanations.

In these informal methods the relationship between teacher and taught is much friendlier than in more formal settings, and communication between them is therefore much more complete and frank. Formal teaching methods often imply omniscience and criticism, and students' energies are directed to combatting these impressions, rather than to evaluating the information given. Communication in these

PARTICIPATION METHODS

circumstances is generally one way only, from the top downwards. The teacher who lectures from a rostrum stands in a position of authority which make the free exchange of ideas and the give and take of discussion difficult. He cannot be sure that all in his audience can see the relevance of what is being taught. ('It's all very interesting, but what's it got to do with me and my job?') The teacher's position of authority may thus make him the focal point for a good deal of resentment. This is shown either in complete disbelief of what is being taught ('That may be so in theory, but it doesn't happen in practice'), or in cynical remarks so often passed between students ('If he knows so much about our jobs why doesn't he come and do them himself?').

These problems are avoided in informal teaching. Here the teacher is not so much an instructor as a guide. He does not seem to sit in authority over the students by virtue of his rank. When he performs the chairman's duties (as he often does) he does so partly because of his acceptability and partly because he has trained himself as a chairman. He is not separated from the group as the teacher is from the class. He is the group leader, the member accepted to lead, and he sits physically and psychologically alongside the other members of the group. Instead of always telling the class what to do he expects the group sometimes to decide for itself what would be most profitable. He attempts to clarify and to interpret the experiences reported by members of the group. Instead of giving out principles, he tries to draw principles from them. By participation in group activity the students learn more thoroughly than they would do otherwise. Because they themselves contribute from their own knowledge and experience, the training is usually directly relevant and its practical implications are clear.

A wide variety of informal methods of teaching, all of which encourage participation and a critical relation of theory to practice, has now been developed. They are discussed in detail in subsequent chapters, and are mentioned here only by way of illustration. One of the most effective is the case study method. By actively participating in the analysis of a problem and the formulation of corrective action, the student practises and develops his critical analytical faculty. He is also able to learn through this technique the importance of the human factor in assessing a situation.

Outside assignments, whether in the form of factory visits, limited practice market research projects, or case studies about his own job, can provide admirable opportunities for the student to gain experience in extracting relevant facts from a particular problem and in analysing them.

The management teacher might also remember that group discussion is a particularly appropriate technique for influencing attitudes. As each person makes his contribution it is examined and evaluated by the others. The outspoken dogmatist is led to modify his remarks by the weight of group opinion and the group's demand for factual evidence, Generalisations and slogan thinking are exposed and more moderate, realistic views prevail. If the group is handled adequately a growing sense of team spirit and a feeling of belonging will consolidate the new ways of thinking.

Informal methods, however, make far more demands on teachers than formal methods. The planning and preparation of a discussion is more difficult than that of a lecture simply because the contributions made by group members make set pieces impossible. In a lecture the facts are produced and organised by the lecturer to give a certain picture. In a discussion it is the group which produces and organises the facts—helped by the discussion leader, who sees that all relevant facts are contributed and considered. The teacher who uses informal methods cannot rely on the comparative immunity to criticism that may go (in fact more often only appears to go) with a role of absolute authority. He cannot rely on the class work remaining within the bounds he has set for his meeting. He must be prepared to handle discussions which may range over the whole field of his subject and which may include detailed consideration of aspects he has not specially prepared. The informality of the situation makes it easier for him to acknowledge ignorance and retain the respect of his class, but this cannot be done too often. Some teachers may think such a possibility offers a blow to their pride which they are not prepared to risk.

The teacher who is prepared to undertake informal methods of instruction must be aware of these problems and must relate them to his subject matter and the quality of his students. He must also relate them to his own feelings of security and to the sincerity with which he means to forego some of his claims to omniscience.

The Discussion Group

'Organised conversation' is the description which the Bureau of Current Affairs applied to the discussion group. It is certainly neither a debate nor an argument, for both these imply antagonism and attempts to convert. Unlike the discussion group they encourage people to maintain their point of view in face of opposition. Debaters and arguers spend comparatively little time listening to what others have to say, for they are much too busy thinking up witty retorts and irrefutable statements. Because of this, and the status that is to be gained by being on the winning side, both these activities usually result in more rigid adherence to established points of view.

A discussion group, on the other hand, has just the opposite objective. It attempts to loosen up inflexibilities of thinking by getting a number of people together to exchange information, opinions and experience. It aims at an integration of views, a broadening of knowledge, at a respect for the other person's opinions, and at a common understanding of problems. Management teachers and trainers will be more aware than most people how important and relevant these objectives are.

In one form or another discussion is an essential part of the teaching methods outlined in this book. It has its place following a lecture, in the case study method, and after a role playing session. It is discussed here as a separate technique both because it can be considered as a teaching method in its own right and because it illustrates an all important attitude to teaching and to those being taught. Its special application to case study and role playing is discussed in later chapters.

Teaching by discussion is to teach with informality and with maximum opportunities for student participation. It has already been suggested how informality can be aided by a suitable layout of the room. Opinions differ about the ideal number in a group. Experience suggests that between six and twelve people is most satisfactory. Above twelve the group leader may have difficulty in chairing the meeting. He may not be able to see that discussion is fairly evenly distributed, nor that each member is encouraged to speak. With less than six, organised conversation may tend to become simply conversation.

The effectiveness of group discussion depends largely on the teacher. In his capacity as chairman he sets the tone of the group by his objectivity, tolerance, courtesy and good humour. These might be said to be the basic essentials of any discussion leader. The authors hope to make clear in the following pages what these basic essentials mean in practice.

Not only does the teacher or chairman determine the tone of the discussion, but he also determines the type of discussion group. Two types might be broadly distinguished. The first, which is the type most frequently used, is the informational discussion group. In this, the teacher uses discussion as a participatory teaching technique to get information across and to assist in its evaluation. The second is the free, problem solving discussion group. The teacher here is not concerned to impart specific information. He hopes by his chairmanship to provide a situation in which problems can be rewardingly discussed. The difference in these two types of discussion, the first of which might be called directed discussion and the second non-directive discussion,[1] centres on the role the teacher imposes on himself, and the objective he has in mind.

Directed Discussion

This is a definite teaching technique. The teacher knows what points he wants the group to discuss and he knows also the conclusions he wishes the students to reach. He could, in fact, give a lecture on the subject, but he decides to use discussion because of the greater possibilities it offers for participation. He prepares his discussion with as much or more care as he would a lecture. He makes notes of the points he wants to emerge, and the discussion is later guided to them by his skilful chairmanship.

Suppose, to take a simple example, that the teacher in the previous chapter had planned to run a discussion on selection methods without giving a preliminary lecture. The points he wants to emerge are (1) the need for careful selection, (2) the need for careful job description, (3) the need for job specification, and (4) some ways of classifying information about the job and the individual so that they can be fairly accurately matched.

He might start by telling a story ... Two weeks after being appointed, a new worker, who has had some difficulty working his machine, approaches his supervisor and asks for his cards. He tells the supervisor he cannot stand the

---

[1] This is a technical term which means that the discussion leader intervenes to clarify and elucidate attitudes rather than to guide. Non-directed discussions would imply a discussion which has no aims or objectives.

noise in the shop because it gives him headaches. In any case, he says, he does not like being put away in the corner of the room. He likes to have people around him for company.

Having told his story the teacher says to the group 'This is a fairly common problem—what are your views about it? Could it have been avoided?' If there is a pause he looks at one member of the group and says 'Mr Peters, would you like to give us your views first?' In this way he encourages general discussion and, at a suitable point, says 'Well, we do seem to be agreed (if they are) that this is a case of poor selection. Perhaps, before we go on to discuss if and how this sort of thing can be avoided, we might pause a minute and assess how much money this particular example of poor selection cost the company. What factors should we take into account?' Further discussion takes place which the teacher sums up before going on to the next point. 'We ought to discuss now how this failure in selection could have been avoided.' Someone is almost certain to mention that the demands of the job were not accurately assessed. If no one does, the teacher might ask a general question, 'What do you think this particular job demands?' He could write the answers up, and each one could be discussed. From this discussion he might develop the idea of job study and job description.

Planning the Discussion

A trainer, who was running courses for foremen within his firm, gave the following somewhat over simplified account of his thoughts in preparing a discussion. He had already talked with key members of the firm and had a fair idea of the weak points in supervisory practice and the reasons for supervisors' failure. He had decided what he wanted to get over and what the group would find helpful and relevant. He began to plan his introductory session of an hour and a half, and his thoughts ran as follows:

PARTICIPATION METHODS

'The subject is the foreman's job. I want a way of analysing the foreman's job so that the later sessions can be related back to it. It must be simple so that the foremen find it of some use in thinking about the job. Training Within Industry has a breakdown of the supervisor's job into two "knowledge" headings and three "skill" headings. I could use that but the technical, organisation and man management breakdown might be more suitable for my purposes. This is the first session so I shall use the guided discussion method of presentation.

'Unguided discussion will come in later sessions with case studies and role playing. Because I am using guided discussion I shall have to plan out carefully how to tackle the three headings. And since this is the first session I shall have to give a small introductory talk so that the students know what the course is about.'

This over simplified recapitulation led to the following plan for the session and for the discussion.

GROUP MEETS

Introduction

See that they all know each other by name, by job and by department.
See that they all know my name.
See that they are all comfortable.
Say how long the session will be.
Say how long the course will last.
Say how important training is in management's eyes.
Say that they are not going to be lectured; that the intention of the course is to discuss supervisors' work, to get the ideas of all supervisors, to arrive at group conclusions about supervisory methods by examining the job and by pooling their experience as supervisors.
Ask how long each has been supervising. Add up the years and say something like 'We have—years of supervisory experience here so we should be able to get some pretty good insight into the job'.

ENDS AND MEANS OF MANAGEMENT EDUCATION

Introduce discussion subject
'Let us start straight away by considering the foreman's job. What does the foreman have to do?' Get answers from the group spontaneously, by probing, by questions.
Sum up. 'Getting production through people.'

Get activities grouped
'Now can we suggest any way of grouping these activities under a few headings?'
By hints, questions, etc, extract the three headings. If they do not come out then say 'Well, what do you think of this classification—Technical, Organisational, Man management?'
Get comments, asking if there is any activity that comes outside the three headings.

Let us look at them in turn
'What comes under the technical?' (Group discusses)
'What comes under the organisational?' (Group discusses)
'What comes under the man management?' (Group discusses)

Analysis
'We shall discuss all of these further as the course goes on, but could we discuss now what sort of knowledge and skill is required under each of these headings if a foreman is to do a competent job?'

Technical
'How much information, how much skill?' (Group discusses)

Organisational
'How much information, how much skill?' (Group discusses)

Man management
'How much information, how much skill?' (Group discusses)

Points to bring out
1 That there are gaps in knowledge and gaps in skill. The trainer should suggest that these will be filled during the course, and note the points so that the course can cover them.
2 That all parts of the foreman's job involve dealing with people—superiors, colleagues, juniors—but still people. The

PARTICIPATION METHODS

foreman's technical knowledge and skill, for instance, is used not for doing the productive job but for helping his workers to do it; he advises, trains, corrects faults, and so on.

'Since the foreman's job is that of dealing with people we shall naturally want to discuss people and how to manage them.'

'But if you are going to manage people you have to know how to manage yourself.' Group discusses. Examples—losing temper, arguments, and so on.

Sum up the argument so far—perhaps suggest the subject for the next meeting.

For some groups of foremen such an introductory session would be far too simple and might savour of talking down. For others this would be a perfectly acceptable approach and a good preparation for getting on to 'meatier' subjects. The next session could well start directly with the problem of training operatives—the use of the foreman's technical skill in conjunction with his man management skill. It might, for instance, start by one of the foremen being asked to demonstrate how to instruct an operative to do a certain task. Or it might start with a case study about a foreman who had let the technical aspect of his job blind him to its other equally or more important aspects.

It must be remembered that the plan in the example is an over simplified statement of the way the material could be arranged and presented. It shows one way a trainer might try to prepare a *guided* group discussion on the foreman's job. It is not the only way, nor necessarily the right way. The right way is the way which reaches its objectives effectively, that is, the way which involves the group in active participation, and makes them think about the subject along worthwhile lines.

In guided discussion the trainer knows what points he wants discussed, and he knows, too, the conclusions the group should reach. He plans a discussion which will cover the ground and emphasise the important points. He sums up at appropriate stages, and then directs discussion to the next point. In this way he makes sure that his students always know where he is going, and that the group is advancing with him. He is not trying to present facts from which his students may draw wrong or biased conclusions. He is hoping to lead them to the most efficient and effective conclusions possible, and he helps the students themselves to make available all the relevant facts which can be mustered.

Quite often the teacher will expect to be asked to give technical information in his role as a specialist. If he thinks this information is already available in the group, perhaps in one student who has so far not volunteered it, he will use this opportunity to encourage him to speak. If the information is not available he will, of course, supply it so that it can be used by the group.

He is not averse to people presenting contradictory views. He encourages all views, in fact, relying on group members to discover false facts and arguments and to correct interpretations which are made without adequate knowledge or experience.

The teacher must himself be assured that if people are given the opportunity to discuss freely and informally their own experiences and the information they each can contribute, they will arrive at moderate, well balanced conclusions. It is for this reason that the content of training has to be carefully thought out. It has to be able to withstand criticism, and to be in line with what the majority of reasonable people will come to decide if they take the trouble to think clearly and objectively. The discussion leader's job is to get his students to do just this.

Plans for a Session

One technical college teacher uses a tape recording to get material for discussion. His course for training interviewers begins with the theory which underlies interviewing, but

PARTICIPATION METHODS

soon moves to practical interviewing sessions. Students are asked to work out a job description for an imaginary but possible job and to decide on a job specification. This work is of course done by discussion groups so that all students are agreed on what is required. Each of them in turn then interviews a number of 'guinea pigs' who have completed an application form in the usual way. These 'guinea pigs', incidentally, are usually employees of the students' company. The trainer sits in on a number of these interviews and arranges for students who are not interviewing at the time to sit in as assessors on the interviews being carried out by their colleagues. Two or three of the interviews are recorded.

At the end of the afternoon the 'guinea pigs' are formed into a discussion group and discuss the way in which they were interviewed. The student interviewers are present at this discussion and gain valuable information about what it felt like to be at the 'other end'. When the 'guinea pigs' have gone the students discuss their suitability for the particular job, using the method of assessment that has already been taught. When they have agreed on an order of merit the teacher briefly comments on the interviews he heard and gets the assessors to do the same.

In the next session the recordings are played back to the group and are once more analysed by group discussion. These recordings, incidentally, are used again in the next interview course as a lively introduction to the problems and techniques of interviewing.

This way of handling instruction in interviewing might well be classified under a number of headings other than group discussion. It is an example of an imaginative and economical teaching method, for every scrap of information gained throughout the afternoon is made available. Everyone is kept busy, in turn interviewing, evaluating the interviews of others, and finally discussing the performance of all members of the group.

Another teacher makes a special point of linking the training and educational functions of discussion by recording the sessions in which his students discuss. The training function is fulfilled in the discussion itself, in which attention is focussed on the application of information learnt in the course. The students might discuss for instance the merits and demerits of different methods of job evaluation. The educational function is carried out when the teacher plays back the recording he has made. This time he directs attention to the way in which the discussion progressed, to the roles played by various members, and to the social skills, or lack of them, displayed. Students often find this method very helpful, for it gives them an all too rare opportunity of hearing themselves in action. They are able to be more objective towards the disembodied voices which few at first recognise as themselves, and are glad of constructive criticism aimed at increasing their effectiveness.

These kinds of discussion are possibly midway between strictly controlled directed discussion and the non-directive discussion. The subjects do not lend themselves to the neat breakdown that characterises the very tightly controlled discussion of Training Within Industry sessions.

The Chairman's Part

Tight control has its own problems and they can be very serious for the discussion leader. He must not be an authoritarian manipulator nor an omniscient mentor who condescendingly chivvies his pupils along. He should not sit impassively and sardonically by, watching his students discuss until one of them produces the answer he wants, nor say 'Yes—that's what I want to hear— that's getting nearer the mark'. Students quite naturally object to being made to perform like circus ponies. After a few preliminary turns under such a ringmaster they would almost certainly give up and refuse to budge. In many cases it is on these grounds

PARTICIPATION METHODS

that Training Within Industry sessions are failures. Students feel considerable resentment towards the trainer who uses discussion simply as a technique to impose his own views on them. Such a trainer has gone through the motions of being 'democratic' and giving up authority while in fact he remains autocratic and overpoweringly in command. It is only fair to add that this criticism seldom applies to the Training Within Industry trainers employed by the Ministry of Labour.

The teacher who performs the duties of a chairman or a group leader should be primarily a guide only. He should use phrases like 'Mr Allsop made an interesting point then; what do others think about it?' To clarify a statement he might say 'Am I interpreting you correctly, Mr Baker, if I say this..?', or 'Could you give me an example to indicate what you mean..?' To sum up, he might say 'Would it be a fair summary of the discussion if I said..?', or 'Are we all agreed that..?' If the group did not agree he should say something like 'Well, how would you like me to modify the statement?' and, later, with the modification applied, 'Will everyone be satisfied if I sum up as follows?'

In general, the group leader should avoid giving his own point of view. Where he wishes to do so, he should make it clear that it is his view as a member of the group and not as a figure of authority—'My own point of view, for what it is worth, is . . .' If one member seems to disagree with the rest he might say 'I think I am right in thinking that you are not satisfied on this point, Mr Collins; would you like to put your point of view again?' He might add later, 'Would anyone like to comment on Mr Collins' statement?' or 'Is there any way we can relate Mr Collins' view to the points some of the others have made?'

The chairman or teacher should act only with group sanction and should not make authoritative or personal statements on his own initiative. His statements as chairman are tentative, until they have been agreed as truly representative of the thinking of the group. The trainer thus carries out his integrating role by encouraging individual members of the group to feel responsibility for the work of the group.

Non-Directive Discussion[1]

This kind of discussion is very helpful in getting information from students about the difficulties they have and the problems they face. As such, of course, it can be used by a teacher or a trainer to discover what his students' needs are, so that he can shape his teaching accordingly. An example was given on page 50 of a teacher who conducted the first session of a course in this way.

A more difficult use of non-directive discussion is for problem solving. Once again the teacher's aim is to get students to discuss their difficulties freely and frankly. Instead of docketing the information about these problems, however, he attempts to get students to work through them. He encourages each member of the group to use himself and other members as sounding boards. In this way he hopes that they will acquire more insight into their problems and thus become able to handle them more objectively.

Unlike the guided discussion group, where the objectives are more or less determined beforehand, this sort of discussion can have no pre-determined end. The trainer will not know the problems the students will produce nor the lines of thought they will follow.

The Teacher's Role

The teacher or trainer might start the session by saying 'We have a couple of hours to discuss together some of the problems you find in your work. This is a confidential discussion and you can speak freely and frankly, for only by people

---

[1] See footnote on page 79.

saying what they really think and feel can we hope to find good answers. This is your session to discuss your problems. I am your chairman, but I am not going to suggest what you talk about. It is entirely for you to decide'.

Having thus given responsibility to the members of the group the trainer must leave it with them. Quite frequently there will be a pause before someone comes forward with a problem. If the trainer feels excessively uncomfortable during the silence, and starts suggesting problems he thinks the group *might* want to discuss, much of the potential value of the situation is lost. It will seem as if the trainer has taken over responsibility and is doing the planning and the guiding for the group. However, if he refuses to initiate discussion, group members will eventually begin to discuss those points which are relevant and important to them.

Sometimes the chairman will think that the problems are neither urgent nor sensible, and he may begin to feel impatient. He should remember that people do not easily discuss matters which may affect them deeply. His patience and success in dealing with a group which discusses trivial matters will give its members sufficient confidence and security to go on and discuss affairs of more importance.

The chairman must be wary of offering solutions or of neatly summarising the problems which are discussed. His job is to help group members to understand the problems in whatever terms they choose to use, and to get them to find suitable solutions. He should restrict himself to giving everyone a fair hearing, and should try to clarify what is being said. He does this by drawing attention to the implications of statements, and he will often use phrases like 'If I understand you, you are saying that . . .', or 'You feel that . . .', 'How do you think that will affect the production planning department?', or 'Now let us hear what this would mean to the purchasing department'. He further stimulates thought by questions like 'How do you suggest we solve this problem?', or 'Can anyone suggest any reasons why this difficulty occurs?'

By dealing with the group's 'practical' problems in this way the training session is directly linked with remedial action. Needless to say the problems discussed must be generally recognised by the group. A training session of this sort is probably not a suitable place to discuss one individual's problem unless it has some generality. The problems might be those which affect the relationship of one department with another. They might be problems of organisation or of relationships, or those arising from the execution of factory policy. It is extremely likely that many of these problems will cause, or will be caused by, poor personal relationships. A free and open examination of the situation in a well chaired discussion group may lead to an understanding and a solution of the difficulties. It should at least result in a more objective and helpful approach to them.

In one discussion group run in this non-directive way a junior manager was able to state the resentment and frustration he felt in his relations with his senior. He complained of his senior's rigid autocratic manner, his extreme sensitivity about his status and his resistance to new ideas. In the friendly and helpful atmosphere of the group the student began to see that his way of reacting to this manager, his persistence in pursuing his own very sensible but novel suggestions, and his emotional response to his failure in getting them accepted, were all forms of behaviour that threatened his senior and put him even more on the defensive. As a result of this insight he became more objective about his relationship with his boss, and more tolerant and understanding. His negative, rather hostile attitude was replaced by a constructive, much more co-operative accepting one. He said later that communication between himself and his senior had considerably improved and that the latter seemed much more flexible than before.

PARTICIPATION METHODS

In another discussion group of this kind, run this time by a firm's trainer, two foremen, who were notoriously antagonistic towards each other, were able to air their hostility and discuss the reasons for it. They came to see that the difficulty lay not within themselves so much as in the relationships they had with each other's departments. As each began to realise the problems the other faced they became much more tolerant. They saw the difficulties of the situation constructively and were able to work out a plan for overcoming them.

Not all sessions of undirected discussion result in such obvious improvements as these; nevertheless the leader will usually find that they go some way towards modifying hostility and reducing inflexibility. Almost invariably such discussions improve communication within the group itself. For these reasons it might well be the aim of a training officer in a firm to get groups of about eight managers or foremen together to discuss the problems they are perpetually finding in their jobs and in their day to day relationships with colleagues, managers and workers. While these discussions can be formally included in a training session they can equally well become part of the ordinary routine of a department, with, say, the departmental manager taking the chair and helping his foremen to clarify their problems. As communication within and between departments is improved, morale improves as well, for each foreman understands more fully what he and others have to do and how he and others fit in as members of a productive team.

Modifying Attitudes

Non-directive discussion is probably the most effective way of modifying attitudes. It often comes as a considerable surprise to people that any other view of a problem is possible than the one they have. As the problem or situation is discussed they become aware of the difference between a fact and the meaning that can be attached to it. They begin to see that facts can be interpreted differently, and that even the facts chosen for interpretation are partly dependent on the observer. They learn, in other words, to recognise their biases and prejudices. Instead of seeing a problem through distorting lenses they begin to see it clearly. Their assessment of the situation becomes more accurate and realistic, and action based on this assessment more truly directed towards solving the problem.

From the chairman, who has helped the group by this acceptance of their views and his patient exploration of the difference between fact and opinion, the group members learn something of the skill of analysis and something of the tolerance which goes with this attitude of non-judgment. Professor Tawney once said that one arrives at impartiality and objectivity not by discussing unimportant matters on which there can be no argument, but by frankly considering controversial issues. He added that members of a discussion group must be prepared to stand by 'the good old democratic principle of according to the revolting absurdities of our neighbours the same tolerance we accord to our own'. The teacher or training officer provides the situation in which this interchange can take place constructively.

Similarities of Method

In writing about directed and non-directive discussions it has been convenient to assume that they are entirely different techniques. This is not so, of course, for each merges into the other. The extremes have been described in order to emphasise their differences rather than their similarities. Some comment should be made on what they have in common.

One of the most important functions the chairman has to perform is to help group members to recognise the difference between fact and opinion. He can do this by questions.

PARTICIPATION METHODS

'Would you like to tell us the facts of the case before you give your interpretation, Mr Edgar?' 'Does anyone have any different views about these facts to put forward?' 'Could these facts be interpreted in any other way?'

Group members often turn to the teacher or chairman for support for their views, or to find out what his opinion is. The approach is sometimes by a direct question, but more often perhaps by an implied question. The chairman should usually avoid giving his opinion. He should turn the question back to the group, 'Perhaps we could hear what others in the group think about that'. Or he can refuse to recognise the implied question and simply restate the member's point. 'Your opinion then, Mr Darby, is that . . . .'

Another important function of the chairman is to clarify the emotion expressed. A student, perhaps a foreman, might generalise his experience of a manager by saying 'Departmental managers don't care what happens as long as you get production out'. Instead of dealing with the manifest content of this (or what the man says) the chairman might well deal with the latent content (or the feeling which lies behind the statement). He might say 'You feel, Mr Fox, you are left to do all the dirty jobs on your own, do you?' This reflective response helps Mr Fox to realise the implications of his remark, and holds it up to inspection by the remainder of the group. If the teacher's remark has been an accurate reflection of Mr Fox's comment, Mr Fox will be able to unburden himself further. In ventilating his hostility and having it understandingly accepted by the trainer and the group, Mr Fox himself will be greatly helped towards an objective understanding of it.

Apart from clarifying the latent content, the chairman must always be ready to clarify the manifest content, if it is stated in such a way as not to be clear to other members.

Finally, the chairman must remember that his job is to stimulate *group* discussion. If one member is very talkative he should not discourage him, but should move the discussion on by asking others for their opinions. If another member remains silent he should encourage him and seek a suitable opportunity to bring him in. 'Mr Howard, we have not heard your views on this point. What do you think about it?' Needless to say, the chairman should not insistently pursue the shy and retiring student, but he should try to get him to talk.

Summary

Any summary of the value of group discussion, particularly non-directive discussion, must take into account the following points.

It provides a situation in which people can participate and work co-operatively together exchanging information, knowledge and experience. It may develop a sense of belonging and common purpose which provides the atmosphere in which members feel secure enough to examine their ways of thinking and feeling. Bias and prejudice are revealed and gently sloughed off in the search for common understanding. Members of the group grow more self reliant, taking over responsibility for the group's activities and its direction from the leader or teacher, but using him to help solve its problems. Individual group members gain insight and learn objectivity and restraint. These claims suggest that group discussion is not only a most valuable and immediate aid in teaching, but that it has far reaching possibilities in education for responsible citizenship.

CHAPTER SIX

ROLE PLAYING

ROLE playing brings up to date the teaching method implied in the old maxim 'learning by doing'. But whereas the maxim refers to training on the job, role playing refers to training in the classroom where mistakes do not matter. It is a practical and participatory technique and it deserves a respected place in the teaching of the social skills of management and supervision.

For some time, role playing under another name, mock trials, has played an important part in the training of law students. More recently the technique has been used in hospitals to accustom nurses to the sight and sounds of injured patients. During the last war it was employed in the USA both as a selection and training device for special service men. In the United Kingdom trade unionists are being taught how to present a case in mock negotiations. Industry has used role playing for training foremen and salesmen particularly, but it has many possibilities for all kinds of industrial and commercial training.

Basically the technique is a very simple one. Two or more members of the class are given roles, or parts, to play. One, for instance, might be told to be a foreman and the other an operative in the foreman's department. The teacher then outlines a situation calling for action on the foreman's part and involving an interview with the workman. He might, for instance, tell the foreman that the workman has been coming in late for the past week, and that the foreman has now decided to bring the workman to his office to talk about it. He then goes on to say that the foreman is to imagine the workman has just knocked at his door and has been told to come in. The foreman now demonstrates how he would deal with the workman, and the workman shows how he would respond, each player developing his role as he thinks fit. The rest of the class are the audience, of course, and they sit and listen. After the scene the class discuss the way the interview was handled and the results the foreman obtained.

Problems in Role Playing and their Solution

In practice the technique is not as easy as it sounds. Charades are never really successful at a party until the guests feel relaxed and agreeably disposed towards each other. The teacher, without the benefit of some of the better known ways of making guests agreeable, has to create a friendly atmosphere in his class so that his students will not feel awkward and nervous when asked to play a part. If charades ended with the opposing team criticising the actors the party spirit might soon evaporate. The teacher however, has to ask the audience to discuss the role playing and, despite this, keep the group friendly. Moreover, he usually asks his students not to act as they would in a charade, but to play roles in the way they would play them in real life. Criticism, therefore, will appear to be directed not so much at imaginary behaviour but at real behaviour in an imaginary situation. The man who plays the foreman in the example given may tend to feel that his supervisory ability is being criticised. This is a very real danger, and the teacher must take special care to deal with it. If he does not, he will find that his students will show a not unnatural reluctance to submit themselves to public scrutiny and comment.

There are a number of ways of overcoming these difficulties. In the first place the teacher should not attempt role playing until his students have settled down into a friendly group. When he starts he should use simple problems, like the one given, which are well within the scope of the members. For the first role playing case he should choose as actors (or,

ROLE PLAYING

better, get to volunteer) the more confident and able of his students. He will find that he gets less embarrassed and artificial role playing if he asks students to play parts about which they have some first hand experience. After the scene he should direct discussion not so much at the quality of the interview as at what happened in it. He can direct attention away from the persons who played the parts and on to the parts which they played by saying something like this:

'Now we have just seen a foreman interview a workman. It was only a demonstration, of course, and it is not easy to give a demonstration in front of a class when the situation is "cold". In some ways it is very much easier to do an interview in real life, so we are not out to criticise the foreman for the way he handled the situation. What we want to do is to examine the interview and see how it works; see how the behaviour of one person affects the behaviour of another. We also want to see how far the foreman got the result he wanted. As a start, then, I am going to ask the foreman what his objectives were and how far he thinks he succeeded in reaching them. After this I would like the workman to give his view about the way he was interviewed and then we shall have some general discussion on it.'

The discussion can be conducted in any way that seems appropriate, although the following points should almost certainly be covered:

1 What was the object of the interview? What did the interviewer want to accomplish?
2 How did he set about it? How successful was he?
3 How did the interviewee react to the interviewer? What sort of remarks seemed to upset him, to be helpful to him, and so on?
4 In what other ways might it have been done? (This sort of question will probably encourage other students to volunteer to demonstrate the way in which they would have handled the situation.)

Another framework for discussion is provided by the questions:
1 What did the interviewer mean to say?
2 What did he actually say?
3 What did the interviewee think he said?
4 What did the interviewee think he meant?
5 What did the interviewer think the interviewee thought?
6 What did the interviewee actually think?

In discussing such questions the class will come to realise the effect of gestures, intonations and ill phrased remarks, and they will learn how important it is to communicate not only facts but attitudes. They should begin to see that communication is not a one way process, but that it involves a sender and a receiver. If these two are not in tune then the message will not be clear, and its intention will be misinterpreted. Foremen or managers who play the 'worker' may also begin to understand why the 'worker' reacts as he does, for they will have experienced the situation from his point of view.

Variations in Role Playing

There are very many variations in the way role playing sessions can be conducted. The situation can be a very simple one, such as that described. After the scene has been briefly sketched by the teacher all he need do is to ask the 'foreman' and the 'workman' to carry on as they think fit. A number of similar situations with which a foreman might have to deal will spring readily to mind—the interview to encourage a worker, the reprimand interview, or the issuing of instructions. The following situation is typical of those which usually produce a lively discussion:

Mr Dark, a recently promoted assistant foreman, started a fortnight ago to work under Mr Miller, one of the older foremen. Mr Dark, who is thought to be a good chap got on the wrong side of Mr Miller, who thought he was treating the men

ROLE PLAYING

too softly. The works manager decided to transfer Mr Dark from Mr Miller's department to Mr Beaton's department. Mr Dark is coming to Mr Beaton's department today and will be knocking at Mr Beaton's office door in three minutes' time. One class member is asked to play Mr Beaton the foreman, and the other Mr Dark the new assistant foreman.

This situation, like the one before, is unscripted and the players develop the parts as they think they would themselves behave.

The parts can, however, be limited by the teacher. He can ask one of the class to play a 'foreman' in an arrogant or ill tempered way. He can give one of the 'characters' a written brief giving specific information about the part he is to play. He can emphasise particular information, saying, for example, that the 'workman' is to imagine that his wife is very sick, but that he is the kind of man who does not like to talk about such things. The man who will play the foreman is sent out of the room and does not know the workman's brief. The 'foreman' is then called in and asked to interview the 'workman' whose work has recently been very poor.

These examples have all stressed the interview as suitable material for role playing. Role playing is not limited to this, of course. Group problems, provided they are well devised, have an advantage over interview situations because more people are involved, and students tend, therefore, to be less self conscious.

One teacher finds this problem a very useful one:

Mr Watson is a departmental manager. Tom Richards, a senior operative who works in one of the sections of the department, has been regarded as the unofficial deputy to the foreman for a number of years. Whenever his section foreman has been absent he has taken charge, and he has performed the job adequately but no more. He applied for promotion three years ago but was not given it, and he has not applied since.

Mr Watson, feeling there was scope for a good young man

in the section, recently started an outstanding new employee called Eddie Frost. Frost is very intelligent, and has a good manner with him, and with Mr Watson's encouragement passed a selection procedure for promotion. Mr Watson then nominated him as the official deputy but did not tell Tom Richards, despite the many opportunities he had to do so.

Yesterday the foreman of the section was absent, and Frost stepped into his shoes. Today Mr Watson hears that the older men in the shop are very resentful. They are complaining that Tom Richards has been unfairly treated and that he should not have been replaced by a younger man who has only been with the firm three or four months. They have apparently said they are thinking of taking the matter up with their union. Mr Watson is disturbed because these men are amongst his most experienced and conscientious workers. When five of them ask if they can come and see him he agrees. He says he will see them at 11.30 am. It is now 11.20 am.

The teacher allocates the roles of Mr Watson and the five older workers. He should give Mr Watson a few minutes to think matters over before beginning the scene. If, as a result of this scene, Mr Watson wishes to interview Tom Richards and Eddie Frost, these roles will also have to be allocated. In all, therefore, eight students will have parts to play.

A number of interesting group role playing situations have been devised by N. R. F. Maier, and are reproduced in his book *Principles of Human Relations*.

Other Situations for Role Playing

Ready made role playing situations exist in practically all case study and filmstrip presentations. These almost always involve problems of human relationships. The case studies presented by the Case Study Writers' Circle (see pages 125, 141 and 183) usually end at a point where action has to be taken by someone. The Industrial Welfare Society's filmstrip series 'Human Problems at Work' outline problems and conclude by asking the audience such questions as 'If

ROLE PLAYING

you were Mr Andrews, what would *you* do?' It is often very rewarding to let the group first discuss the case study or filmstrip and later to suggest that they play out some of the roles. Almost invariably there are differences of opinion about what should be done. Most students tend to describe in general terms the action to be taken. 'Mr Andrews should call the foreman in and tell him that he thinks . . . , and should then see the worker and tell him . . .', or 'Mr Andrews should persuade the shop steward . . .' These are all suitable openings for the teacher. He can step in and say 'Fine, now would you like to give us a demonstration of that? Will you be Mr Andrews? Who will play the part of the foreman?' In this way students are asked to practice communicating, and learn that it is usually far easier to say what should be done than to do it effectively. By working out the problem in action students begin to learn how to act in the situation in addition to learning how to think about it.

Some teachers report unsatisfactory results from role playing. They say that students remain constantly embarrassed at being asked to act out a part. At some time or other this has probably been the experience of most teachers who have used the method. In the face of this evidence it would be both inaccurate and unwise to claim more for role playing than that it *can* be very successful in teaching social skills. In general it seems most successful when students are asked to play roles which they normally play in real life, or about which they have first hand experience. Management trainees who have had little experience of industry should not usually be asked to play the part of a foreman. If they are given such a role, they often act in the way they think foremen behave, and they do no more than reproduce music hall stereotypes which may entertain, but which are so far from real life that they are useless for teaching purposes. Management trainees should be asked to play roles as management trainees or junior managers. Foremen can usually be asked to play roles as workmen, shop stewards or managers, in addition to those of foremen, because they have had sufficient experience to model their behaviour on real life. If these precautions are taken, and if the group is friendly, role playing can be both realistic and instructive.

Plays and Playlets

A variation on role playing is to use a fully scripted brief, or play or playlet. These provide, incidentally, a good introduction to the kind of role playing already discussed. Students gain confidence in appearing in front of the group and they feel less embarrassment in reading a part than in extempore performance. Here is an example of a playlet used by one management teacher.

'IT'S THE MANAGEMENT'

A Playlet in One Scene

Characters

JIM FERGUSON	An operator
BILL GAGE	A chargehand
MR WYATT	An inspector
SCENE	The foreman's office
TIME	The present

SCENE ONE The foreman's office

On one side of the table sits *BILL GAGE,* the chargehand. On the other side sits *JIM FERGUSON,* an operator. On the table lie papers, drawings, and three holding-down bolts.

BILL Well, Jim, what did he say to you?
JIM   Oh! He cursed me up and down properly. Said I was a slacker and wasn't keen on my work, and all that.
BILL But why the hell didn't you say in the first place why you wanted the afternoon off? To go and pretend you're ill, and just shoot off after the dinner hour is

ROLE PLAYING

JIM damn silly! You might have guessed you'd have been found out!

JIM But I had to get away that afternoon, Bill. If I hadn't, I'd have missed that house altogether. For the last three months I've been walking round and round trying to get a place for me and the missus, and I couldn't afford to lose the chance.

BILL But you only had to say what you wanted it for. You'd have got leave.

JIM Would I! I know what they'd have said! 'Oh, it's very difficult just now, the job you're on must be finished tonight...'—all that sort of stuff. And then I'd have to wait for another three months before the next chance came along.

BILL Oh, rubbish, Jim. You know as well as I do that you could have got special permission if only they'd known about the house. I heard them speaking about it yesterday, and your name cropped up. I heard them say if only you'd asked permission in the ordinary way, the whole thing would have been OK. Anyway this job of yours that you did, yesterday, is what I really want to see you about.

JIM I must say I didn't feel much like work yesterday after all that cursing. What's the matter with the job, anyway?

BILL The matter is that I've had to scrap these holding-down bolts. They won't do, Jim. They just won't do! I'm afraid there's going to be trouble over this. It's an important job.

JIM Well, that's not my fault. That's the blasted fixture!

BILL How d'you make that out?

JIM Why, the fixture for the final boring has always been faulty.

BILL If it's always been faulty, why the blazes haven't you said so? What's the good of turning out stuff like this, which is just waste of time!

JIM Here! Wait a minute, Bill! I have told you about the fixture.

BILL Told *me* about it? You certainly have not!

JIM I tell you I did!
BILL When?
JIM Last week, of course; I told you last Friday. And I told you about it the week before, too.
BILL Oh, no, you didn't. Last Friday you said you thought the fixture wanted re-bushing. I remember that very well, and I remember looking it over at the time. It didn't need re-bushing, as a matter of fact. But you didn't tell me anything else about it. If you had, I'd have done something about it, damn quick!
JIM (with irritation) Oh, I don't know. I thought I told you about it.
BILL Look here, Jim, something's biting you. It has been for days. Now, what's the bother? Was it being on the carpet for taking that half day, or what?
JIM Oh, I suppose so. I dunno really what it was. I just feel bloody well fed up!
BILL Then for God's sake forget about the blasted half day! This rotten stuff you're turning out is much more serious.
JIM But look here, Bill. Why didn't the inspector stop me on the job? He ought to have known if there was anything wrong. It's his job to know, isn't it?

(*the door opens and* MR WYATT *enters*)

BILL Oh, Mr Wyatt. I've just been telling Jim about these bolts being no use. I've had to scrap the lot.

(*The inspector comes to table.*)

WYATT Yes. The first ones were all right, but it looks to me as though the lathe needs a thorough overhaul.
BILL It is a bit old, certainly.
WYATT Half the plant in the whole ruddy place wants chucking out, in my opinion!
JIM Hear, hear!
BILL Shut up, Jim! What the hell do you know about it, anyway?
JIM All right, all right, I'm only agreeing with Mr Wyatt. The trouble is, the ruddy management doesn't know its job.

BILL   As a matter of fact, I do think that fixture's badly designed.
WYATT Yes. If the drawing office had to use their own fixtures they'd soon learn how rottenly designed they are.
JIM   Ah, that's it, Mr Wyatt, that's it. If they had to use them—that would teach them something. It's all the fault of the management, really.
WYATT D'you remember, Bill, when old Smithy was here as works manager? He was a wizard for fixtures.
BILL   That's right. He wouldn't let the drawing office go one inch from the design laid down. Not a flippin' inch.
JIM   Good old Smithy.
BILL   Things aren't the same, now.
WYATT I'd say they're not. What was that fellow's name who was always going round with Smithy? ... Dicks? ... Dickson ... some name like that. He left the same time as Smithy. He was a good chap, too.
BILL   Things were different, then, Mr Wyatt. Seemed smoother, somehow ... if you know what I mean?
JIM   If you want my opinion ...
WYATT I don't think we do!
JIM   All right, all right! I was only going to say that if you want my opinion ... the whole ruddy place has gone to the flippin' dogs!

BLACKOUT

After this playlet has been read and acted it can form the basis of a discussion in the same way as might an unscripted role playing scene. It will be obvious that this particular example involves a good deal more than simply a discussion of the social skill of the characters.

Committee Work

In all the examples so far given the emphasis has been on

teaching social skills, but role playing can be used for developing other skills as well. In Chapter Ten, for example, it will be seen how a group was formed into a board of directors in order to solve policy problems described in a case study. A group of students can also be formed into a committee and asked to discuss a practical management problem. They might be told, for instance, to imagine themselves as a sub-committee of a larger committee. They have to make recommendations about introducing a merit rating scheme, or about a projected move to a new factory, or about a work's outing. They will need some information before they can profitably discuss such matters and the teacher will have to provide a brief. In some cases, such as the work's outing or the new factory project, this brief might run to two or three pages.

Here, for instance, is a brief used by one training officer:

The company, of which you are a member, manufactures sweets, and has a factory at Portsmouth and its head office in London. At head office 200 people are employed, 120 of them women. At the factory in Portsmouth, 1,200 workers are employed. The managing director of the company has just returned from his first conference on human relations and is very keen on the idea of getting all the office personnel to see over the factory since he believes this will increase their interest, and improve the already satisfactory relationships at head office. He has asked the committee of departmental managers at head office to discuss this idea and to make a report to him. He wants to know, firstly, whether they think it is a good idea or not, and, secondly, if they agree with it, how it will be best carried out.

This is a simple brief for a quite complicated problem. Apart from the general principle involved in the idea of a visit there are a number of administrative points which require to be settled. Will everyone be sent, or volunteers only? How will the office be run? How will the visitors travel—by coach or by train? What about food? Will they go in office time or on a Saturday? Will they be asked to pay anything or not? What will it cost? How will they be shown round?

As a second example, here is a somewhat more detailed brief of a project to set up a new factory. It involves a choice between two sites. An imaginary map of the area showing roads and railways provides more talking points and adds to the interest value of the brief.

ONCLEY ENGINEERING COMPANY[1]

Our company, which was established in 1911, manufactures light engineering components and assemblies (eg, carburettors, oil cleaning units, car heaters, windscreen wipers, de-icers, fuel injector units, etc) for the motor and aero industries. Our head office and factory are in East London on the site where the founder of the company had his original workshop. There we employ approximately 4,000 in the factory (1,000 men and 3,000 women) on two shifts, with about 250 clerical and management staff. We have no other factories in the UK but at the end of the war we established a small one on the continent which, like the parent factory, is working to capacity. During the war we evacuated our head office to Patton, a country estate, and there set up a dispersal factory; this has since been maintained on a much smaller scale purely as a research station.

During the last year or so we have been faced with a steadily increased demand for our products both at home and overseas, and now have full order books for at least two years ahead. We have tried to meet our commitments by working overtime and operating two shifts, but these moves have not been popular, nor have they enabled us to maintain our delivery schedules. If we are to cope with the expected volume of new business it is urgently necessary to obtain increased output as soon as possible. It is not possible to expand our existing factory, nor have we been able to find sub-contractors who could help us on a temporary basis.

The board is therefore considering setting up a factory in South Wales, a Development Area where there is abundant

[1] This brief was prepared by P. G. H. Lewison.

labour, we are told, and where the government is anxious to establish new industries. Taryton, with a population of 120,000 has been suggested as a suitable centre, since it has good rail communication with London, Bristol and the Midlands where our main customers are situated. It is only fifteen miles by road or rail from Carport, where there are good shipping facilities.

At Taryton we have the choice of Site A, a twenty year old two storey factory building in good repair and with ample space, which is situated near the town centre. This we could rent for 21 years at £9,750 pa or for a longer period up to 99 years at £6,300 pa. The terms of that lease would be the usual rack rent lease terms, whereby we would be responsible for rates, taxes and internal repairs, while the landlord would pay insurance on the building and the cost of external maintenance. Its rateable value is £5,750 and local rates are 21s 6d in the £. The conversion to our requirements would take six months to complete and cost approximately £100,000.

Alternatively, we have been offered Site B which is twenty minutes' bus ride (between five and six miles) from the town centre, and which we could buy in order to build a new factory. The total cost of the building (including the site) would be £500,000 and it would be completed within nine to twelve months. Its rateable value is likely to be £8,500 and rates are the same as in Taryton.

Our financial state is such that we anticipate no difficulty in being able to raise the necessary bank loans for either project at the usual charge of one per cent over the current bank rate. At the same time, our financial director is known to be conservatively minded and does not view with favour any expenditure beyond the bare minimum. Our chairman, who inherited the position from his father, the founder, spends much of his time abroad, being mainly interested in possible overseas developments, particularly in those countries where big game abounds. The expansion of the business at home has been entirely due to our go ahead general manager, John Edwardson, who will almost certainly succeed the present managing director when the latter retires at the end of the year.

Other factors to consider are as follows:

ROLE PLAYING

1 We understand that transport in Taryton is overcrowded, and that housing anywhere is likely to be difficult, though we have not yet made full enquiries on either point.
2 The target labour force for the new factory is 500 men and 1,500 women, excluding supervisory and office staff. Of the men not more than ten per cent need to be fully skilled tradesmen. Experience in London has taught us that it takes an untrained operative approximately three to six months to reach normal efficiency.
3 In the main, our work is light engineering on mass production lines. Apart from the fact that some of the work is extremely dirty, there are no special health hazards.
4 Owing to past economic depression and other causes, there is a strong local tradition of unhappy industrial relations including some suspicion of 'foreigners'. Most of the labour we are likely to recruit will probably be strong trade unionists.
5 When 'Operation Taryton' was first discussed, one or two members of the board, impressed by the success of wartime evacuation to Patton, raised the question of transferring the whole works from London to Taryton. But the question was left for consideration by the sub-committee of which you are a member, which has been appointed to decide between Sites A and B.

The committee might be given an hour to reach a decision on the above problem. At a subsequent session a further committee might be set up to consider the following problem.

RECRUITMENT AND TRAINING SUB-COMMITTEE

Now that the site committee's recommendation has been accepted, the board feels that the next step is to make arrangements for the recruitment and training of the necessary labour and staff for the new factory, particularly in view of possible difficulties to be anticipated in local industrial relations. Your sub-committee has therefore been appointed to examine the whole question. Among other factors you will probably need to consider, and on which the board will certainly be interested to have your views, are the following:

(a) Methods of counteracting the defensive attitude of local unions.
(b) Suggestions for breaking down local suspicions of us as 'foreigners'.
(c) Hours and conditions of service for office and workpeople.
(d) Rate of salary and pay—to be related to local conditions or those prevailing in parent factory and office?
(e) Method and rate of recruitment—from Taryton or London? When to start—before, during or after completion of factory?
(f) Method of training, at London or Taryton?
(g) Supervisors from London or Taryton?
(h) What, if anything, should be done about reported local housing difficulties?

The training officer who uses these problems in a course for management trainees splits his class, which usually consists of twenty students, into two groups, corresponding to two committees. The committee dealing with the problem sits out in front on three sides of a large table, and the remainder of the class become the audience. The committee handles its problem as it thinks fit, and when the committee has reached its decisions—it is allowed one hour only—the audience is given the opportunity to ask questions and make comments. After this the trainer makes his comments, and another outside observer adds his own.

The Trainer's Part

The outside observer, who is a member of the personnel department, tends to restrict his comments to the matter discussed. He criticises the decisions the committee reached, puts forward alternative suggestions and points out some of the difficulties and problems the committee may have overlooked.

The training officer deals more with the manner in which the committee worked. He keeps an account of all the contributions made, and is able to say how many times each committee member has spoken. He discusses the way members put forward their suggestions, and gives verbatim examples of socially skilled and socially unskilled presentation. For instance, some members may be particularly destructive and have little to offer constructively. He draws attention to the effect which certain remarks have, pointing out that the member who says 'What you seem to have overlooked is ...', or 'That's a most superficial argument' is likely to cause resentment and hostility. Sometimes the group does not elect a chairman and its discussion wanders aimlessly. Sometimes the chairman is ineffective or shows lack of tact, or is too autocratic to carry his committee with him. Sometimes a member uses the chairman to push his own ideas, accepting the chair's rule when it suits him and going on strike when it does not. The trainer also points out how voting effectively silences a minority, but does not necessarily resolve a difference. When the difference is acute, he can usually find verbatim examples of its coming to the surface long after a vote was taken on the contested point.

In highlighting the manner of the committee's discussion, the trainer has to display considerable social skill, and his touch should be a light one. He nevertheless attempts to indicate the interplay of personalities so that the students become more aware of the problems of communication, and of the importance of building up an atmosphere in which good communication can take place. Committee work of this sort thus not only provides a situation in which students' information and knowledge can be actively employed, but it also gives them an opportunity of learning how to apply knowledge effectively and in co-operation with their fellows. Few lessons perhaps are so well worth learning.

PART II
THE CASE STUDY APPROACH TO MANAGEMENT EDUCATION

INTRODUCTION

DR BOWIE clearly recognised the potential value of the case study method. In 1930, he wrote[1] 'The typical function of the manager in action is the solving of problems and, therefore, there is much to be said for giving students actual practice in the art. It provides valuable training in the study and analysis of actual business situations and whether the result of the student's diagnosis be good or bad, and no doubt often enough it will be bad, the practice in selecting, relating and comparing the data involved, in arranging the factors in order of importance, just as the manager must do, is of prime importance, for only through actual doing can one learn to do . . .

'No knowledge is really secure to the individual unless he has in some measure discovered it for himself. Where the student is given a set of facts and is required to study them so as to be able to discuss them intelligently, his active reasoning faculties will be evoked. He will be better prepared to tackle actual business situations as they arise than if he merely listened to lectures or read the usual textbooks which consist largely of arbitrary statements.

'But if the case method teaches the student to examine and analyse, it also impels him to draw conclusions and to decide. The distinction is not unimportant. Some men have almost too keen an analytical mind; like Hamlet they overthink things and find it difficult to come down definitely on one side or the other. The methods and conditions of university teaching are too apt to encourage this type of ability at the expense of the executive type. Lectures and textbooks present the students with ready-made conclusions which they are expected to be able to justify. But in business the

---
[1] Bowie *Op cit*.

INTRODUCTION

process is reversed. The manager is presented with a miscellaneous and often incomplete array of facts from which he has rapidly to forge a judgment. The case method is the classroom's way of reproducing this.'

The following section describes the case study method in considerable detail, showing what a case study is, how it is written, and how it can be used most effectively. The case study has definite limitations and these are examined as carefully as its advantages. For example, it is clear to the authors that the case study method is more useful for students who have extensive experience in industry on which to base their contributions to the discussion than for those who are fresh from university. That is not to say, however, that cases are not also valuable for the inexperienced. They do, in fact, provide some insight into the real life industrial atmosphere and give essential training in the method of approach to problems which will inevitably be encountered in the course of the student's career.

The authors also recognise that teaching time is limited and inexperienced students frequently will not benefit as much from group discussion as from a straightforward presentation of facts. Student attitudes must similarly be taken into consideration. The evening student wants a solid take-home and he may feel cheated if he is not given information which will enable him to fill several pages of his notebook. Here, it is up to the teacher or training officer to try to alter the student's attitude and make the relative value of facts and techniques clear. Obviously there is not only room but a basic need for practical instruction, for imparting factual information in such tool subjects as purchasing, accounting, work study, statistics etc. The teacher and training officer in addition to conveying this 'know how' must also explain the 'know why', those principles of organisation, of higher control, of psychology, which have been distilled and abstracted from a long tradition of industrial experience.

However, the instructor's task will not be complete unless he makes his students aware of the importance of the human factor and equips them as far as possible with the skills for dealing with human relations problems, for here the 'know how' and the 'know why' merge to become the real life function of management.

The task is a difficult one as the readers will perceive as they work through the cases that follow. However, those who do so will experience what the student undergoes and will see precisely what the case study method sets out to achieve.

CHAPTER SEVEN
WHAT IS A CASE STUDY?

THERE is a wide divergence of opinion about the case study in management education. Some advance it as a completely new and self sufficient teaching system, a substitute for such traditional techniques as the lecture, question and answer examination, and outside reading. Others feel that it is no more than a teaching aid (or at most a teaching method) which can be used with greatest effect when combined with other methods of instruction. A few regard it as a spoonfeeding device and a sugar coated debasement of tested academic techniques.

However, it would be inappropriate to consider the relative merits of these differing points of view about case studies without first providing evidence.

What is a 'case study'? The name is a blanket term describing a selection of facts, either fictitious or drawn from real life, describing a technical or human relations situation, usually in an industrial or commercial setting. It is a segment of history or a piece of reporting, and like both history and journalism depends on selection and condensation for its effect. If history is the art of making a complex truth into a simple lie, so is the case study, even within its more circumscribed, episodic framework.[1]

Brief Illustrations

The simplest method of classifying cases is by length and

[1] The term 'case study' is generally associated with those cases involving human relations or technical problems which are analysed by means of group discussion. However, because specific examples can play a useful part in the teaching process, regardless of their length and complexity, the definition has been interpreted in its broadest sense.

use. At one end of the scale is the brief illustration. For example, an instructor might be discussing techniques of public relations and refer to the part played by 'Mr Cube' in the campaign to prevent nationalisation of the sugar industry. In the course of a lecture on the importance of the human relations factor in technical problems of productivity, the teacher might also call his students' attention to the famous experiment at the Western Electric Company's Hawthorne factory, where the late Professor Elton Mayo scientifically established a relationship between the social attitudes in the group and productivity. These simple examples serve to reinforce a general point by giving it practical relevance and by enabling the student to appreciate it in terms of his own frame of reference.

The 'Success Story'

The 'success story' and the 'dramatic statement' define the limits of the second category. The following extract from *Target,* the government's monthly bulletin on productivity, is typical of the 'success story':

A far reaching change in production methods at the Thornliebank (Renfrewshire) factory of the Brook Manufacturing Co (Northampton) Ltd, helped girl operatives to double their output of finished ladies dresses.

Making a dress was a one girl job, or at most a three girl operation, but Thornliebank manager, Mr D. V. Emmerton, considered output could be speeded up considerably if instead of each girl being asked to learn the complete routine of dressmaking, the manufacturing process was broken down into eight to ten operations. This was a variant of the synchro-flow methods recommended by the Working Parties in 1946.

Within a very short time of introducing this system of dressmaking by easy stages, six girls had increased their weekly output from eighty to 180 dresses. A team of five girls has, on an average, increased their weekly output of dresses from ninety to 180, a 100 per cent increase.

WHAT IS A CASE STUDY?

Under the new system each operation is studied separately before a particular piece rate is applied. On one particular operation a learner machinist, who had previously failed to earn on piece work the minimum rate of 8¼d per hour, increased her hourly earnings to 1s 4d. A more experienced girl increased her earnings from 11½d to 1s 7d per hour, while yet another girl raised her earnings from 1s 1d to 2s 4d per hour.

An interesting point about the system is that it follows on an experiment in assembly line manufacture of garments where it was found that practice did not coincide with theory. One girl on the bench might be off-colour, or one worker was possibly more adept than another, consequently there was no smooth follow-through. Under the new system allowance is made for these human factors. The normal number of workers in a team is five, and the normal number of operations is ten.

Each worker (employees number 100—all women) is allotted an average of two operations. Small stocks are allowed to accumulate between workers, and a girl making very rapid progress may, if necessary, take over one operation from a slower worker, with only a minimum amount of readjustment.

For each new style, fresh time and motion study had to be made. The girls' earnings are checked each morning and afternoon and under a tear off card system, which itemises the operative's number, the specific operations, and the number of the garment, the management is kept in constant touch with the work in progress.

The uses of this type of case are apparent. Fundamentally it is propaganda, proof that better methods mean higher output. The report could be used in a course on production methods as an example of the advantages of specialisation. However, it does not include sufficient details to be used as a source of technical information for a class in time and motion study, line production methods or incentive schemes. For example, the report says that 'the manufacturing process was broken down into eight or ten operations', but does not explain how it was done or what they were. Later, it points out 'On one particular operation a learner machinist, who had previously failed to earn on piece work the minimum rate of 8¼d per hour increased her hourly earnings to 1s 4d.' The reader can deduce that the scheme was successful, but is left with a number of unanswered questions. Why was the girl unable to earn her minimum rate on piece work? Was the job badly time studied or was the girl inefficient? How was she selected for the job? If she can earn so much on the new system, is the basis of payment at fault? and so on. Again the article refers to special allowances being made for the human factors which interfered with the successful application of the new system, without supplying the data essential for any useful analysis. However, as propaganda and as a starting point for discussion based on the students' own more detailed experience of similar problems, this type of case has its value.

The teacher can make similar use of the out of context dramatic statement. One teacher cited with great effect the comments of a department head about his division manager to illustrate the importance of following the established channels of communication and lines of authority. The department head had said 'I detest my boss. He is one of these impulsive, insecure, power hungry men that you find in business. He is anxious to get ahead and does not care whose face he tramples on in the process. When I do a job well he never thanks me. He takes it for granted. But if the higher ups like it he takes all the credit. When anything goes wrong, even if it is his fault for not giving complete and accurate information, I am the scapegoat. If I tell him that he did not let me have the full instructions he says that I should know by now what he meant. I can barely manage to put up with that, but what really outrages me is his habit of checking with my subordinates to see how they are getting on with the work I have assigned them to do. They must really think I am incompetent; it's no wonder they don't appear to have much respect for my authority. If he

WHAT IS A CASE STUDY?

rings one of them again without consulting me and asks them to speed up a job for him, I swear I'll chuck the job'.

Such a statement is not really adequate to give insight into the personalities and problems involved in that particular situation, but like the 'success story' it does provide a useful basis for discussing questions of organisation, authority and communications in terms of the students' experiences.

The Limited Objective Case

The term 'case study' is most generally associated with the next two categories: problem cases. *Anders Ltd*[1] (1953) is an excellent example of the limited objective case, in which a problem is described in brief, with enough facts to launch a discussion but with insufficient data for a lengthy analysis without considerable speculation about the background of the company concerned and the personalities involved.

This is the Anders case:

1   Tom Whitford, works manager of Anders Ltd, a small manufacturing company of 200 people, instructs the manufacturing foreman to have a day's run on Pine disinfectant, one of sixteen products. Whitford also tells West, foreman of the filling department. Pine disinfectant, after manufacture, is filled into G size bottles. The rate of filling is approximately 23,000 per day.
1.1 Vernon, manufacturing foreman, goes ahead with mixing the materials.
1.2 West, filling foreman, requisitions 23,000 G size bottles.
1.3 Andrews, stores foreman, on receipt of this requisition, telephones to report that there are only 3,000 G size bottles in stock.
2.1 Questioned about the situation, Andrews, stores foreman, says:
2.1.1 The month's quota of G size bottles was almost used up a week ago.

[1] Reproduced by kind permission of the author, Norman C. Rimmer.

CASE STUDY APPROACH TO MANAGEMENT EDUCATION

2.1.2 He doesn't know when more are expected.
2.1.3 As a normal routine, he always notifies the buyer of the stocks and a copy of this statement goes to the works manager.
2.2 Asked whether he does not feel that it is his duty to give special notice to the works manager when a particular stock gets to a point when it is below a 'day's run', he says
2.2.1 The works manager should ask the buyer.
2.2.2 The works manager already has the information.
2.2.3 He has never regarded anything as a danger point.
2.2.4 His job is to receive stores and issue them
3 In the face of the situation described, Andrews, stores foreman, rings the buyer urgently and reports the predicament of the manufacturing and filling departments.

The buyer chases the bottle suppliers, who agree to send later the same day 5,200 G size bottles.

Andrews reports this to the works manager with distinct satisfaction.

The case above describes in the briefest possible terms a stores problem, reflecting (in the author's words) 'ineffectiveness due to lack of top management co-ordination'. There are five people involved. All facts are numbered to assist the discussion. There is no history of the firm or details about personalities. From the expression 'with distinct satisfaction', which appears in the final sentence of the case, it might be possible to infer either that the stores foreman disliked the works manager or that he was quite complacent about the whole thing and did not understand what was required of him. However, enough information is provided to justify brief critical comments on the method of production planning, re-order points and the stock control system. Anything further must involve conjecture on the student's part, based on his own experience. Thus, limited objective cases provide a focal point for the brief analysis of a specific problem followed by discussion on more general lines.

WHAT IS A CASE STUDY?

The Industrial Welfare Society produces film strips of limited objective cases. One of them[1] describes a consultation problem, as follows:

Cast:

Mr Lane	Works manager
Harry Andrews	Stores foreman
Tom Long	Stores labourer
Bill Smart	Maintenance foreman
Managing director	
Works committee representative	

'The stores foreman, Harry Andrews, has two labourers using hand trucks in his department. One labourer, Tom Long, has been complaining about the state of his truck. When Andrews takes the matter up with the maintenance foreman, Bill Smart, he is told that to repair the old truck would cost almost as much as buying a new one. Bill suggests he tackles the works manager, Mr Lane, about a replacement.

Soon afterwards, Mr Lane comes into the stores and Andrews asks him about the truck. Mr Lane is very busy and suggests that the truck is all right—it's Long that's the trouble. Long overhears this and takes the matter up with his works committee representative.

The representative raises the matter at the next meeting and the managing director orders the works engineer to deal with it the next day.

The next day when Andrews tells Tom Long to move some material—Tom says that his truck has been taken away by the maintenance men for repair. Andrews sees the maintenance foreman immediately who says that he was told by the works engineer to collect the truck and repair it.

WHAT SHOULD HARRY ANDREWS DO?

The case includes a number of questions which the group is asked to answer in addition to considering:
(a) How could the situation have been avoided and what mistakes were made?

---

[1] Reproduced by the kind permission of the Industrial Welfare Society.

(b) How can the problem be solved?

The following questions are useful as a guide in discussion but the list is by no means comprehensive.

1 Why hadn't the maintenance department reported the truck beyond reasonable repair?
2 Should Mr Lane have taken more notice of Harry Andrews' request?
3 Should the works committee representative have accepted Tom Long's complaint without reference to the foreman?
4 Should the managing director have asked Mr Lane's opinion of the state of the truck at the meeting?
5 Should some arrangement have been in operation to inform Andrews of the committee's decision?
6 Should the maintenance foreman have told Andrews before taking the truck to be repaired?
7 Can Andrews rectify the mistakes made in any way and also restore his status in the department?

The real question is how many of these can be answered by more than a straightforward 'yes' or 'no' without adding facts and information which are not provided in the case. Thus, the student must speculate, and when he gives his answers they are based on many unspoken personal assumptions of which the rest of the group is unaware.

However, this type of case is extremely valuable for groups unfamiliar with group discussion and critical analysis, or for students lacking the educational background which often helps in the comprehension of a more complex and difficult problem. It also lends itself to role playing, as has been mentioned in the previous chapter. The interview situation, for example, can be role played, recorded and discussed on playback as a follow-up to the film strip. For these reasons many teachers have found the 'limited objective' case well suited to the foremanship level, at least in the early stages of a group's introduction to the case study method.

The foregoing examples, as well as playlets (an example of which, *It's the Management*, was given in the previous

WHAT IS A CASE STUDY?

chapter), require the student to draw on his own experience, and the success of the discussion depends on the quality of the contributions. The cases serve as a stimulus for discussion, most of the facts being supplied by the participants. They are not therefore much of an exercise in diagnosing a problem, collecting all the relevant facts and making a decision on the basis of the evidence. They provide an effective method of introducing a discussion on certain prescribed lines, based chiefly on an exchange of personal views and experience. Accepting this limitation, the teacher can make valuable use of these various cases.

The three remaining categories differ fundamentally from the others. They are complete within themselves. They provide an objective set of facts available to the entire group, instead of depending on a number of personal points of reference.

Human Relations and Technical Problem Cases

The human relations and technical problem cases are effective for teaching purposes at higher foremanship and middle management levels. They are based on the principle that each case must provide sufficient information to enable the student to analyse the situation, diagnose the problems, and see the general implications of his conclusions in relation to the particular case and its personalities. The following example, in which wilful damage to a dipping tank is the central thread in a highly complex situation, is a good example of this type of case study. (This case and those following should be read carefully and in their entirety.)

THE EDWARDS CASE[1]

A Problem of Reinstatement

Diptanks Limited is a medium sized manufacturing concern

---

[1] Prepared by the Case Study Writers' Circle and reproduced by the kind permission of the publishers, Newman Neame Ltd.

situated outside a large midlands city. The company was founded in 1948, with the full backing of a financial syndicate, by a group of production engineers experienced in the rubber industry. Factory No 1 manufactured job order lots of special purpose rubber shapes for industrial use; Factory No 2 mass produced hot water bottles.

George Barry, the production manager of Factory No 2, was in charge of 170 employees. They worked two twelve-hour shifts over a five day week, alternating fortnightly between day and night work.

Dipping was the main operation in this continuous manufacturing process. The water bottle shapes were given a thin coating of rubber by being dipped into tanks of rubber solution. One operative, known as a dipper, attended a number of these machines. The most important part of his job was controlling the temperature of the solution. If the temperature was too high, the rubber coating was too thin and contained bubbles. The tanks were therefore fitted with water jackets, a double wall through which water circulated, for cooling the solution. At lower temperature the solution became more viscous. It produced a thicker, more uniform coating on the frames, but it required greater care and attention from the operative.

Because each tank reacted in a slightly different manner, the dipper had to decide when the solution needed cooling. Every tank was fitted with a small hand valve which controlled the flow of the water into the jacket. The water passed through a drain pipe, emptying into a ditch outside the factory wall.

Malcolm Yates was the permanent night foreman; he had been promoted from the factory because of his leadership qualities. In one annual report on his foremen, Mr Barry, the production manager, described him as 'a big, strapping disciplinarian who is liked by the chaps and is accepted as being fair'. Mr Barry had only once had a disagreement with Yates—when he discovered that for two years Yates had been giving the men extra time for their tea break.

Trouble with Edwards

Yates had recently been having some trouble with one of his men, Jeff Edwards, who had failed to turn on the water when

WHAT IS A CASE STUDY?

the solution needed cooling. Edwards complained that the day shift man left the water on all the time, with the result that by the beginning of the night shift the solution was almost impossible to use. He said he had complained, with no result, and finally had been forced to take the valve handle off at night, so that the day man could not turn the water on again. Even that move had not proved successful, he admitted, because the day man found a substitute handle.

One night the inspector who checked the shapes as they came out of the tanks brought Yates a number of bottles which had been rejected because of bubbles in the rubber. He said that there had been an unusually large number of them during the previous week and they had all come from Jeff Edwards' tanks. Yates was very upset. He immediately checked Edwards' tanks and found that the taps were turned off. He bawled Edwards out and ordered him to open the valve at once. Although Edwards complied he did not seem very concerned about the whole matter.

Yates mentioned to Mr Barry that he was not getting much co-operation from Edwards. 'Well, what do you expect from an illiterate old soldier type like him?' Mr Barry asked. 'He has a grudge against the world and will go out of his way to dodge work.' He explained that Edwards would never have been given a job if labour had not been so scarce, and would not have been kept on if other men could have been found to replace him. He then recalled two episodes which he felt showed Edwards up in his true colours.

The first concerned the canteen dart board. The workers used a dart board in the canteen at break times and lunch periods, and by custom the chairs in front of the board were never used. When Edwards arrived, however, he proceeded to use the chairs. Despite complaints from his co-workers and several polite requests to move, he refused to budge and, finally, they had to move the dart board.

On another occasion it had proved necessary to cut overtime hours during a period of reconstruction in the factory. Edwards had demanded an interview and said that his wage must not be lowered because he had five children and that 'by law, the firm was responsible for them'.

Two nights after his talk with the production manager about Edwards, Yates was checking the water jackets of Edwards' tanks. When he found that the water was off, he turned it on in Edwards' presence and removed the handle to ensure that the water would stay on.

Edwards' Dismissal

Some time later that night, Edwards came up to Yates and told him that one of his tanks had burst. Yates found the floor covered with 250 gallons of highly inflammable treacle-like solution. One side of the tank had buckled where the water jacket had burst from too much pressure. He turned off the water at the nearest main in order to stop the flow and ordered Edwards and two others to clean up the mess, which they did for the rest of the shift while Yates watched them.

When the production manager arrived the next morning Yates told him what had happened. Mr Barry took a very serious view of the matter and immediately checked the tank. He found nothing to cause the buckling until he unscrewed a curved section of the drain pipe outside the factory wall and there he discovered a rag treated with rubber solution, which obviously caused the damage.

He sent for the three dippers just before they left the factory at nine o'clock in the morning. Yates was present at the interviews. He saw them one at a time, leaving Edwards until the last. The stories of the first two tallied completely. They said that they had not noticed anything unusual until the tank burst. They had seen Edwards go outside, but he often did so 'to get a breath of fresh air', as he put it. Edwards was then interviewed. In reply to Mr Barry's first question Edwards said that he got on 'quite well' with the other dippers. He was then asked if he could account for the burst tank. He said he had no idea how it happened.

Mr Barry then reached into his drawer and tossed the plug on to the desk. 'Have you ever seen this before?' he asked. Edwards did not bat an eyelid and said no. Mr Barry explained that it had been found in the exhaust pipe of the tank that had burst. 'It wasn't me,' Edwards said. 'If it had been I should have got rid of it.'

WHAT IS A CASE STUDY?

Mr Barry realised that the evidence, although convincing, was only circumstantial. He told Yates that he had decided to sack Edwards on the grounds of his previous failures to obey, rather than for what he was convinced was wilful damage to the dipping tank.

After Edwards had left, the production manager interviewed the two shop stewards and informed them of his action. This was a courtesy interview and was not part of any union agreement. He was told by the shop stewards that they were fully satisfied with the action taken, one of them saying, 'He has had far too many chances already'.

Edwards, however, did not pay his union dues to the collector in Factory No 2. He still paid them at another local factory where he had been employed two years before. On being dismissed he proceeded to his old firm, saw the union representative there and complained of unlawful dismissal. Officials of the central branch of the union were notified by telephone and they in turn contacted the Union Secretary at Diptanks, John Challiner.

Challiner was a young trade union member in No 1 Factory, who had recently been promoted to secretary. He had never been in Factory No 2. The Edwards case was the first serious problem in his new position. His only previous training had been on a Training Within Industry course, which he had attended three months before his appointment. The relationship between the shop stewards and the management had been quite friendly. About half the workers at Diptanks Limited were union members.

The Union Secretary Takes up the Case

On the afternoon of Edwards' dismissal Challiner saw the Production Manager and asked that Edwards be reinstated. He said that Edwards had reassured him that there was no proof that he had caused the damage to the tank and that it was a frame up. The production manager assured Challiner that a full investigation had been carried out and that, whilst there was no proof of Edwards' guilt in this instance, he was being dismissed for a number of matters, some of which had come to light as a result of the incident. He gave as an example the persistent turning off of the water.

The production manager suggested to Challiner that he investigate the matter himself in the factory and talk to the local shop stewards before starting to defend Edwards. Challiner said he would do so, but it was apparent by his attitude that he saw in this case the possibility of 'fighting the bosses' and thus showing what a keen new secretary the union had. When asked on what ground he objected to Edwards' dismissal he stated that it wasn't right for any man to have the power of life and death over workmen. When asked to clarify this statement he said the union's permission should be obtained before any man was dismissed and he proposed to see that this procedure was followed.

The whole of the incident and the interviews up to this stage were verbally reported to the general manager who agreed with the action being taken but said, 'I hope to God we're not going to have a fight with the unions'. He was assured by Mr Barry that there would be no fight because employees and shop stewards in Factory No 2 would support the dismissal of this man.

The following day Mr Barry received a message asking him to call at the general manager's office. When he arrived there he found the general manager, the works manager, Challiner and the secretary of the trade union's central branch, in conference. Edwards was outside the office. The general manager explained that the central branch secretary had called with reference to the dismissal of Edwards and was asking for the matter to be reconsidered. The secretary then informed Mr Barry, the production manager, that whilst he did not exactly disagree with the action that had been taken, he must point out that no witnesses had been produced to say that Edwards put the plug in the pipe. The production manager again indicated that it had been made very clear that Edwards had not been dismissed for that particular offence. The company had decided to dispense with his services because he was generally unsuitable. On that very morning, he said, a factory maintenance man had reported that all the grease nipples were missing from the machines previously operated by Edwards. He added that the man had actually seen Edwards knocking these off with an iron bar, after he had bumped his elbow on the grease cup.

The secretary objected very strongly to this kind of statement which had only come to the production manager's attention

WHAT IS A CASE STUDY?

after Edwards had been dismissed. Mr Barry stated that he was only giving this as an illustration of Edwards' general unsuitability; many instances had been known previous to his dismissal, and many more had come to light from subsequent enquiries.

The secretary then asked Challiner to state his views. Challiner said that he felt that it was a simple case of victimisation and exploitation of the working man. After all, it was only hearsay evidence and Edwards' version of the story had just as much right to be believed as the production manager's. The general manager suggested that Edwards be asked to come in and present his own case. Edwards restated what had already been said by the trade union representatives on his behalf and requested another chance. The general manager then turned to Edwards and asked, 'Did you plug the drain pipe?' Edwards answered, 'No, I did not', and repeated the charge that he had been framed.

The general manager then turned to Mr Barry and said that it looked as if they would have to reinstate Edwards. Barry seemed very upset at this and pointed out that it would be very awkward for Edwards to come back and work under him after this incident. Edwards interrupted to say that he did not want to transfer to No 1 Factory, since he would have less opportunity to earn overtime pay and that he was not afraid of being victimised if he returned to his old job.

The general manager accepted this statement at its face value and told all present that he felt they had worked out a satisfactory solution from every point of view. He said that they would give Edwards another chance and because he showed the courage to return to his job without fear of recrimination, he would be allowed to do so.

QUESTIONS

THE EDWARDS CASE

Analysis of the situation

1 Do you agree with the general manager that he has worked out a satisfactory solution of the problem from every point of view?

2 What are your views about Mr Barry's reaction to the general manager's first statement that he had to reinstate Edwards?
3 At the final meeting between management and the local trade union authorities, what is your opinion of the case made:
   (a) by the union representatives?
   (b) by the management representatives?
4 What do you think of the way in which Mr Barry handled Challiner after the dismissal?
5 What do you think of the action taken by Mr Barry to determine the cause of damage to the dipping tank, after Yates had reported the incident to him? What do you think of:
   (a) the way he timed the meeting?
   (b) his arranging to see the other dippers first?
   (c) his keeping Yates in the room?
6 What picture does the case give of Yates' ability as a foreman?
7 What evidence in the case helps you to understand Jeff Edwards' personality?
8 What factors contribute to the state of discipline at Diptanks? Why did some of Edwards' inefficiencies come to light only after his dismissal?
9 What problems may arise when Edwards returns to Factory No 2?
10 What does this case tell you about the dismissal procedure at Diptanks?
11 What do you think of Challiner's work as local union secretary? What problems, if any, are raised for the union by
   (a) Challiner?
   (b) the shop stewards?
   (c) its branch secretary?

Unlike the limited objective cases, in order to answer these questions, the student must dig out the facts on his own initiative and decide which are relevant to the points at issue.

WHAT IS A CASE STUDY?

Action Questions

Regardless of the size or complexity of a case, a student is in effect role playing when he answers action questions beginning: 'If you were Mr So and so . . .'. There will almost inevitably be a difference of opinion no matter what action is proposed. However, the problem case contains the body of facts which is common knowledge to the group. When someone disagrees with a proposal and the attitude it represents he can produce evidence to support his argument. In limited objective cases it is a matter of one man's opinions against another's.

It is at this stage of the discussion that the case study method can have its greatest and most lasting effect on the individual.

This point can be seen more clearly in relation to the action questions of the Edwards case.

Action

1 If you had been the foreman what action would you have taken
   (a) when Edwards first complained?
   (b) when Edwards flaunted your authority after your talk with Mr Barry?
   (c) when the inspector reported the increase in rejects from Edwards' tanks?
   (d) when Edwards reported that the tank had burst?
2 If you had been Mr Barry, the production manager, what action would you have taken:
   (a) when Yates mentioned that he was not getting much co-operation from Edwards?
   (b) when Yates reported the bursting of the tank?
   (c) when dealing with the union and Challiner after interviewing Edwards?
3 What action should Mr Barry take, confronted as he is with the decision to reinstate Edwards?
4 If you had been the general manager, what action would you have taken:

(a) when Mr Barry reported the bursting of the tank and the subsequent interviews?
(b) when approached by the Secretary of the trade union's central branch?
(c) when told by Mr Barry that it would be very awkward for Edwards to come back to Factory No 2?

General Implications Questions

A man was walking with his wife one fine but windy day. He looked at her and said 'Surely you aren't cold. With the temperature where it is, the one sweater you are wearing should keep you warm.' 'My dear,' she said, 'that is an example of inductive reasoning and where human beings are concerned it is worse than useless. This is a case for deductive reasoning,' she continued. 'The proper reasoning is: I am wearing one sweater, I am cold. Therefore one sweater is not enough for me in this kind of weather.'

The general implications questions in a self contained problem case study operate on this same principle. They are intended to promote discussion of wider issues arising from the case as well as from the individual's experience. The Edwards Case questions are typical.

General Implications

1 What are some of the problems of the union's reinstatement of an operative who has been sacked by a foreman?
2 What are the requirements of an effective dismissal procedure? What part should the union play? Should the foreman be free to dismiss without consulting:
   (a) his manager?
   (b) his shop steward?
3 What effect does full employment have on a supervisor's relationship with his operatives?
4 What should be the responsibilities of a union secretary in a company? How can he best be trained to assume these responsibilities? What are the functions of the secretary in contrast to those of the shop stewards?

WHAT IS A CASE STUDY?

5 Does this case suggest any general problems in the physical separation of factories in the same organisation?
6 What problems are likely to arise when some workers in a factory habitually earn overtime pay? How can the difficulties be overcome?
7 What methods may be adopted in assigning workers to different shifts, if a company finds it desirable to operate on a twenty-four hour basis?
8 From the evidence presented in this case, how may technical problems reflect on human relations, and *vice versa?*

Technical Cases

A purely technical case is one describing a process, technique, procedure or system without introducing the human factor. Problems of finance and accounting, production techniques and processes, storage, stock control and office systems lend themselves to this type of treatment. They are of the greatest practical value, especially in courses on technical subjects, because they provide an opportunity for students to apply the data they have learned.

The two examples which follow illustrate the nature and scope of this type of case.

PRODUCTION PROCEDURE AT THE FACTORY OF ELECTRIC SWITCHGEAR CO LTD[1]

The Birmingham factory of the Electric Switchgear Co Ltd—manufacturers of worldwide repute—makes switchgear and control panels for all types of power application—from portable generating sets to power station and sub-station installations.

Each contract received is for specially arranged switches and control panels to suit the special requirements of individual installations.

The detailed specifications and production drawings for each contract are prepared by a drawing office attached to the

[1] Reproduced by the kind permission of the Department of Industrial Administration, Birmingham College of Technology.

contracts department at the head office of the company, which is in London.

Some of the parts specified are common to many different contracts—such as standard relays, resistances, nuts, bolts, screws, etc; these are termed 'stock' items.

There are many parts on each contract which are required only for that contract—these are termed 'special' parts.

Delivery promises are made by the contracts department in London in relation to the amount of time it is estimated the factory will need to supply the 'special' parts—it being assumed that 'stock' items will always be to hand off running orders or from finished stores.

The works manager divides his responsibilities as follows:

factory engineer	— plant and factory maintenance
works superintendent	— supervision of factory labour
planning engineer	— processes, jigs and tools, piece rates
chief inspector	— quality control
chief storekeeper	— supply, handling and custody of all factory materials
progress	— definition of production programme and ensuring its achievement

A cost accountant is attached to the factory but reports to the chief accountant who is at the head office of the company. The cost department is also responsible for the factory payroll and wages payment.

The factory, which employs 1,500 direct workers, is divided into the following departments:

light machine shop
heavy machine shop
fabrication shop — welding, cutting, sheet metal, sandblasting, painting, plating, etc
control panel assembly shop
switchgear assembly shop

WHAT IS A CASE STUDY?

The efficiency of each shop is measured on a budgetary system from the total value in sterling of shop orders completed each month.

Responsibility for initiating production on each contract rests with the progress office which operates under the personal supervision of the works manager.

In view of the many changes to specification which have to be countenanced after production has been put in hand, it is necessary for one individual to be fully conversant with the requirements and progress of each contract. This difficulty has been overcome by appointing a senior production man to control manufacture of a specified range of equipment. The progress office has six such men; each has a small group of clerical staff and progress chasers.

Routine control of stocks and issue of works orders for individual batches of work are carried out by a centralised stores control office under the chief storekeeper.

The stores control office acts under production programme instructions issued in writing by each sectional production man. Detailed shop orders are issued quoting required completion dates in conformity with these instructions.

The sequence of manufacturing operations and piece work prices are also quoted on each factory order from information supplied by the planning department.

All the orders for the 'special' parts on one contract are issued to the factory as soon as possible after contract details have been received from head office—this is one of the matters closely supervised by the works manager. 'Stock' items are controlled on a consumption basis.

Shop foremen arrange for work to be done as and when materials and new tools (if these are necessary) become available. They give priority to certain work at the request of the progress staff.

Shop foremen are given copies of all correspondence regarding production programme, for the achievement of which they are held jointly responsible with the progress office. The managing director of the company personally watches output achievement from figures supplied to him by the chief accountant for each department of the factory.

CASE STUDY APPROACH TO MANAGEMENT EDUCATION

NEW PLANT FOR EXTRUDED METALS LTD

Mr Jackson, the cost accountant of Extruded Metals Ltd, was recently faced with the necessity for making a decision concerning cost allocation. Since there was some difference of opinion between himself and the rest of the management upon the subject, he decided to obtain an unbiased ruling by writing to the secretary of the Association of Extruded Metal Manufacturers of which his firm was a member.

This was the letter to the association secretary:

Dear Sir,

The main equipment of our works comprises eleven extrusion presses. These were installed at varying dates between 1920 and 1939 and had an original cost of around £1,700 each. I might mention here that the value of these presses has been written down judiciously each year to cover depreciation, until at the present time they are represented in the books by only a nominal sum.

It was decided three years ago that it would be advantageous to replace three of our extrusion presses with one new, fully mechanised machine of modern design which, although costing some £42,000, would be much more economic in operation and have a far higher rate of output than the machines it replaced.

This new press was in due course ordered and is now due to be delivered in a month's time. Meanwhile work is proceeding on the removal of the old machine and the preparation of the bed for the new one.

The cost of taking out the old press and installing the new one will be considerable—over £2,500—which on its own is more than normal shop maintenance expenses for a whole year in the section in which the machine will operate.

I feel that this cost should be charged as part of normal maintenance overhead expenses, but others in the organisation, particularly the works manager, maintain that it should be set up as a capital charge in the books as part of the value of the new machine.

WHAT IS A CASE STUDY?

I shall be very grateful for any information with which you can furnish me regarding the correct way of dealing with this expenditure in the accounts.

Yours faithfully, GEORGE J. JACKSON

The association secretary did not reply with his own opinion but thought it preferable to contact several leading accountants in the industry upon the subject. In due course their comments were received and passed on to Mr Jackson who found, however, upon studying them that there was a considerable divergence of views between them. The five opinions submitted were as follows:

Accountant No 1

The cost of dismantling the old machine should not be included with the cost of installing the new machine, but should be provided for in the depreciation of the old press. In other words, depreciation is the difference between the original installed cost of the old machine and its final salvage value, so would include dismantling costs.

The expense incurred in installing the new machine, on the other hand, should be added to its cost to make up its original capital value in the books of the firm, since it can have no value until it is installed.

The line of distinction should be just as clear as though, in the one case, the old machine had been discarded and not replaced, and in the other case, the new machine was being installed as a new project and not a replacement.

Accountant No 2

In my opinion the proper method of handling the cost of taking out the old machine is to charge this expense against the machine's salvage value. If the expense exceeds the salvage return then the excess should be considered as an item of current expense along with the cost of installing the new machine.

Accountant No 3

The cost of removing a machine, or its replacement, as well as the cost of installing the new machine, should be included with the cost of the new machine. However, if the old machine is still retained for use, but in a different location, then the cost of its removal and re-installation should be charged to shop expense.

Accountant No 4

I do not believe it is good accounting practice to set up on your books the cost of dismantling or installing such a piece of large equipment.

These charges are purely items of expense and should, if unusually high, be charged as an exceptional expense direct to the profit and loss account, in order to avoid short term distortion of the shop expense account.

Accountant No 5

The cost of removing old machines, large or small, is not a proper addition to the cost of a new machine replacing the old one. Such cost is properly charged to shop expenses, as would be the cost of moving a machine from one location to another.

It is permissible, however, to reduce these removal charges against shop expenses by an amount representing the value of the foundation, etc, for the new installation, and this value can be included with other installation charges in the capital value of the new machine.

In the light of these comments from experts on costing matters, how would you advise Mr Jackson to deal with his problem?

A Combined Human Relations and Technical Case

However, the closest approximation to the real life situation is a case study which combines the human and technical elements. The case of Truckshops Limited is a good example, because while the case describes in detail the firm's personnel selection procedure and presents the application form used, the verbatim transcription of the interview inevitably throws light on both the interviewer and the candidate.

WHAT IS A CASE STUDY?

TRUCKSHOPS LIMITED[1]

As a result of an advertisement in a well-known and respected daily newspaper Truckshops Limited received 200 letters of application for the post of management trainee. Of these 200, the Directors rejected 120 as unsuitable. To the remaining 80 they sent off application forms along with the description of the job (shown on page 148). Only 46 candidates returned application forms, and of these 22 were invited to interview. J. H. Patterson (whose application form is on page 149), was one of these. He was interviewed on the 26th September 1952 by the Junior Director of Truckshops, Mr Matthews, who was responsible for the engaging of staff. A transcription of the interview forms the subject for this case study.

An interview

(I is the interviewer; C the candidate)

I   Good morning, Mr Patterson, my name is Matthews. Please sit down and help yourself to a cigarette.

C   Thank you, sir.

I   You're just out of the army, I see. You're on leave now are you?

C   Yes, sir. I was demobbed a fortnight ago and I have still got another fortnight to do.

I   Well, I think a good place to start is with your National Service. Would you like to run over what happened to you there?

C   Right, sir. Well, I was called up in September 1950, and after taking a Unit Selection Board went up for WOSB and passed that, and then went to OCTU.

I   Sorry to interrupt you, but could we go a bit slower? You went into the Gunners, didn't you? Did you choose that?

C   Yes, sir, I did.

I   Why was that?

C   Well, no reason really, I suppose, but the chaps at school

[1] Prepared by the Case Study Writers' Circle and reproduced by the kind permission of the publishers, Newman Neame Ltd.

were keen on the Gunners and I thought it was better than the Infantry or the Service Corps.
I Better?
C Well, it has got more status in a way—it's better socially.
I Right, we've got to your passing the WOSB. Was that the first time?
C No, actually, it wasn't. I got 'Fail Watch' the first time. They said I was a bit immature or something, but I could try again in three months' time.
I And that time you got through. What about OCTU? Did you enjoy that?
C Not really, I suppose, but then I don't think anyone does. It was better than the training unit and you were with a better set.
I In what way?
C Well they were all keen, and many of them were public school boys and so you had someone to talk to.
I Oh yes. You were commissioned, I see, in August 1951. What happened then?
C I was posted to an AA Regiment in Bessex. I didn't really want this because I don't think the AA is so good as Field Artillery. However, we couldn't choose. I put down for a posting to Austria, but it didn't make much difference to the army.
I Why did you want Austria particularly?
C It's supposed to be one of the best stations—bags of sport and lovely countryside, and I thought I might as well try and do some travelling at the Government's expense—see the world and all that.
I What is involved in your job in Bessex?
C Not much really. I am a troop subaltern, but you don't get nearly so much to do as in the Field Artillery. So much of it is automatic. There's a certain amount of man-management —looking after the men and sorting out their problems. Then you've got all the equipment and vehicles on charge.
I Do you like the job?
C It's all right, I suppose, but it's rather boring. There's too

WHAT IS A CASE STUDY?

much red tape and petty discipline in the army altogether, and while it would not be too bad if you had good sergeants, a lot of this sort of work falls on the officers.

I   You didn't feel that the sergeants were up to their jobs.

C   It's pretty general in the army, I think. In the old days it was different I'm told, but today many of the sergeants are very young and don't know much, and the old ones are more often than not just waiting for their pensions.

I   What about the men?

C   Most of them are National Service men, of course, so they didn't see much point in it. Mine weren't too bad, I suppose. You have to be pretty strict with them, and you can't expect them to show much initiative, but beyond that they were okay.

I   And what about the officers. Did you have a good set in the mess?

C   Well, the subalterns were mostly National Service men like myself so we got on all right together. Most of the captains and above were living out so we didn't see much of them socially, and then I used to go out visiting quite a bit because one or two of my school friends live around Panton and I used to go and see their people.

I   So a good deal of your spare time was spent away from the camp.

C   Oh yes. Of course, I played cricket for the regiment when I started there, but we didn't have much of a team so I joined a club in Bartlett, about 20 miles away, and used to go there at weekends. I have got an old car to do the journey and that is another thing that takes up a lot of time. I like tinkering with the engine and I have also built a new body for it since I have been at the camp.

I   That sounds a big job.

C   Well it isn't as big as all that. I had the idea of what I wanted and then I got the local garage man to cut the metal from old scrap I collected. It's fairly easy after that. The engine's much more interesting though. I've done some pretty considerable improvements to that. I do all my own maintenance.

I   What does that mean?

CASE STUDY APPROACH TO MANAGEMENT EDUCATION

C Greasing, and last week I fitted a new gasket. Then I've had some trouble with the wiring and I've done all that myself. I have had plenty of practice on this sort of thing at home because my father's got a car and he's very interested in working on it, and most evenings you will find us in the garage.

I I imagine the car's a pretty useful social asset at the camp.

C Well, I don't know about that. Mine's pretty often in bits. Anyhow, the other subalterns seem to prefer hanging around the mess or on the tennis courts, so we don't go out on pub crawls if that's what you mean.

I Right. Did you ever think of staying in the army?

C Funnily enough I did at first, but OCTU cured me of that, and since I've been commissioned I'm sure I'm right. There's no future in the army. You're pushed around a good deal and you can't use your own initiative. You're always on duty and you never know when you're going to be sent for and told to do something. Then when you get married you can't live where you want to, and at 45 you're as likely as not to be told that the army has no further use for you. By that time you're not fit for anything else. You will have learnt nothing except slack habits. The big trouble is that there is no keenness. Everyone is 'nine to fivish'. You can work as hard as you like and you never get on, and in your spare time you aren't paid enough to live in the ways officers should. The Regular Army is not worth much socially any more, I don't think, though I suppose we can't blame the Labour Government for that.

I You feel there are many things you can blame them for?

C No, I don't mean that exactly, but they do seem to be responsible for the levelling down that has gone on, and I can't help feeling that they've made an awful mess of things right from the start. Everything they have nationalised has had to be denationalised to make it work. Still, you can expect muddle from people not used to govern. I am not interested in politics actually, but my father is very bitter against the labourites and I suppose I have taken his views.

I What does your father do? What sort of engineer is he?

C He's a civil engineer in a large contracting firm.

WHAT IS A CASE STUDY?

I   Oh yes. Did he want you to go in for that?
C   Yes he did really, but I didn't do well enough at school and since I didn't stand a chance of a scholarship I didn't expect him to send me to a University.
I   Did he want to?
C   Yes. He said he thought it gave people a good start in life, but I'm not so sure myself. It's all right if you go to Oxford or Cambridge, but I wasn't very keen on going to a redbrick University. So I told him I would try the army and see if I liked that and, if not, try to get a job as a trainee when I left.
I   Are you the only one in the family, incidentally?
C   No. I've got one sister. She's 23. Works as a secretary in some clothing firm. We don't like the job there though, and my father is trying to persuade her to leave.
I   Why is that?
C   He doesn't like the people she works for primarily, but we want to move to Guildford which is a much better area and he thinks she ought not to live away from home. She's young for her age, you see, and then my mother's an invalid.
I   Oh, I'm sorry to hear that. What's the matter?
C   Some sort of nervous complaint which began in the war. She gets very worried about things. She didn't like me going into the army, as a matter of fact.
I   What does she think about your applying for this job?
C   Oh, that's okay. She leaves those sort of decisions to father and me. As long as the job leads somewhere and gets me into a good position she'll be happy.
I   Well, we've discussed the army a bit, will you tell me something about school. You left in July 1951. Did you do anything between then and call-up?
C   No. I had a holiday that's all, and helped look after my mother actually.
I   Now about school.
C   From the start?
I   Yes please.
C   I went to a private school near home in which I passed Common Entrance and went into St Kit's.
I   As a boarder?

CASE STUDY APPROACH TO MANAGEMENT EDUCATION

C No. It wasn't far to go because the school was evacuated. That's one of the reasons I went there really because mother wasn't keen for me to leave home.

I I see. Things went on straightforwardly for you after that.

C Yes. I took the School Certificate at 16 and got through okay.

I Almost 17 weren't you? Was that the usual age?

C No. I was a bit older than some because I didn't seem to get the hang of maths very well. I was okay on the arithmetic but algebra never seemed to make much sense. I think the teaching had something to do with it too.

I Anyway, you got through all right and managed a credit. Was that at the first attempt?

C No, it wasn't. I took it twice. Once again in December.

I Fine. Now you stayed on at school for a couple more years. What about the Higher Schools Certificate?

C Well, the exam system had changed by then to the G.C.E. I took chemistry and physics at the advance level and maths at the ordinary level. Unfortunately, I got physics only at the ordinary level.

I Yes, I see. Apart from work, what sort of things were you interested in?

C Games particularly, I suppose, but I didn't like football or cricket at school. I used to play tennis for the school and I did quite well at athletics, especially cross-country. In the winter I used to play a good deal of golf at our home club. My father managed to persuade the Headmaster to let me off the compulsory Saturday games provided I played golf. I still play quite a bit.

I I notice you became a house prefect but not a school prefect. Why was that?

C I don't know, but I suppose golf had something to do with it—that and my not too successful school work.

I You did pretty well in the CCF.

C Yes. I was one of the few who seemed to like it. If you were keen the corps officer naturally pushed you on.

I Summing up, would you say you enjoyed school?

C It's a difficult question to answer. I should say on balance that I did, but I wasn't sorry to leave.

WHAT IS A CASE STUDY?

I Yes. I wonder if you would like to fill out on these interests you have put down. We've discussed the car and golf. You aren't playing very much these days, I understand.

C No, not since I began National Service, but I hope to take it up later if there is a good club near where I am working.

I Yes, I see you put down reading on the form. What do you mean by that?

C I'm very keen on it, especially biographies and travel books.

I These are your favourites, are they? Done much recently?

C Not in the army, of course, you can't settle down to read properly there.

I And you like to get really immersed in a book?

C Oh yes.

I Can you remember any book you particularly liked?

C Ummmm. I can never remember names when I want them. I know, the 'Winged Dagger' by that commando chap who was sent a bomb.

I Oh yes. Well, Mr Patterson, I don't think there are any more questions I would like to ask you. Are there any you would like to ask me? You will have read the description of the job, but perhaps there are some points you are not clear about.

C Yes. At least there were when I was coming along in the train, but I can't remember exactly what they were now. The description you sent me makes things pretty plain actually. I don't think there are any questions I would like to ask you.

I Fine. If there are, you can always get in touch with me here. I shan't be able to give an answer today about this appointment, of course, because I have got some other candidates to see. However, I hope to be able to let you know in a fortnight's time. When would you want to start?

C Any time now, sir.

I Well, Mr Patterson, thank you very much for coming along. I will let you know the result in a fortnight. Good morning.

CASE STUDY APPROACH TO MANAGEMENT EDUCATION

A DESCRIPTION OF TRUCKSHOPS LTD
MAIN STREET, BIRMINGHAM

Truckshops is a retail grocery and provision business situated in Birmingham. It sells mainly to middle and working class customers and employs 160 workers, 100 of whom are women shop assistants. It has eight shops distributed in the suburbs, and only the Head Office and the Warehouse are at the address shown on this letter.

The directors of Truckshops have decided that the time is now ripe to take on two Management Trainees. These trainees will be given extensive training lasting about two years in the different branches of the Company's work. During this time they will be expected to learn the practical as well as the theoretical aspects of the business. They will serve on the counters as shop assistants, then in the offices as clerks, and later in the shops as supervisors and managers. They may also be required to travel around with the directors attending business meetings and conferences. At the end of the training the trainees will be given managerial positions in the fields in which they have shown most aptitude. Some of the jobs the directors have in mind are:

> General Manager of a set of four shops
> Transport Manager
> Manager of the Warehouse.

Hours in the retail trade are long—from 8.30 am to 6.00 pm with half day on Wednesday. Saturday is treated as a normal working day.

The training salary will be between £375 and £450 pa according to age. On appointment to manager this salary will be raised to about £650 pa. The directors are planning to expand the firm considerably in the next ten years and, depending on the efforts and ability of the successful applicants, an eventual salary of between £1200 and £1800 can be expected.

Candidates between the ages of 21 and 24, and physically fit, must have completed or be exempt from National Service.

WHAT IS A CASE STUDY?

APPLICATION FORM

Surname PATTERSON   *Christian names* John Henry
Address 21, Xenophon Road, ACTON
Date of birth 2nd July 1931
Father's occupation Engineer

Education

Name of school	No of boys	Leaving age	Highest form
St Luke's Private	50	11	Top form
St Kit's (Public school)	450	18	VIth

Examinations

Name of examination	Subjects taken and results	Age
School Cert.	Credits in English, French, Maths, Physics-and-Chemistry	16
G.C.E.	Chemistry 'A' level Physics, Maths 'O' level	18

Did you hold any positions of responsibility at school?
(Give details)
  I was a House Prefect and Sgt. in the C.C.F.

What games did you play at school? (Details of colours, etc)
  School colours for tennis and cross country running.
  Golf (privately).

What are your interests and hobbies now?
  Maintenance of cars, Golf, Reading

National Service (Give dates, ranks held, duties, etc)
  Called up in September 1950. Commissioned as 2nd Lieutenant in Royal Artillery. Served in L.A.A. Regiment in Bessex as Troop Officer. Demobilised in September 1952.

Business experience. None

If there is any additional information you would like to give please use this space

Referees (Give two or three names and positions held)
  J. Brown Esq M.A. Headmaster, St Kits
  Lt-Col Williams R.A. My O.C. during National Service

CASE STUDY APPROACH TO MANAGEMENT EDUCATION

QUESTIONS (TRUCKSHOPS LIMITED)

Analysis of the situation

1 What is the interviewer trying to find out in this interview? Is he successful?
2 What discrepancies are there, if any, between the information on the application form and the candidate's replies in the interview?
3 Which are the most effective questions? Why?
4 Which are the least effective questions? Why?
5 What do you think of the way the interviewer begins the interview? What do you think of the way he closes the interview?
6 Does the interview seem to flow easily from topic to topic? If so, how is this achieved? If not, why not?
7 From this interview, what estimate do you form of Mr Patterson's intelligence? What picture do you gain of the part he plays in a social situation? What aptitudes does he have? What are his interests?
8 What can be learned from the picture given in this interview of Mr Patterson's family background? Of his school career? Of his army record?
9 Does Mr Patterson show any consistent attitudes in describing different aspects of his experience?
10 Does the interview give any information about the attitudes of the interviewer? If so, how? If not, why not?

Action

1 Should Mr Matthews take on Mr Patterson for (a) the position advertised (b) another position? If (b), what other position might he offer him? On what grounds do you think Mr Matthews should accept or reject this applicant?
2 How should Mr Matthews inform Mr Patterson of his decision? What sort of a letter should he write? If he writes a letter of rejection, what reasons should he give, if any?
3 Should Mr Matthews have gained more information on any particular topic? If so, which topic, and what questions should he have asked?

WHAT IS A CASE STUDY?

4 If you had been in Mr Matthews' position, would you have called Mr Patterson for an interview on the basis of his application form?
5 Should any alterations be made in the application form in the light of this interview? If so, what?
6 Should any alteration be made to the selection procedure? If so, what, and why?

General Implications

1 What is the value of the interview in a selection procedure? Does it yield any information which cannot be obtained in other ways? What are the difficulties or disadvantages of an interview?
2 What general rules and principles of interviewing are demonstrated in this case?
3 Why is it useful to ask an applicant for a job about (a) his interests (b) his school career (c) any time he has spent in the services (d) his feelings about different groups he has worked with?
4 Should an interviewer make his own attitudes apparent to the applicant? If so, why? If not, why not?
5 What are the requirements of an application form?
6 Is a firm of the size of Truckshops justified in introducing a management training scheme of the sort described here? What are the advantages and disadvantages of such a scheme to a small company? What implications does a management training scheme have for other workers in an organisation like Truckshops? Can the disadvantages, if any, of such a scheme be overcome?
7 What selection procedures are suitable to a small firm attempting to fill the position of management trainee? Are the same procedures suitable for filling the positions of (a) shop assistant (b) clerk (c) shop manager? If not, what procedures would be suitable for filling these positions?

SUGGESTIONS FOR THE TEACHER

From the job description it should be possible to get the group to compile a job specification. The interview can then be investigated to see how far it covers the requirements of the job specification, and the candidate can be assessed to see how far he matches up to what is wanted.

To make the interview more lifelike it is suggested that two members of the group should sit in front of the desk, each reading one of the parts.

Descriptive Cases

The last type is not primarily a teaching case, although it contains material which is suited for longer term syndicate or project assignments as well as for background reading.

The study of the London docks[1] by R. P. Lynton and S. D. M. King is one example of a case which attempts, by describing the history, social background and everyday conditions of work in an industry, to explain the reasons for the high incidence of strikes among dockers.

The studies made by Scott and Lynton are in the same category.[2] Sir Charles Renold's survey of the development of joint consultation in his own firm[3] over three decades provides a wealth of material for studying the consultative process and many of the problems connected with it.

The exhaustive and scholarly study of the experiments in gaining sanction from the workers for the exercise of management authority at the Glacier Metal Company[4] poses enough basic questions to keep a class profitably occupied for at least a year.

Novels describing human relations problems in an industrial setting, such as Walter Allen's *Dead Man Over All,* Winston Clewes' *Men at Work,* Nigel Balchin's *Sundry Creditors,* and Cameron Hawley's *Executive Suite* also fall in this category.

---

[1] *The London Docks; a framework for study:* R. P. Lynton & S. D. M. King: BIM May 1950 (Duplicated).
[2] *Three Studies in Management:* Jerome F. Scott and R. P. Lynton Routledge and Kegan Paul, 1952.
[3] *Joint Consultation over Thirty Years: a case study:* Sir Charles G. Renold: London, Allen and Unwin, 1950.
[4] *Changing Culture of a Factory,* Elliott Jaques, Tavistock Publications, 1951.

WHAT IS A CASE STUDY?

How can the management teacher or training officer make the best use of this case material, which most closely approximates to the real life situation with its vast complexity, its entrenched traditions, its subtly conflicting personalities?

In the first place he can assign the books or selected parts of them for general background reading. He can then select specific episodes from the books, like the changeover from piece rates to flat rates in the Glacier Company's service department or the move of one entire division of the Renold works from Manchester to Cardiff as case studies for discussion. However, he must be aware that in each of these full length accounts the analysis of the problem is an essential part of the study. The problems, which are rarely described in great detail, are juxtaposed with their solutions. The comments of the class are therefore usually restricted to appraisal, rather than critical analysis.

These cases undoubtedly provide a rich source of material for general discussion of broad psychological, sociological and economic issues, but they do not provide the training officer or management teacher with an easy tool for sharpening his students' critical faculty or their capacity to collect and analyse the facts relevant to a specific problem.

Different Uses for Different Cases

It is possible to discern a pattern of sorts in the relationship between the length of the various kinds of case studies and their uses.

The brief illustration is suitable for any level of management and is an essential ingredient of the lecture method. It is as valuable in explaining principles of management and their practical application as it is in pointing out some of the problems in evolving a successful incentive scheme based on time and motion study. The only limit to the number used and the time devoted to them is imposed by the experience and enterprise of the teacher.

CASE STUDY APPROACH TO MANAGEMENT EDUCATION

The success story, personal statement and limited objective case are primarily intended to stimulate discussion. The first two can be considered elaborate examples to illustrate points in a lecture and therefore can be used as successfully with young students, inexperienced in industry, as with lower levels of management, for whom such examples will help to give the lecture a sense of realism and relevance. The limited objective case, however, depends for its effect to such an extent on the amount of information which the student can contribute to the discussion that it is suitable only for those whose experience falls into the same frame of reference as the case itself.

The longer problem cases are best for the middle and higher levels of management. In addition they can perform a useful function for the inexperienced student by providing him indirectly with considerable technical information about a number of specialised subjects in a wide variety of industries. This is one of the principles on which the Harvard Graduate School of Business Administration operates, since most of MBA degree students have come directly from university.

Proceeding with the rough correlation between complexity and students' level, one can conclude that the comprehensive studies and surveys which come closest to the real life situation are most effective for top management and university students.

However, it is the teacher's responsibility to decide which type of case will best suit the needs of the group. As Norman C. Rimmer has pointed out, the management teacher, like the golfer who varies his clubs to fit the situation, must choose his case on the basis of the attainments of the group, his relationship to the group, the requirements of the syllabus, his own ability to present the case and his intentions in doing so.

With the completion of this brief account of the various categories of case studies and their application, it is possible

WHAT IS A CASE STUDY?

to return to the problem of evaluation. How good are case studies really?

The Case for Case Studies

Those who have used the case study method successfully feel that it is the best answer produced so far to the students' problem of applying classroom theories to on-the-job practical difficulties.

The case study philosophy rejects the traditional views
(a) that there is value in abstracting the management skills and teaching them theoretically, and
(b) that management is scientific where it deals with human problems.

In other words, the case study enthusiasts feel that management is no more scientific than the Industrial Revolution was a revolution. Management is not an exact science in the same sense as mathematics, engineering and chemistry. Human beings are involved and their reactions do not follow any exact predictable pattern. Professor Erwin Schell of the Massachusetts Institute of Technology emphasised the implications of this point when he said 'A young man may hesitate to undertake responsibilities involving business administration after training in science unless he has received a proper induction into these less exact fields of endeavour during his formalised training. The business problem has the disadvantage of moving data, of the presence of important intangibles and of the competitive unknown, all of which tend to disturb the scientific mind, which has been trained only in the more precise sciences. We consider it our function to teach the student of scientific and technical background the possibilities of the scientific method as it applies in these less precise areas. We find that once the distinction is seen and its limitations understood, the distinguished student finds as great fascination in administration as in science'.

CASE STUDY APPROACH TO MANAGEMENT EDUCATION

The belief that management skills can be abstracted is the other myth which the supporters of the case study method think must be exploded before the teaching problem can be seen in its proper perspective. On both sides of the Atlantic it has become customary for highly successful executives to write text books on general management based on their experience. The generalities which are produced as the quintessence of thirty years or more in business have relevance, but only to the author, who sees the principles as a logical outgrowth of experience. The reader finds himself very much in the same position as a motorist just about to set out on a journey who asks his friends at tea for directions. The churches, turns, distances, etc, which they mention as landmarks (with directional gestures) all have meaning to them, but to the prospective traveller it is usually gibberish and only rarely helpful.

One American textbook (and a multitude of similar examples could be quoted from British works) lists the following 'operating fundamentals':

'1 the development of an adequate system;
2 the establishment of adequate records to implement the system and to use as a basis of control;
3 the laying down of proper operating rules and regulations within the established organisation in keeping with the established policies;
4 the exercise of effective leadership.'

One other fundamental might have been added: viz, that in each business in each industry, these objectives are reached in different ways. After reading a number of these books, a disgruntled student, when asked what he had learned, replied that he had finally worked out a suitable definition of management studies—'an elaborate pseudo-scientific amplification of the obvious'. Management deals with human beings, and teaching general principles only is not enough.

WHAT IS A CASE STUDY?

Nor is teaching efficiency expertise enough, as F. W. Taylor said fifty years ago.

Taylor knew, as did the management pioneers, that approach and attitude of mind are the important considerations; ability to recognise and to act on what Mary Parker Follett called the 'law of the situation'.

Most people agree that experience is by far the best teacher, and is the most effective way to learn. But can one learn best by absorbing the worst practices or even by learning a tiny segment of the best?

It is also generally agreed that the purposes of education for management can be deduced only from the practical requirements of the job. Like a doctor, the manager must be able to recognise symptoms of trouble; like a barrister, he must be able to extract all the relevant evidence. Finally, like any competent executive, he must be prepared to make a decision and, if required, act on what he has found.

In the opinion of the converted, the case study more than any other teaching method achieves these ends.

Although it is difficult to disprove the logic of this argument, there is no reason to conclude that the case study is faultless and should be the sole instrument of instruction.

Limitations of Case Studies

Case studies have a number of limitations which must be recognised before a balanced judgment about the value of the method can be made.

First, a teacher cannot hope to cover all the material in his course by using case studies alone. Not only are they very time consuming but they do not lend themselves to systematic and thorough coverage of technical information. In fact, some essential points will be completely missed in the cases used and others will be given an importance that is excessive in relation to the whole programme of study.

Secondly, and perhaps more important, skill in dealing with case studies is by no means a sure indication of skill in management.

Thirdly, no matter how detailed and comprehensive the information, a case cannot hope to impart the knowledge of a company's background and the personalities involved which a person in the real situation would have absorbed long before and taken for granted. In this sense the student is at a disadvantage, although, of course, in the case study learning-by-doing method, what he is doing is far less important than how he is doing it.

It has been claimed that prolonged exposure to case studies can develop too critical and negative an approach, a habit of looking for what is wrong, rather than instilling a more positive and constructive outlook. An allied complaint is that the method gives the student an exaggerated idea of his own importance. Because he has been dealing with case problems at the board or top management level he feels that he is frustrated, and that his managerial potential is not recognised when he returns to his job and is not immediately promoted. This view gave rise at one time in American business circles to the quip 'You can always tell a Harvard Business School graduate—but you can't tell him much!' Both of these criticisms appear to stem from the divorce in case study sessions of responsibility from the exercise of authority. A student can blithely recommend a course of corrective action in a problem situation without any real fear of the consequences.

There are also several technical limitations to case studies. Their success may depend to a surprising extent, especially in the early stages of training, on the ability of the teacher as a case study leader. An inept leader can reduce a case study session to an exercise in pointless prolixity.

WHAT IS A CASE STUDY?

The Balance Drawn

However, it should be pointed out that most of these criticisms could be levelled with at least as much justification at every other teaching method. The case study method has limitations as a substitute for real life experience, but it has some marked advantages as a teaching method.

No other method provides a closer approximation to the real life situation than the case study. There is the same pressure of time, incomplete data, conflicting personalities, complexity and inter-dependence of factors. Most students recognise this and respond to it, feeling that a case is practical work and is related to what they will encounter in their jobs.

Because group discussion is an essential part of the case study system, most students learn not only to analyse given material but also to reach a solution in collaboration with others, an exact parallel to the situation in business.

The case study gives students a broad view of business, and serves to remind them that any organisation is a group of inter-dependent parts, and to introduce them to a variety of systems and techniques in use in a wide range of industries.

Case study work can develop in students the speaking and writing skill needed to sell their ideas to colleagues and other levels of management.

At least when competently conducted, case discussions encourage a new approach to problems, whereby each situation is handled on its own merits, and irrelevant principles or 'standard' solutions are avoided.

Finally, the case study convinces students, as no other method can, of the crucial importance of the human factor in management, and case study sessions may give the more perceptive among them insight into their own attitudes as well.

CASE STUDY APPROACH TO MANAGEMENT EDUCATION

If, however, case studies succeeded only in teaching the inexperienced student that nine-tenths of management is not according to the textbook, but is illogical and emotional, and if they only developed some skill for coping with this paradox, they would still be too valuable not to include as one of the essential instruments of education.

CHAPTER EIGHT
WRITING A CASE STUDY

TRAINING officers and teachers who are tempted to experiment with case studies are often discouraged because they do not know where to get them or how to use them when they do.

Although there are now several organisations producing problem cases for teaching purposes, budget considerations in a training department or a technical college can on occasion rule out such expenditure. There are also instances where a case with a special industrial background may be wanted, although the particular setting of a case is incidental to its training function.

In these circumstances the best solution may well be for the instructor to write his own case, if he can find the time. Unfortunately it is usually easier to find the sources of information for the case than it is to find the time.

A case study of a case study in preparation may throw some light on the technique of preparing the case. The Edwards case, which was cited as an example of an effective problem case study, had its beginnings as a report writing assignment in a technical college class on the Nature of Management. The student had been asked to write a case from his own experience and then to make a report on it as if to higher management. In his report he was to include his recommendations for solving the problems he had set out in the case study.

The Original Version
This was the original version of the case, suitably disguised to prevent identity of the company or the individuals described in it.

CASE STUDY APPROACH TO MANAGEMENT EDUCATION

DAMAGE TO EQUIPMENT

In a certain department of a rubber factory each operative, named a 'dipper', works a number of dipping machines, operating each one in turn in a particular cycle. Each machine includes a large tank, the sides and bottom of which are 'water jacketed' ie there is a double wall with a space through which cooling water circulates. The tanks each contain about 200 gallons of rubber solution.

Certain atmospheric conditions affect the solution and products made whilst the solution is in this condition contain a high percentage of rejects. The cooling of the solution tends to minimise this consequence but unfortunately makes it more difficult to work with. The dippers have to take more care over the manufacturing process and for this reason one or two dippers do not like using the cooling water. It was common knowledge in the department that Jeff Edwards came in this category.

As the solution in each tank acts differently it is necessary that each dipper should be allowed to decide when the solution requires cooling. Each tank is therefore fitted with a small hand valve by which the dipper can control the flow of water into the jacket—the water leaving the tank through a pipe which passes through the outer wall of the factory (on to which the tank abuts) and discharges into a flume. The pipe is open ended and at floor level.

The dippers in this department work in two twelve hour shifts and Jeff Edwards' relief on the opposite shift was J. Jones.

For some days previous to the incident in question conditions had been bad and Jones (who was working the day shift) had had the water turned on at a particular tank, No B4, throughout each day, which meant that Edwards came in each night to cool solution—which caused a certain amount of grumbling on his part. When Jones came in each morning he found, though conditions were still bad, that the water was turned off at this machine.

Two or three days passed and then one morning Jones found that the valve handle at B4 was missing (the water being turned off); he procured another handle and continued to leave the water turned on. He removed the handle each night.

On recommencing his shift a few days later Jones found the stud on which the handle turned had been broken off with the water turned off. Later that day he reported the matter to the day foreman who called a fitter and had the valve opened with a special tool (which the fitter took away with him). To make sure that the valve had been correctly opened both foreman and fitter checked the end of the discharge pipe and found water to be flowing from same. This was immediately prior to the end of the day shift.

Edwards then came on night duty and at 3.00 am reported to his foreman, Malcolm Yates, that something was wrong with B4 tank. Yates found that the tank was completely buckled under internal pressure and the machine unworkable. He turned off the water at the nearest main valve and reported the whole matter on the following morning.

On being informed, Mr Barry, the production manager, examined the tank, had the water turned on and, on finding that it was not discharging, instructed fitters to probe the pipe at the discharge end. After half an hour's work and considerable difficulty, two plugs, made from cloth and cured rubber, were extracted from this pipe.

An enquiry was then held (at which the above facts were obtained), special regard being paid to the question of whether or not Jones, or any other employee, has reason to wish Edwards harm. As far as could be ascertained (and this was later agreed by Edwards) there was no one.

Other facts brought to light at the enquiry, whilst not directly relevant to the incident, tended to show the outlook of Edwards. After knocking his elbow on a grease cup on a dipping machine he had been seen to forcibly break off this equipment and throw it away. There were other similar incidents.

Mr Barry, the production manager, then sent for Edwards and asked for his account of the night's events. He made no denial of, nor attempt to account for, the previously missing handle and broken off stud, but with regard to the blocking of the pipe he stated that if he had have been responsible he would have removed the plugs after the tank ruptured; that he liked working with cool solution; that he couldn't have gone outside to block the pipe (it had been determined that he frequently went outside in the vicinity of the pipe 'for a breath of fresh air'); that no one had seen him do anything and it was unfair to blame him.

He was informed that whilst it was true that there was no direct evidence in this case, a number of other matters had come to light and the company therefore intended to terminate his engagement. He did not query what the other reasons were. He was given a week's wages in lieu of notice and discharged.

Whilst this is a fitting place to leave this history it did not end there—the dismissal was countermanded, Edwards reinstated and he is still working for the particular company in the same capacity.

The report read as follows:

To: The General Manager   Copies to: Chief Engineer
From: Production Manager   Personnel Officer

WILFUL DAMAGE TO DIPPING TANK NO 2 FACTORY

The solution dipping tanks in No 2 Factory have water jackets for cooling purposes, the water discharging through an open ended pipe into the flume outside the factory.

At 3.00 am this morning, November 7th, one of the tanks collapsed due to internal water pressure and the discharge pipe was found to have been blocked with a plug of rubber and cloth.

Whilst there is no direct evidence that the employee in charge of the machine, 797 J. Edwards, was responsible, for various reasons (outlined in the attached Confidential Personnel Report) he has been paid a week's wages in lieu of notice and dismissed. He had been in our employment two years.

There was no injury to any employee. The tank was not a pressure vessel within the regulations and the factory inspector has not been notified.

It is expected that the loss to the company will be £120 (for a new tank and fitting of same), and it is estimated that loss of turnover during the four days required for refitting will be in the region of £x.

WRITING A CASE STUDY

The following recommendations are made:
1 That the discharge ends of all cooling pipes be screened, to prevent either wilful or accidental blockage of same.
2 That water jackets be fitted with some form of safety device to prevent development of pressure.
3 That one extra solution dipping tank (Drawing No V724/8) be obtained and held as spare.

November 7th 1910. App: Confidential Personnel Report 39.

The teacher made these comments on the student's case and report:

Case Study

This has the makings of a very interesting case. The real problem of course is contained in the last sentence. Who countermanded the order? Why? What was the effect on his coworkers? How did the production manager react to having his authority undermined? I hope you can see that these are the facts which anyone would have to know before reaching the 'analysis' stage and most certainly before recommending corrective action.

Critical Report

I am afraid you have missed the whole point of the report. First, let us consider content. The recommendations you make represent a sizable expense and there is no real need for them. With the exception of this particular incident, the problem is unlikely to arise again. Your proposals should have dealt with the question of grievance machinery and dismissal procedure.

As far as the form is concerned you should have begun with a very brief statement of the gravity of the problem. Then you should have summarised your recommendations. This should have been followed by an amplification of the problem, an elaboration of the recommendations, and finally a resumé of the main arguments favouring your proposals.

This is not meant to suggest that the type of report you presented is valueless. For certain purposes, it is adequate. For a more general management policy problem the form suggested above is usually more suitable.

The First Draft and Final Alterations

The next stage was a three hour interview with the student, the production manager in the case. He described the background of the company and explained in great detail the sequence of events in the wilful damage to the dipping tank. The teacher took longhand notes of most of the information. He learned that the part played by Jones in the original version had been greatly exaggerated and that several other points had been inaccurately presented. On the basis of the additional information he prepared a first draft.

This version was then revised into its final form which appears in Chapter Seven. The first section was altered to increase the clarity of the background information. Unnecessary sentences such as ' "Night shift was not punishment", Barry explained, "He asked for it as a permanent assignment" ' were eliminated because they added nothing to the case.

In the *Trouble with Edwards* section an introductory paragraph beginning 'Yates had recently been having some trouble . . .' was inserted so that the specific incident about the water bottles rejected because of bubbles in the rubber would be seen in its proper perspective.

The first paragraph in the *Edwards' Dismissal* section which read as follows was omitted.

'Yates was in a difficult position. He realised that Edwards held the trump cards. He was not afraid of dismissal, since he could have his pick of many other jobs in the area. Secondly, although the dipping department operated on a group bonus based on the quantity of output, Edwards seemed indifferent to the attitude of his fellow workers, who were hostile to him because his rejects were costing them part of their bonus money. Nevertheless, Yates decided to report this incident and the previous one to the production manager but he did not tell Edwards of his intention to do so.'

WRITING A CASE STUDY

As can be seen, there was no real evidence for determining Yates' views on the matter and it would have appeared to be pure conjecture. Other minor changes were made in this section to tighten the narrative and reference to Barry's experience in Naval Intelligence were eliminated as unnecessary.

The final section was given the same editorial treatment. Since there was a statement in it that Edwards repeated a charge that he had been framed, it was necessary to insert a reference to a 'frame-up' in the second sentence of the section.

Several examples will help to explain the revisions which were made in the questions between the first and final drafts.

One question in the first version 'How effective was Mr Barry's handling of Challiner after the dismissal?' was felt to be too leading and was accordingly revised to read 'What do you think of the way in which Mr Barry handled Challiner after the dismissal?'. For the same reason the following question 'Who was to blame for the troubles in the relationship between Edwards and Yates?' was altered to 'What evidence in the case helps you to understand Jeff Edwards' personality?'.

Another question was changed because the original version seemed unsuitable for the *General Implications* section. 'Can any of the problems in this case be ascribed to the physical separation of the two factories?' was rephrased as follows: 'Does this case suggest any general problems in the physical separation of factories in the same organisation?'.

Another question in this section 'Can you see any significant connection between the technical aspect of temperature control in this case and the problem that developed?' was reworded for greater clarity to 'From the evidence presented in this case, what conclusion would you draw about the effect, if any, of technical problems on human relations, and *vice versa?*'.

CASE STUDY APPROACH TO MANAGEMENT EDUCATION

The teacher decided that it would be helpful to include a postcript on what happened after the end of the case. If he wanted to prolong the session he could introduce it as a basis for further discussion. Otherwise he could simply satisfy his students' curiosity about the aftermath of the episode, or if he preferred, make no use of it at all.

ADDITIONAL INFORMATION FOR THE CASE STUDY TEACHER

Mr Barry held his tongue with great effort after the general manager's decision to reinstate Edwards and decided that he would have to handle the situation with great care. He called together his night shift foremen and told them that regardless of provocation they were not to reprimand Edwards but merely to write down a detailed account of every misdemeanour. When they had sufficient evidence, he explained, they would then be in a position to give Edwards the sack without union interference.

The foremen reported to Mr Barry that every week Challiner arranged a meeting with Edwards to see if he were being victimised.

Six months later, Mr Barry came to work early one morning and noticed one of the workers behind a bush outside the factory reading a paper and smoking. It was Edwards. He sacked him on the spot. Edwards went to his shop stewards and complained, but they told him that they would take no action since he had 'only got what was coming to him'.

Some Pitfalls

There are certain pitfalls in the writing of a case which can best be described by examples. One teacher heard from a student about an aeroplane company which had a number of problems to deal with. The student said that labour turnover was high; there was no drawing office attached to the jig and tool department; there was too much responsibility and reliance on jig and tool operators; the line system was not used in departments producing details; there was no

WRITING A CASE STUDY

proper selection system or plan for training employees for higher grade jobs; finally, there was a lack of co-ordination of effort in the production departments.

The student was asked to supply the relevant details about these various problems and on the basis of this information, the teacher prepared the following case.

SAFETY AEROPLANE COMPANY

This firm specialises in the manufacture of air frames. The majority of orders are to government specifications.

The company extends over a large site on the outskirts of a midland city. The number of employees now totals 5,000.

During the slump of 1932 to 1935 the firm ran into financial difficulties and had to sell the adjoining airfield to house builders. The flying field is situated twenty miles from the parent firm.

Due to the distance between the flying field and parent firm, a system of split construction was pioneered and introduced. Aircraft are now designed so that construction can be divided into nineteen main units. This greatly assisted transport to the airfield.

Other benefits derived from this system of split construction are greater ease of manufacture due to increased accessability, greater division of labour and, most important, a substantial reduction in the cost of aircraft.

All tools, jigs and fixtures are produced in the jig and tool department. These tools, etc, are designed by the operators themselves to standard production drawings. There is no jig and tool drawing office.

Both line and functional systems of manufacture are used.

Most details, both machine parts and hand operated parts, are made in departments using the functional system, as quantities are usually small. Assembly of fuselage (forward and aft), centre section, wings, elevators, rudders, etc, are manufactured under the line system.

Planning is responsible for the sequence of operations. It frequently occurs that different departments and sections are held up through lack of certain materials and machine parts.

Most of the foregoing difficulties in production are caused through difficulty in receiving delivery dates for castings and materials.

Selection is left to departmental chiefs, and procuring a better job is through the time honoured principle of whom you know, not what you know.

The managing director is responsible to the chairman board of directors. He is responsible for the co-ordination of all works effort and has responsible to him the seven senior administration staff, viz labour superintendent, works superintendent, chief designer, secretary, sales manager, buying manager and manager flying field. The labour superintendent is responsible for the rate fixing department, personnel, inspection, training and transport.

Responsibilities of the works superintendent, assisted by an assistant, are heavy. He is primarily responsible for planning under whose jurisdiction are the departments of jig and tool, progress, shop layout, production development, and manufacture.

The chief designer is in charge of research, testing, drawing office and lofting, and the accounts, costing, estimating and bonus sections are under the secretary.

Sales and public relations are very small but important departments. The buying department is directly responsible for ordering all materials, component parts and sub-contracting. Both stores (in) and the tool stores are under the buying department.

The manager flying field is in charge of final assembly workshops; an inspection department (which also has access to the managing director in case of a dispute between the manager and inspection); chief test pilot and an experimental department. There are three further sections under the experimental department: research, workshops, and design and drawing office. There is complete liaison between the manager flying field and the parent firm on all matters.

The labour turnover averages roughly twenty per cent each year.

WRITING A CASE STUDY

The firm have a contract with salvage merchants for the removal of all scrap.

The case study above was accompanied by a detailed organisation chart (see overleaf).

How successful was the case? The teacher found that his class had a lively discussion about the various problems but only in terms of their own company's practices on such questions as personnel selection, production methods, etc. He was also bombarded with questions about details in the case and even more often about information not included. He was unable to answer most of these and suggested that the class would have to assume certain facts which they made up as they went along.

No Focal Point

What was wrong with the case? In the first place, although the teacher was quite right in recognising that the problems could make a very useful case, he made a mistake in trying to deal with all of them at once. If, for example, he had picked the turnover rate and provided considerable information about it, the other problems might have emerged in the course of analysing it. Alternatively, he could have decided to make it primarily a technical case by using the production delays as the central theme. This is a problem which almost always confronts the case writer at the initial stage and he must choose the element which is to be the focal point of the case structure.

The *Safety Aeroplane* case illustrates what can happen when the writer fails to make that decision. It is absolutely formless. It is a brief recital of incomplete facts, most of which are already covered in the organisation chart. On the face of it, there would also appear to be some plainly misleading information. The writer says that the company was forced to sell its adjoining flying field and bought one twenty miles away. He says that therefore the aircraft had

ORGANISATION CHART OF THE SAFETY AEROPLANE COMPANY

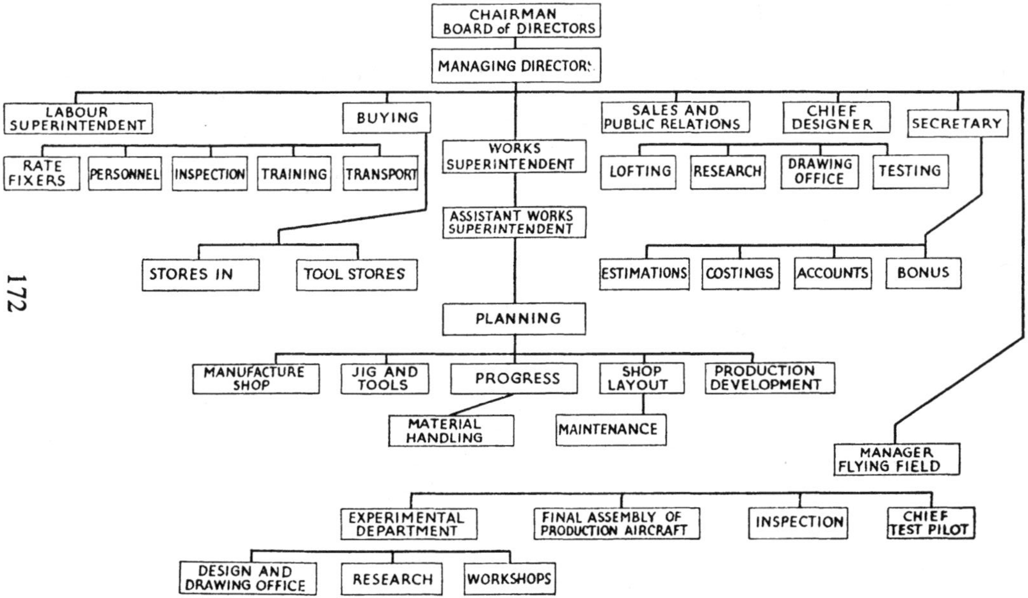

to be constructed in smaller units. 'This,' he says, 'greatly assisted transport to the airfield,' and he then continues by citing other benefits derived from this system of split construction. None of these so-called benefits seems logical or attributable to split construction and the implication that the new method of construction and the transport to the distant airfield are an improvement over the original system is ridiculous. Other statements are meaningless as they stand, eg 'The labour turnover averages twenty per cent each year'. If that turnover is in the most junior personnel, then it is not a figure to cause worry. If, on the other hand, it is among the more senior personnel who are disgruntled with the promotion policy, then there is cause for concern. Similarly the next sentence in the case, 'The firm have a contract with salvage merchants for the removal of all scrap', has no meaning unless it was made quite clear that the scrap was inordinately large.

The style makes the case difficult to read. The writer has also broken every major commonsense writing rule. His language is loose and inexact, eg 'government specifications' (para 1), 'other benefits' (para 5), 'increased accessability' (para 5), 'hand operated parts', 'quantities are usually small' (para 8), 'procuring a better job' (para 11), 'assisted by an assistant' (para 13), 'directly responsible' (para 15), 'complete liaison' (para 16).

The writer has fallen into two other traps. He has used technical expressions peculiar to one industry without explaining them: 'details' (para 8) and 'lofting' (para 14). He has also committed the sin of editorialising in a supposedly objective account of the facts of the situation, viz 'procuring a better job is through the time honoured principle of whom you know, not what you know'.

Subjectivity

Because of its importance in the construction of a case

study, this point deserves special consideration. There are two choices open to the writer. He can present the facts from the point of view of an outsider, in which case he must be scrupulously careful to avoid personal judgments or editorial opinion. This is not meant to suggest that such observations need to be excluded completely. In a human relations case such a policy would defeat the purpose of the exercise. Whenever comment is made, it must be made by a person in the case. Alternatively, the writer can present the case from only one person's point of view. Then it is essential that the writer's intention is made clear to the reader.

To illustrate the point from the *Safety Aeroplane* case, it would have been quite in order if the writer had suggested the discontent with the promotion procedure by giving the source of the comment about the 'time honoured principle'. It might have come, for instance, from the assistant works superintendent or any other disgruntled members of middle management. Alternatively, he could have written the entire case from the assistant works superintendent's point of view, in the form either of his comments or by reproducing his written report on the situation.

The *Safety Aeroplane* case just escapes being an atrocity story, the kind of case in which unbelievably bad conditions exist and inconceivable mistakes are made. For example, one atrocity case described a situation in an old established electrical equipment manufacturing firm, where the only purchasing and stores records consisted of a loose leaf book of suppliers' names. Competitive estimates, quality control, storage systems, bulk orders, in fact the most elementary principles of effective purchasing and stores procedures were unheard of. Although this case and others like it are taken from life they strain the credulity of students and are of limited value for teaching purposes because the solutions are too obvious. On the other hand a case which offers

WRITING A CASE STUDY

several delicately balanced alternative courses of action, leads to a much more useful discussion.

Insufficient Detailed Information

A tutor at a residential centre experimenting in foremanship courses decided that he would like to introduce the case study method. He had compiled some notes on an interesting problem of post-war adjustment in a manufacturing firm, related to him by a member of a previous foremanship course. On the basis of this information he prepared the following case. (The case should be read carefully and in its entirety before the reader continues with the chapter.)

XL COMPONENTS LTD

Common with wartime practice, a large manufacturing concern was directed early in the last war to devote a percentage of labour and factory space, principally to further processing the main factory products. To enable this task to be carried out, a foreman and a chargehand were upgraded from existing main factory personnel, and a superintendent in charge of other small departments was elected from members of the technical development staff. The choosing of these people was made by selecting the most enterprising employees from the main factory.

The new work entailed quite a lot of development work, followed by full scale production in a very short space of time. Much credit can be given to the supervisory staff for their keen interest in an obviously difficult but successful venture, and the department grew to employ some 120 male and female operatives.

But, with the termination of hostilities the wartime devices became unwanted, and whilst there were peacetime applications for similar products, the idea of keeping the department open was frowned upon by the works manager (an elderly fellow). Orders, though on a reduced scale, continued to come in and such had been the firm's reputation that it was difficult to turn orders down. No financial assistance was forthcoming to the department in order to maintain existing plant and buy new tools and small machines for revised production.

This state of affairs continued for a few years and with occasional assistance from the technical resources of the firm, some degree of quality and development was maintained, most of it unknown to the disinterested works manager. It could not be put over to the works manager that a fair quantity of extra material was being 'sold' by this department, material that would otherwise not be sold in its 'raw' state. So little was the interest shown, that no credit was given for selling this material on behalf of the main factory, and only the perseverance of the departmental heads kept the section alive. The superintendent was withdrawn from having any major say in the department and the foreman assumed full charge, responsible to the main factory superintendent. The main factory superintendent was responsible to the works manager.

With the appointment of a new manager, senior to the works manager, more interest began to be taken in the department. He realised that the department in question could become an asset to the firm, from a financial and prestige angle.

An investigation was carried out into the workings of the section and nothing very conclusive or very detrimental was discovered. There were, it was found, a considerable amount of rejected articles which in many cases were unrecoverable and only had a scrap value. A lot of this proved to be due to lack of proper tools and this was put right. The layout of the plant was revised for better working conditions and comparative production figures were taken at regular intervals. A new foreman had been introduced prior to this investigation and the previous foreman had been upgraded to production superintendent, but a feeling of incompetence reflected badly on him. This was shown in the higher management's attitude towards him.

Further changes in staff took place and the superintendent was relieved of his production post, and though not downgraded, was given a development design and liaison job, still in the same section. The investigator who had been appointed to take the check up on the workings of the section was promoted production superintendent, and the departmental draughtsman appointed as assistant to him. Two other male staff members were engaged in the capacity of draughtsman and technical assistant.

For about twelve months things went fairly smoothly and with a large order book it seemed that the department had been rescued. Time study experts probed every job and costings were based on these figures and passed on to the customer with the usual overhead allowances. Instead of arriving at separate overhead allowances, the overheads of the main factory were changed and this brought some articles to an 'unsaleable' high level.

In the effort to make a large profit from the further processing of what was normally sold raw to the customer, it appeared that the effect had been to discourage sales, at least by judgment of the current order book. Instead of being satisfied with making a small profit from the further processing operation and the usual from the 'raw' material, short sightedness still prevailed, and the fact was that the company did not realise that the department sold goods for them which they would not otherwise have sold, not counting the prestige value.

The writer of the above case has avoided the fundamental mistake made in the *Safety Aeroplane* case and has concentrated on one issue, the problem of the post-war fate of a processing department set up to meet wartime requirements.

However he is guilty of other equally serious faults. There are nine men in the case, but none comes alive to the reader because of insufficient information about them. He has not even given them names. As a case study in human relations it is almost useless.

Once again the writer has fallen into the trap of slipshod expressions, contradictory statements, incomplete data. What is meant by 'principally to further processing the main factory products', or 'some degree of quality and development was maintained', or 'a feeling of incompetence reflected badly on him'? Lack of care is also reflected by such confusing and ambiguous statements as 'such had been the firm's reputation that it was difficult to turn orders down'.

The proof reading was also careless. The author presumably meant to say that 'a superintendent was selected', not elected' (para 1) and that 'overheads of the main factory were charged'—not 'changed' (penultimate para). The latter mistake leads to much confusion.

The writer has omitted a number of details which are of importance to the successful analysis of the case. It is impossible for the reader to deduce from the case the following points (to mention only a few):

1 Who selected the supervisory staff of the new department and how were they selected?
2 How much assistance was given to the department from the technical resources of the firm and how was it given?
3 What efforts were made to sell the works manager on the value of the department. By whom?
4 Who authorised the investigation of the department? What form did it take? What reactions did it arouse?
5 What are the details of the withdrawal of the original superintendent and the upgrading of the first foreman? How was higher management's attitude to him expressed?
6 What are the details surrounding the other staff changes in the department?
7 What were the circumstances of the decision to charge the main factory overheads to the department's products?
8 How seriously had the increase in the overhead loading affected sales?
9 What did the factory make? (This omission arouses unnecessary curiosity and leads the student to waste time speculating on this irrelevant point.)

In style the case is subject to almost as serious criticisms as the *Safety Aeroplane* case. There are a number of inexact phrases and mistakes in grammar. The writer says that 'the wartime devices became unwanted'. He refers to the works manager as 'an elderly fellow', instead of stating his age. The structure of some of his sentences is awkward, eg 'So little was the interest shown that no credit was given for selling this material on behalf of the main factory'.

The writer is also guilty of injecting his personal views into a supposedly objective account, first when he says 'Much credit can be given to the supervisory staff for their keen interest in an obviously difficult but successful venture', and later when he concludes that 'short sightedness still prevailed, and the fact was that the company did not realise that the department sold goods for them which they would not otherwise have sold, not counting the prestige value'.

Other Inadequacies

The following were among the questions students were asked to answer about the case. They serve to highlight the inadequacy of the material:

1 Was the works manager right in taking the attitude he did in suggesting closing of the department immediately after the war?

(Insufficient evidence in the case for an answer.)

2 Do you think his lack of enthusiasm was because this was a new field and something in which he felt out of his depth?

(There is no evidence in the case to indicate 'lack of enthusiasm' or motives for his action. Furthermore, the question prejudices the issue by suggesting an answer. It would have been more effective if written: 'How would you explain the works manager's attitude towards the department?'.)

3 How fully should the production investigation have been carried out and by whom? (Own personnel or independent?)

(The case does not give any information about the investigation or the reasons for it. Therefore any answer would have to be pure hypothesis. Once again, the

question is awkward. A better phrasing would be: 'What are your views on the investigation of the department and the way in which it was conducted?'.)
4 Was the new manager (senior) keen because he was a 'new broom'?
(No evidence at all in the case.)
5 The feeling between the new design and development superintendent, the production superintendent and his assistant were somewhat strained. How could this be overcome?
(These 'strained feelings' are mentioned for the first time in the question, and do not appear in the case. Once again there is insufficient evidence in the case so that answers would have to be largely personal speculation.)
6 Do you think that independent overhead charges should have been worked out and put into operation?
(Insufficient evidence in the case.)
7 Do you think a department should exist if only paying its way by reason of being an unpaid salesman for the main factory? Or should it be sold (on paper) the raw material on a reduced profit basis and allowed to work independently as far as its own profit is due?
(It is not quite clear whether the writer is suggesting in the second sentence that the department should be converted into a subsidiary company. The student could express his opinion on the alternatives, drawing from his own experience and making assumptions about the meaning of the questions, but he would find little material in the case to use in substantiating his argument.)
8 How far back in higher management should decisions about policy and the company's products be decided?
(Unless the writer is trying to get the students to suggest that it was the board's responsibility to decide about the fate of the wartime processing department,

the question is too vague. If he is attempting to bring the role of the board into the discussion, the question would have been more objective if it had been framed as follows: 'What do you think of the policy making machinery at XL? In general? As it affected the processing department?')

Common Sense Rules for Case Writers

From these three cases it is possible to extract certain common sense rules which can help to guide the inexperienced case writer along the right line.

1 Find a problem suitable for case study treatment, keeping in mind the audience that will use it and the purpose which it is intended to serve.
2 Make certain that there is a central problem around which related problems can be woven, and which offers a nicely balanced set of alternative courses of action for its solution. This type of problem provides the greatest scope for fruitful discussion.
3 Try to relate complexity both in terms of contents and number of persons involved to the length of the case. Short cases should be simple.
4 If the case is primarily concerned with human relations problems, be sure to provide enough anecdotes, incidents and quotations (not descriptions) to make the personalities come alive.
5 Let the characters in the case reveal themselves through their own actions and/or comments or through the actions and comments of others.
6 Do not let personal views intrude into the case and avoid any editorial comments.
7 Before writing the case, outline the proposed structure of the case beginning with the background data (of the organisation or problem), then introduce the problem and develop it in the narrative, then lead finally to the

unresolved crisis. The case need not end on such a note but can describe the company's solution to the problem and move on to present other difficulties arising from or related to the solution. The more complex the case the more logical it is to include a number of problems, some explicitly stated, others implied.
8. While writing the case, keep in mind the three kinds of questions which will have to be asked: analysis of the situation; action; general implications.
9. Avoid inexact terms, technical jargon, grammatical errors and do not make the clues too obvious or pointed.
10. Arrange for others to read the case and the questions in draft and conduct a trial session with the case before committing it to its final form.

CHAPTER NINE

RUNNING A CASE STUDY SESSION

THE time was immediately after lunch on a day in January.[1] The place was Manchester. The group consisted of about 35 managers, a majority of whom were managing directors or company directors. The session was designed to acquaint the group with the case study technique. Copies of the case had been circulated to the participants a week before with a request that the case should be studied for discussion at the meeting.

The Case

The case, called *Mainstays Limited,* dealt with problems arising from the company's transition from skilled to semi-skilled production.

MAINSTAYS LIMITED[2]

Transition from Skilled to Semi-skilled Production

Now in its fiftieth year, Mainstays is one of the most reliable engineering works in the Midlands. It employs just over 1,000 workers. Like many old firms, its working conditions are not ideal. As the firm expanded shops were added or enlarged, and extensive rebuilding in the middle thirties brought with it many improvements in layout and lighting.

These improvements marked the handover of the firm to its present managing director, the eldest son of the founder, Mr Westaway. Mr Westaway, Senior, had won a reputation as an

---
[1] This is a case study of a case study session.
[2] Prepared by The Case Study Writers' Circle and reproduced by kind permission of the publishers, Newman Neame Ltd.

excellent man to work for. He had recognised the trade unions early and had fully approved of their closed shop policy.

Promotion has been largely from within and ten of the present fourteen foremen are ex-apprentices who still hold honorary membership of their union. Mr Morrison, the present works manager, a man in his early fifties, was himself promoted from machine shop foreman and is as popular and energetic in his new role as he was in his old.

Mr Westaway, Junior, has a degree in engineering and worked in the various shops for a couple of years before he took the firm over. He has the same enlightened views as his father, but increased administrative work has prevented his spending much time on the shop floor. He chairs works committee meetings, however, and actively supports the firm's social activities.

Mass Production Techniques Introduced

Together with Mr Morrison, Mr Westaway, Junior, had re-planned the factory so that modified mass production techniques could be employed without interfering with the steady demand for jobbing work on which the firm had originally built its reputation. Today the firm is still moving towards further mechanisation and works simplification.

The machine shop is one of the busiest at Mainstays. It employs seventy skilled and ten semi-skilled men, five labourers and two clerks. The ten semi-skilled men work on semi-automatic machines which are grouped together in the middle of the shop. Around them are the skilled turners, millers and drillers.

The first of the semi-automatic machines was introduced five years ago. They are used on long runs for making standard parts, such as bolts. They require comparatively little attention and their operatives are able to move about and chat. All the machines operated by the skilled workers require constant attention.

Bob Corrigan has been foreman of the machine shop for six years. He is thirty-six and was an apprentice and an operative with Mainstays before he was promoted.

Like the other foremen, Corrigan is directly responsible to

the works manager for the effective running of his shop. He engages his own operatives, though he is not allowed to dismiss them without consulting the works manager. There is no personnel department at Mainstays because Mr Morrison thinks it important to keep responsibility for employees in the hands of the people who supervise them.

Corrigan has always been enthusiastic about new production techniques. It was partly through his efforts, in fact, that the semi-automatic machines were introduced. His ideal is a shop full of semi-automatic machines in which he can employ semi-skilled men with only a few skilled setters. He had been riding this hobby horse at a foremen's meeting only a few months ago. 'We might need more detailed planning and a larger planning staff but we'd get higher production and pay less out in wages,' he said. 'A good many of my skilled men who are on long runs feel the work is too easy for them as it is. They often ask for transfers to the toolmaking shop and I have to tell them there are no vacancies. Then they get fed up and leave. I've lost five like that in the last year. It's sad to see them go, especially after I've worked with them for fifteen years at least, but let's face it —we just don't need these skills any more.'

Three more skilled workers left the machine shop soon after this meeting. Since they were old friends of Corrigan's they talked to him freely about why they were going. One said that he had found a job where he could earn more money. Another who had been with the firm for twenty years said that it did not feel the same any more—there was not the same team spirit, and there were too many arguments and too many bosses. The third said it was his eyes and he kept on getting headaches. Although his sight has recently been tested, he thought it must be getting weaker. In any case the lighting did not help, and if that was the best the lighting consultants could do the place was better left as it was in the old days.

Two semi-skilled men also left at this time. Corrigan was not on such friendly terms with them, and he had to ask them why they were leaving. One said he thought the canteen food was too dear and the quality too low. The other said he could not get on with the shop steward, Matthews. 'He's a troublemaker,' he added.

CASE STUDY APPROACH TO MANAGEMENT EDUCATION

The Work of the Machine Shop Foremen

Corrigan has his own office in the machine shop and next to it is the shop's administrative office. Here Corrigan's two clerks receive the programmes from the planning department and hand out job cards to the operatives. Production programmes are issued fortnightly by the planning department, and give production figures and some general notes on production method for each machine in the shop.

The production programme is based on minimum piecework rates but since most operatives are earning well above these there is usually a good deal of spare time for each machine. This is filled by urgent additional orders, or by special requests from other departments, or sometimes by tool making. Skilled workers in the machine shop are put on to tool making when—as sometimes happens—the tool room can no longer keep pace with the demands for new tools, jigs and fixtures and for repair work. For this work the machine workers are paid on tool rate. Bob Corrigan is responsible for allocating all work not on the planning department programme. He leaves the routine allocation of work to the clerks, who also see that correct materials are received from stores at the right time and in the right quantity.

Very little of Corrigan's time is taken up with inspection since the inspection department adjoins the machine shop and, in addition, a roving inspector, responsible to the chief inspector, continually moves around the floor. This inspector is an ex-tradesman, and is encouraged to advise and help operatives. He not only inspects parts to see that sizes and finishes are correct but also suggests how the operatives can best do the job. On occasions he has corrected mistakes made by the drawing office.

If it were not for the roving inspector and for his clerks, Corrigan would not be free to consult with the technical departments as often as he does. He is frequently asked to advise the planning department about production methods, and the toolroom foremen about the design of tools for his shop, and the works manager over costing and pricing new orders.

A pile of blueprints is always prominent on Corrigan's desk awaiting his comments. Much of this work he does at lunchtime and after the factory closes. It has become a standard joke in the machine shop that Corrigan is never in his office for two minutes before the telephone rings and he is called away to see somebody.

The New Shop Steward

Matthews, the shop steward in the machine shop, has been with the firm for six years and is one of the semi-skilled operatives. He was one of the first to try out a semi-automatic machine and requested successfully to be kept on the job. He was first elected steward three years ago after an aggressive campaign in which he easily defeated the other candidate, a friendly, easy going tradesman who had held the post for the previous ten years. At the time this defeat irked the old employees in the shop, though they had done little to prevent it. During the campaign they had regarded Matthews and his 'modern' fiery views with an amused tolerance tinged with contempt. 'He's not much good with his hands so he makes up for it with his mouth,' was one tradesman's comment.

In the three years of his stewardship Matthews has won close support from his fellow workers on the ten semi-automatic machines. Seven of them are 'new' men and under his guidance they have become quick to spot possibilities of victimisation and departures from trade union rules. Whenever he is told of a case, Matthews quickly lodges a complaint with Corrigan. Twice when he received an answer he thought unsatisfactory he and his colleagues canvassed the shop and brought it to the verge of an unofficial strike. Each time the works manager was called in to speak to the shop. His point of view was accepted by the majority of the shop, and the strikes were averted.

Matthews is as eager to discipline workers as management. He makes operatives obey the terms of the union's agreement to the letter. He is particularly strict over hours and work breaks, and his colleagues are bitterly sarcastic to operatives who work during rest pauses. Once Matthews referred the case of an inveterate offender to the local branch of the union, and the man was reprimanded and fined for not stopping his machine when the tea waggon appeared. His defence—that he was in the middle of a five minute operation which could not be interrupted—was dismissed when Matthews insisted that his was not an isolated instance.

Matthews is particularly relentless in his battles with Corrigan over the rates. It is in Corrigan's jurisdiction to alter these where he thinks them inappropriate. By persistent arguing and by finding difficulties in the work Matthews has managed to push the rates up on a number of jobs, most of them performed by the semi-skilled men. There is now often little difference in the 'take home' of the skilled and semi-skilled men, although the skilled men complain that the others have an easy time 'tram driving'.

One Operative's View

One morning, when Mr Morrison was in Corrigan's office discussing the drawing, a young semi-skilled workman named McCormack knocked and entered. He was very angry and asked for his cards. He said he had been working on his semi-automatic when Matthews tapped him on the shoulder and told him he was doing too much work. McCormack went on to say that he had stood out against Matthews' communist claptrap ever since he came three months ago but he had just about had enough. 'I've got a wife and a couple of kids to support,' he added, 'and if I can't get on with my work without being called a boss's man, I'll go somewhere else where I can.'

The Teacher's Notes

While he was reading the case and preparing for the session in Manchester the teacher underlined all the factual statements which he felt might be relevant in the analysis. He then drew up the following notes summarising the major problems he saw in the case.

Implications of Growth and Specialisation

1 Effect on Group Relations
   (a) Break-up of old status values
   (b) New groups formed by antagonisms and/or new skills
   (c) Blockage for ambition: no promotion, no contact with foremen or management

RUNNING A CASE STUDY SESSION

- (d) Apathy and insecurity of old workers
- (e) Changing functions of management, eg Westaway, Jr, and Corrigan as compared with Westaway, Sr, and Morrison
- (f) Loss of sense of loyalty with nothing to replace it
- (g) Unfortunate effects of too much autonomy

2 New Organisational Problems
- (a) Incomplete switchover to semi-skilled production
- (b) Inadequacies of planning production programmes, methods of work, rates, labour, material
- (c) Paradox in position of supervisory personnel who were performing administrative, middle management functions
- (d) Bad working conditions: overcrowding, inappropriate position of semi-skilled operatives
- (e) Too wide a span of control; too many people under one supervisor
- (f) Lack of supervision, or supervision by non-management personnel

3 Effect on Foremanship
- (a) Changing needs from technical man and administrator to expert in social skills and human relations
- (b) Greater emphasis on foreman as interpreter of management policies and formulator of attitudes

4 Effect on Role of Union
- (a) Increased opportunities for disparities and irregularities to appear
- (b) Added function as representatives of new semi-skilled groups
- (c) Growing role as catalyst in altering management views
- (d) Conflicting interests as representatives of both old guard and new groups, whose interests and attitudes were fundamentally different

A Few of the Many Possible Solutions

1 More supervisory personnel
2 Establishment of a personnel department
3 Setting up of a training course for foremen, to train them for jobs with greater responsibility higher up in the management scale, and also to improve their social skills

4 Adoption of an information policy
5 Board level discussion on switch-over policy
6 Expansion and reorganisation of planning department
7 Revision of layout of machine shop to isolate semi-skilled men
8 Upgrading of Corrigan

Others to be added by group in discussion.

The leader's next step was to study the questions and become familiar enough with them so that he could produce a relevant one whenever the discussion flagged.

The questions supplied with the case, and the diagrams showing the layout of the machine shop and the work flow and communications between machine shop and other departments, were as follows:

QUESTIONS: MAINSTAYS LIMITED

Analysis of the Situation

1 What do you think are the major problems in the machine shop?
2 In what ways has the introduction of semi-automatic machines affected the old skilled employees?
3 If other semi-automatic machines were introduced into the machine shop what do you think it would 'mean' to:
   (a) Corrigan, the foreman?
   (b) Matthews, the shop steward?
   (c) The skilled tradesmen?
   (d) The semi-skilled men?
   (e) The works manager?
4 Has the layout of the machine shop any influence on the problem?
5 What do you think about the way the planning department does its work and about the way work is allocated to the operatives?
6 What do you think of the job that Corrigan performs? Does it have any bearing on the problems of the machine shop?
7 What do you think of the way inspection is done? Do you

think that the roving inspector is a good idea? Do you see any difficulties he might have, or problems he might cause?
8 With Mainstays' long history of good union relationships, why do you think it is having difficulties with the shop steward in the machine shop?
9 Why do you think the old skilled workers have not replaced Matthews as shop steward?

Action

1 Faced with McCormack's demand for his cards what would you do if you were:
(a) the foreman?
(b) the works manager?
How would the action affect the workers in the machine shop?
2 What action, if any, would you take with the shop steward?
3 What action would you take as works manager to prevent further problems like that of McCormack's?
4 As a consultant would you have any recommendations to make about the re-organisation of duties in the machine shop? Would you have any suggestions to make about Corrigan? Would you consider any re-organisation in the planning department and in its relationship with the machine shop?

General Implications

1 Are the problems in the machine shop inevitable in a process of change to mass production methods or can they be avoided? What ways do you suggest could be used to bring about change?
2 In what ways does a change to mass production affect the job of a supervisor? What aspects of his job become particularly important?
3 What do you think of the works manager's views on personnel departments? Do you think it is possible to introduce a personnel department without taking away the foreman's responsibility for his workers? If so, how?
4 What do you think of the job Mainstays expects the machine shop foreman to perform? Do you think this is the sort of

job foremen should perform? Do you thing that the foreman has too much power in this case?
5 Does this case suggest any principles about the span of control?
6 Does this case throw any light on the way groups are formed and the way attitudes are built up and maintained?

Diagram for the blackboard (2)

	Machine shop foreman	Admin office		Tool room foreman
X X	X X X	Tool room
X X	X X X
X X	X X X
X X	X X X
X X	X X X
X X	X X X
X X	X X X
O O	O O O
O O	O O O
X X	X X X	Tool room stores
X X	X X X
X X	X X X
X X	X X X
X X	X X X
X X	X X X
X X	X X X

X Machines of skilled men
O Semi-automatic machines

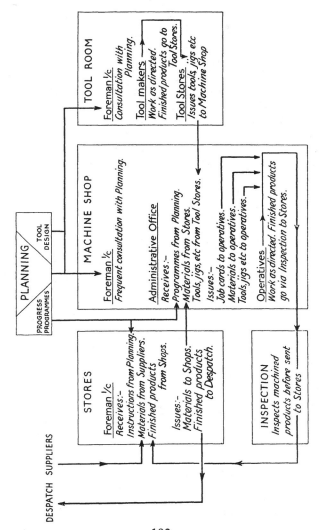

CASE STUDY APPROACH TO MANAGEMENT EDUCATION

When the case study leader arranged to have a copy of the case sent one week beforehand to everyone expected at the Manchester meeting, he did not include the questions because he felt that with such a high level of management these would oversimplify the problems. Before the meeting he prepared two visual aids, which consisted of the diagrams drawn in two colours on large pieces of cardboard, three feet by four feet. He then felt satisfied that he had taken all possible preliminary action to ensure a successful session.

The Discussion

On the appointed day after luncheon, the group moved from the table to seats at the end of the room.

As he was being introduced to the group, the leader reviewed in his own mind the plan of action he proposed. He thought he would devote about an hour and a quarter to the discussion, summarise it and then, in the last quarter of an hour, review how the case study technique had worked in practice.

He began as follows:

Gentlemen, you are here to see how a case study works and there is no better way than to try one out. He asked if everyone had a copy, handed out several extra ones which he had brought with him and next read through the case aloud. He then said, *Now gentlemen, my task is done. From now on, it is up to you.*

There was a moment of silence and then a member of the group said that he had read the case and had made a list of forty-two things which were wrong with it. He said that he did not believe that the company had a closed shop (para 2), he did not agree that Westaway, Senior and Junior, had 'enlightened views' (para 4). In fact, he thought that they did not know what they were doing, especially since there were at least three instances in the case of contravention of the York Engineering Agreement.

RUNNING A CASE STUDY SESSION

The leader, a non-technical man, had never heard of the York Agreement and also realised that the first speaker had put his finger on some editorialising in the text. He was rattled, and suggested that the group might care to discuss the objections one at a time. After a brief exchange about the possibility that there might be an engineering company with a closed rather than a union shop, someone suggested that they were not there to decide whether they agreed with the facts in the case or the attitudes of the people described. The point was to analyse the various problems and try to agree on a solution.

The discussion veered back on course and a number of speakers suggested what they would do to solve the problem. The contributions were in no way connected with one another and each one was addressed to the leader. He in turn raised a number of questions, trying with some success to direct the discussion to the analysis of the situation. He realised that he could never cover the main points in the first two question sections in time; so he was faced with the problem of how to conclude the session. He decided to interrupt the discussion offering shortage of time as his excuse, and read out the questions which had not been covered.

Lessons in Retrospect

Clearly, very few of the advantages expected from the case study method had been realised at this meeting. The case study leader studied what had happened in retrospect, to see what lessons could be learned from the experiment. He concluded that there were at least six.

1 With a group unfamiliar with case studies, it is advisable to make a few introductory remarks about the method. For example he might have said something like this:

> In many ways the case study method of teaching is equivalent to the clinical method of training doctors. One learns how to examine a human situation, to collect evidence, to

recognise symptoms and to make progressively more accurate and more refined diagnoses. One also learns to suggest more effective remedies, and to develop more practical plans for getting the remedies accepted.

Doctors are fortunate in having patients brought to them in the training hospital. Unfortunately, it is impossible to take members of a discussion group into an actual situation, and so a situation must be brought to the group. This situation could be fictitious, but experience has shown that an accurate and objective description of real life generally contains more complexity than fiction can invent. There is rarely a single right answer to a case, and seeking the answer is not the main point. What is important is that we should think through the situation and analyse it and discuss it. If we can make an effective analysis of a problem situation, then the action we take should be reasonably effective. But the action I take will be different from the action you take, however similar our analysis, simply because we are different people.

We can learn something else from case studies, too. The information they give is the same for all of us, but we shall discover that each of us puts different interpretations on this information. Perhaps as we go on discussing the case we shall begin to realise that it is not only the facts that are important, but the way we see them. Perhaps, too, we shall begin to realise that we may always be seeing them in the same way, that we are not really objective, but that we are prejudiced and are projecting our own wishes and fears into a supposedly objective analysis of the situation. This is an important insight, and it carries with it the key to successful management.

2 It might have been better after all to have distributed the questions with the cases. The longer people have been away from an academic setting, the more difficult it is for them to approach the analysis of a case study in a logical and organised manner. Alternatively, a few introductory remarks on the way the case was to be discussed, ie first analysis of the situation, then views on the action to be taken and finally consideration of the general implica-

tions, would have helped to get the session started on the right lines. This is a useful point to bear in mind with any group trying case studies for the first time.
3 The importance of the effect of the number in a discussion group and the setting for the session had been very much underestimated. If the leader has to sit at a table and the chairs are arranged as they would normally be for a lecture or class, the conditioned response of the group is passive. If the group contains more than twenty or at the most twenty-five, it is difficult to range the members around a table or to create the informal, committee meeting atmosphere necessary to overcome this psychological obstacle.
4 The case was much too long for the ninety minutes available. Either a shorter case should have been used, or a careful selection made of those questions which could have been covered in the time and which would have illustrated the analysis-action-implications aspects of the case study technique. This was due partly to an inaccurate estimate of the speed of the group and further to the fact that it was the first time the case study leader had used the case. When working on a tight schedule, the case study leader should try to use a case which he has used before and knows well.
5 The pattern of speaking and the nature of the contributions made to the discussion were typical of the performance of a group new to the technique. At every level the pattern tends to be the same; first a number of quick, easy 'solutions' quite unrelated to one another, followed by an equally unconnected series of partial comments on the problem. The leader is called upon to play a far more active role in order to give the discussion any kind of form and direction at this early stage. The extent of his participation also tends to increase in direct proportion to the size of the group, since the larger the group, the

less members seem willing to argue points out among themselves without reference to the 'chair'.
6 The initial attack on the case could have been anticipated. The person who attacks the case or the method at the outset is by no means a rare phenomenon and he provides the case study leader with a readymade opportunity to win the confidence of the group, or equally, to alienate them. It is a challenge which the leader must be prepared to meet. In this instance, the leader was fortunate to have a member of the group produce the correct argument, but in most circumstances the leader must be ready with the answer. Gentle handling of the heckler or session-saboteur, preferably with a touch of humour, is essential to avoid arousing the group's sympathy with him. At another case study meeting of senior management the case study was subjected to violent criticism by one of the members on the grounds that it did not contain enough detailed material for useful discussion. The leader said 'Well, you are probably right, but since we are all here and this is the only case we have available, why don't we see what we can do with it? Do you all agree?' Two hours later at the end of a most interesting and lively discussion, it was quite clear to everyone that the challenger had been thoroughly but gently vanquished. This initial attack reminded the case study leader of a related problem in conducting cases. Quite often a leader finds himself confronted by a member or by an entire group who express frank disbelief that any company could make the elementary mistakes described. In these instances it becomes very important to assure the group of the accuracy and validity of the case and to remind them that cases are descriptions of actual experience—often the experience of very successful companies. A group loses confidence and interest very quickly if members become persuaded that they are studying an impossible or make-believe situation.

RUNNING A CASE STUDY SESSION

Group Variations

The same case study leader also used the *Mainstays Case* with three other groups, one consisting of a very mixed representation from the higher levels of industry and commerce gathered together for a case study exercise, the second composed of middle management members in an executive development course, and the third comprising a more technical group with a large proportion of supervisors attending a residential course.

A comparison of the composition, teaching conditions and reactions of the three groups sheds light on some of the factors which play such an essential part in the handling of a case study.

There were fifteen members in the first group drawn from such diverse industries as printing, nationalised airlines, chemicals, book trade, oil, industrial consultancy, coal. Only two had previous experience of the case method. After a few explanatory remarks on the case study method, the leader asked the members of the group to introduce themselves and state briefly their occupations. As they did so, he drew a plan of the U-shaped table and noted their names and jobs. He then read the case aloud, passed out the questions and opened the discussion. Time—evening; length of session—two hours.

The second group consisted of twenty-one members of an executive development course. They were familiar with the case study method. There were four production men, seven from sales and the remaining ten were from a variety of middle management positions. The group was arranged in four semi-circular rows of easy chairs in a hotel lounge, with the leader at a table in the centre. He had a seating plan and had studied the class list several days before to give him time to decide which members could be called on to provide specialised information or to answer certain of the more technical questions. No questions were distributed. He was introduced to the group and after reading the case through opened the discussion. Time—late afternoon; length of session—ninety minutes.

The third group, attending a residential course, had never used case studies before. Six out of eighteen were supervisors, and six more were in works management. The session was held in a lecture room where the two rows of metal chairs were arranged in a semi-circle close to the leader's table. He introduced himself and asked the members of the group to follow suit. As they spoke he drew up a seating plan. He then spoke briefly on the case study method and explained the procedure he proposed to adopt. Instead of handing out the questions he briefed the group on the three-stage sequence which the discussion ought to follow. After reading the case aloud, he opened the discussion. Time—late afternoon and early evening; length of session —three hours.

Conclusions to be Drawn

The case study leader drew certain conclusions from these three teaching experiences.
1 They confirmed his impression that arranging the group round a table encourages continuous logical discussion.
2 They showed him that it is very helpful indeed to have a seating plan which indicates the members' names, jobs and industries. It enables the leader to establish a more personal relationship with the group. It also provides him with the opportunity to note some of the points made and the name of the person who made them. Such notes are invaluable for referring back to the source of a contribution and avoiding unnecessary repetition. A comment such as: 'In other words, what you are saying is really another way of putting the point which Mr Martyn made earlier in the discussion' can reduce waste of time

without offending any feelings. It also enables the leader to call on some of the shyer members of the group who otherwise might hesitate to enter the discussion. The case study session at the residential centre provided an interesting example of this situation. Although the case contained a considerable amount of material about supervision, not one of the six foremen in the group took part in the first half hour of the discussion which was dominated by seven members who were either managers or held administrative positions. The leader finally induced one of the foremen to give his views and the rest followed. In this instance shyness, combined with a feeling of social and educational inferiority, appeared to be the cause of the initial unwillingness to participate. As mentioned before, the seating plan helps the leader to call on the 'expert' in the group to answer technical questions. There is a danger here, however, unless the case study leader is also able to answer such questions. This is best illustrated by an incident in the session with the executive development course. The case leader called on one of the production men to explain what was meant by the sentence: 'The production programme is based on minimum piecework rates, but since most operatives are earning well above these there is usually a good deal of spare time for each machine.' The 'expert' did not give a clear explanation and so it was up to the case study leader to provide the examples which would make the statement understandable to the non-technical members of the group. The explanation he produced was no better and the seed may have been planted in the minds of one or two members of the group that he did not know what he was talking about.

3 In the first of the three sessions, the case study leader supplied a set of questions with each copy of the case. He discovered that in attempting to deal with the questions in

order, he was stifling the discussion. While he was trying to ask: 'In what ways has the introduction of semi-automatic machines affected the old skilled employees?' two members of the group were analysing the faults of the layout of the machine shop. Rather than interfere, he let the discussion take its own course. However, there are occasions when the discussion is dead and can only be revived by the artificial stimulus of formal questions. There are other occasions, such as the Manchester senior management session, where other considerations indicate that the questions should be given to the members of the group for their guidance. The case itself should always be circulated well in advance to ensure that members of the group are familiar with the problems to be discussed. This was done for all the four sessions described.

4 The second group had been working and living together for some period before the case study session while the third group had been formed only two days before. The former group was already thoroughly integrated, that is, they knew each other, had lost their shyness and were no longer concerned with working out their individual relationship to the group, but looked upon themselves as members of the group. This was reflected in the readiness of members to disagree with opinions expressed by their colleagues and by their willingness to consider the one point under discussion rather than introduce an unrelated fact and break the continuity of thought. The degree of a group's integration has a very important effect on its performance in a case study session. It generally means that less time is occupied by the inconsequential views of different individuals, before any real discussion begins to get under way. It also encourages lively and constructive discussion rather than destructive commentary.

RUNNING A CASE STUDY SESSION

5 A further relationship between the composition of the group and the course of the discussion emerged from the case study leader's experience with all four groups, although it was most noticeable with the last two. The case had a certain technical element, a production engineering machine shop setting, and was concerned primarily with the supervisory level. It therefore appeared that the closer the elements of the case to the experience of the group, the greater the intellectual and emotional interest and degree of participation. Thus, it was quite logical that the residential centre group with its larger proportion of foremen and production personnel, should make the best showing. It was also clear that the non-technical background of the case study leader was not a serious handicap to running a technical case.

6 Management teachers often find themselves teaching cases which involve technical problems about which they may know very little. In fact this is what happened to the teacher in the four sessions described. He realised that the greatest danger he faced on this score sprang from his own fear that he might be asked a technical question he could not answer. However, he knew in any crisis he could fall back on two devices: first, calling on the 'experts' in the class for their opinion and secondly, pointing out that the question, although interesting in itself, did not really affect the case or its problems. He also knew that, provided he had shown competence in conducting the case, he could exploit his lack of technical knowledge and create closer *rapport* with the class as well as establish a friendlier, more informal atmosphere by surrendering his position of authority. This could be done quite simply by admitting his ignorance and telling the group that he would have to depend on them for guidance.

The Role of the Teacher

Further analysis of the last two sessions gave the case study leader some additional ideas on the conduct of a case and the role of the leader himself.

A misogynist once described the conversation at a ladies' tea party as 'an endless series of monologues which were unheard because each person present was fully occupied deciding what to say when the next lull occurred.' The similarity to the first part of a case study session has already been pointed out, but the leader now felt he had learned how to use this period to good advantage. In the last two of the four sessions just described, he had noted the comments that were made during the first part of the session and the names of the speakers. At the executive development session, the first ten comments covered the following points:

1 In effect there was no foreman
2 The problem would be solved by setting up a personnel department
3 The semi-automatic machines in the machine shop were misplaced
4 Works study was the key to the problem
5 Corrigan talked too much
6 The company would soon get a bad reputation because so many of its staff were leaving
7 The roving inspector should never be allowed to perform supervisory functions
8 Better planning was needed
9 Written orders should be introduced to reduce all the time wasted on meetings and telephone calls
10 The main weakness was in the lack of a management policy.

At the residential centre, these were the first eleven contributions:

1 The organisation was all wrong and Westaway, Junior, was to blame

RUNNING A CASE STUDY SESSION

2 Corrigan had too much to do and should not have been giving advice to other departments
3 Time was being wasted on the semi-automatic machines
4 Tools should have been made in the tool room not in the machine shop
5 Lighting was bad, layout was bad, and Corrigan should be made works manager
6 It was a family business which had lost the personal touch. Corrigan was a technician, not a foreman. Foremen should be introduced into the shop. Clerks should not allocate work. Reasons for quitting given by employees were bogus. Not enough skill demanded by jobs. There should be one operator for two semi-automatics. There was no one for the operator to turn to except Matthews
7 A personnel department should be set up
8 A works study department should be organised and separate production programmes prepared for the semi-automatic machines. Skilled and semi-skilled workers should be in different parts of the works
9 A training policy is needed to ensure the success of the switchover policy. No information or consultation
10 Corrigan was too keen on new techniques and should concentrate his attention on improving the organisation of paper work
11 Solution to the problem lies in the history of the company

By the time the case study leader called a halt, comments in both groups had ranged over the entire case with most of its major problems, and he had achieved the following:

1 He had given the group free rein and had intervened as little as possible, thus giving the impression that success of the discussion depended on the group and not on him.
2 He had gained some idea about the members of the group: which ones were likely to dominate the discussion, which to make the intelligent contributions, and so on.
3 He had put himself in the ideal position of being able to select any one of the points raised and to direct the discussion towards it.

4 He had also given himself an opportunity to assess the speed at which the group was capable of covering the essential points in the case. This should have enabled him to confirm his original timetable or to alter it accordingly. Judging from the initial comments of the two groups, he might have concluded that the former would be able to complete the case in the time allotted, because they would have to be guided more and were not sufficiently interested to get involved in lengthy arguments among themselves. Similarly, he might have foreseen that the second group would have great difficulty in conforming to the schedule, since they appeared to have greater initial appreciation of the problems and reflected such different backgrounds and attitudes.

Through the process of assessing the group's views on procedure, he realised that he had learned the true role of the leader and the value of the persuasive approach. He was there only to guide them, to exercise a watching brief, to make clear to them what was happening and what had been said. For example with the Executive Development group, at the end of the first fifteen contributions, the leader reviewed the ten points that had been made and asked which they would prefer to discuss first. With the residential centre class he followed the same procedure but gave them guidance by suggesting that the comments seemed to fall logically under five main headings:

Foremanship
Organisation
Planning and production
Human relations in the factory
Trade union functions

He then asked the group in which order they would like to consider these problems. As he had anticipated, the group chose the order in which he had listed them. He also used the same technique when the group met for its second ses-

RUNNING A CASE STUDY SESSION

sion after dinner. Most of the first period had been devoted to analysis of the situation. The group had covered almost all of the salient points except the relationship between the history of the company and the social problems which had recently developed. They were given the choice of continuing in the search for this one basic factor in the problem or adjourning into their syndicates to decide on the action to be taken (for this they were given copies of the questions). They chose to curtail their syndicate period and, after reporting their recommendations, to devote the final ten minutes to completing their analysis. This approach gave them a sense of participation in the session which could not have been achieved in any other way.

There are also times when it is inadvisable to ask the group's advice. For example, at the beginning of the Manchester course if the leader had asked the class whether they would have liked to discuss the forty-two points mentioned by the first speaker, inexperienced as they were with the method, they might well have said 'yes'. However, the leader might have got the answer he wanted if he had put the question in this way: 'Would the group like to discuss these forty-two points now or would you prefer to get on with the main problems in the case and then return to these detailed criticisms if there is time later on?' As a rule of thumb, the leader decided that so long as he did not give the group the impression that he was asking their advice because he did not know what to do next, the technique was a useful one.

He also concluded that it is essential for the case study leader to maintain discipline and control, preferably as unobtrusively as possible. The reactions in Manchester over Mainstays' policy towards trade unions and the emotional arguments in one of the other sessions between top management and supervisory personnel, underlined the need for strong discipline from the 'chair', when the discussion becomes irrational and irrelevant to the discussion. A few words from the leader such as 'Excuse me, for interrupting, gentlemen, but I am not sure that this argument is relevant to the case. If you feel it is, would you show the rest of us how it is important. If not, could we return to the main subject matter.' A humorous aside to the rest of the group may also have the desired effect, but it is dangerous unless the leader knows his group intimately.

Visual Aids

In two of the four sessions, the visual aids were hung in the background and were referred to by the leader only once, when he was reading the case aloud before the discussion began. In one session, a member of the group, at the leader's invitation, went up to the diagram of the machine shop layout to show how he proposed to rearrange the machines.

At the residential centre course, the discussion about organisation became so heated that one of the group asked the leader if he could use the blackboard to sketch the chain of responsibility as it was described in the case. It was also used by several others to show the changes they suggested in the organisation chart. The flow diagram was not used at all, probably because it was confusing and lacking in detail, while the machine shop layout served the same purpose as it did for the executive development group.

HOW THE TEACHER PLAYS HIS PART

In one respect, namely that he was a stranger to all four groups, this teacher's experience is not typical. When a teacher has worked with a class for a time, many of the obstacles described above would have been overcome. The group would be integrated. The teacher would know the names and special interests of his students. They would be familiar with, or at least more receptive to, the case study technique. He could select cases suitable for the group. However, it is usually the first case with a new group which discourages the teacher from employing the case study method regardless of its theoretical merits. Therefore, it might be helpful to review some of the important points which should be borne in mind when learning how to run a case study session.

There are differences in the interpretation of the role played by the teacher. In the educational theory of the Harvard Graduate School of Business Administration, in accordance with much that is known about the psychology of education, learning takes place through participation. Criticism or guidance from one's peers is educative, criticism from a superior is not. At Harvard, therefore, where the case study method was pioneered and has been used for more than thirty years, the teacher does little more than provide a situation in which discussion can take place. He himself is not a discussion leader; he does not point out principles; he does not bring discussion to a point; he does not keep the noisy ones back or encourage the shy ones to come forward. On the other hand, he clarifies both the statements that are made, and the emotion behind the statements. He may also summarise as the discussion goes along.

Others have found it advisable to play a slightly more active role than the Harvard teacher. This role can be broadly summarised under six headings.

Providing the Situation

The teacher's job is not to give his views of the case but to get the discussion of those in the group. The group itself ideally should consist of probably no more than twelve members so that each has many opportunities to speak. The teacher does very little talking and in a good discussion is hardly ever heard at all.

Starting the Discussion

Members of the group should have ample time to study the

case before they meet. When they are all comfortably sitting down the trainer can say something like 'What seem to be the major problems in the case?' At first there will probably be an embarrassing silence which may last for a minute or so or even longer. Then someone will make a contribution and he will usually address his remarks to the trainer. The trainer might take some non-committal comment and then say 'Has anybody else got any views on this?' In this way the trainer encourages group discussion and prevents 'one to one' conversation developing between himself and individual members of the group.

With new groups not used to the case study method it is sometimes helpful to start with an action question—'What would you do if you were Mr X in the case?' After the group has discussed this for three or four minutes the trainer might well break in and say something like 'Well, we have had a number of suggestions for action. If any action is to be effective, of course, it must be based on good analysis. Can we go ahead and analyse the case first? What seem to be the major problems here?' Alternatively, as indicated on page 204, he can let the group ramble for a time and then summarise the points covered and decide on the direction he would like the discussion to take.

Inexperienced groups find action questions easier to deal with, usually because they have not considered all the relevant factors in the case. It is always very important, therefore, to stress the analysis of the case, for, if students have made a good analysis of the problems, the action they base on it has more chance of being effective. The action one member would take, of course, might well differ from the action another member would take, simply because of the differences in their personalities. The analysis of the situation, however, should remain roughly the same for both.

Clarifying Views

One of the trainer's jobs is to clarify statements and the

RUNNING A CASE STUDY SESSION

feelings behind statements. He can do this by re-stating a member's contribution in another way, 'So your opinion, Mr Able, is ...', or 'You feel that ...' He can also do it by reflection. If a group member says 'The only thing wrong with this firm (in the case) is that it employs Mr X', the trainer might respond 'So you feel, Mr Peters, that the firm's problems would be solved if Mr X were dismissed?' This may not seem a particularly worthwhile comment, but in fact it allows Mr Peters to look at his statement again and to realise its implications. It also holds the statement up for examination by the group. The trainer must also clarify the meaning of words. If, for instance, a student says 'The works manager should see the foreman and tell him ...' the trainer might ask 'What do you mean by the words "see" and "tell", Mr Browning? Would you like to say what actual behaviour these words stand for? How will the works manager "see" the foreman and how will he "tell" him?'

Seeking Evidence

It is the trainer's job to expose generalisations and to get specific evidence for conclusions. He can do this by such remarks as 'Would you like to tell us how you arrive at that conclusion?', or 'Would you like to give us the evidence for that statement, Mr Fox?' If someone says 'We had an exactly similar case to this in the factory the other day', the trainer might say, 'Would you like to tell us about it Mr Williams, so that we can see what the similarities are?' When the student has finished his description the trainer might ask the group 'Now is this an exactly similar instance or are there any differences?' Remarks such as these ensure that the group considers the particular case in point, rather than generalisations of some of the problems it may contain.

Fresh Leads

At times the trainer will want to direct attention to parts of the case which have not had sufficient consideration. He can do this by such words as 'Can we consider the situation from the foreman's point of view?', or 'What do you think of the way ...?' If a student has made a point which the group has neglected, or which the trainer thinks is important, he can draw attention to it later by saying something like 'Mr Browning made a point recently and said that ... What do the others think of this?' If the group feels that there is a lack of evidence in the case, the trainer can say 'What evidence do you feel you want before you can come to any conclusions?' When this evidence is listed he can ask the group 'Do we have any evidence on these points?' Often it will be found that there is some evidence in the case which the group has neglected.

This last point introduces an important consideration. It is one of the rules of good human relations and of good decision-making to get all the facts. It is unfortunately true, however, that it is seldom possible to get all the facts, and many decisions have to be taken on the facts that are available. It is important, nevertheless, for managers to know what facts they have not got when they take a decision. As one training authority has put it, decisions must be taken on the best available facts, but a manager should know which facts he does not know.

Summarising

When the group seems to have arrived at a conclusion on any particular point in the case study, the trainer does a service by summarising. He can do this by saying 'The group seem to be agreed that ...' If there are two or more points of view he might summarise by saying 'We have had these two opposite points of view put forward. Is there any way we can relate them or are they incompatible?'

A good summary will help the group on to the next stage of the discussion. A bad summary will interrupt the group's

RUNNING A CASE STUDY SESSION

discussion and may meet with some criticism from the group.

The trainer does not make evaluative comments such as 'Good, I wanted someone to say that', or 'Surely you don't feel that's right?' He accepts all contributions as if they were of equal merit. While he is accepting, however, he also questions, directing attention at the specific situation and at the need for evidence.

He does not try to get the group to arrive at a final decision. He encourages different points of view and different interpretations in the hope that the group will agree on a sound analysis of the particular situation. He is careful always to obtain the group's sanction, never stating more than the group has decided and never pushing his own point of view in front of or over that of the group.

The trainer is not supposed to be a textbook, nor an authority on the case, nor an omniscient oracle. He is there to provide a situation in which discussion can take place in a friendly atmosphere and his job is to stimulate thought. People do not learn to think by being told how to, but by getting practice in thinking. One of the trainer's main functions is to give them this practice.

CHAPTER TEN

CASE STUDY IN THE COURSE

EVEN after the teacher has become familiar with the types of case studies and has learned how to run a case study session as well as to write his own cases, he is still left with a major problem. How can he best use cases in the planning and execution of a course?

One of the most interesting examples of an original and energetic approach to this problem is provided by a recent management practice course in a technical college.

The teacher used the Suggested Syllabus for a Final Examination in General Management (Urwick Syllabus) as his starting point.

MANAGEMENT PRACTICE

Purpose—to provide a review of the responsibilities and practice of management, with special reference to the higher levels. It should link together the functional aspects of management discussed separately in other parts of the course.

The Structure of Organisation—Determining, defining and directing executive and supervisory responsibilities. Establishing the structure. Charts and manuals.

The Formulation and Interpretation of Policy—relation of functional and sectional policies to general policy. The issue of instructions. Delegation of responsibility. Standard practices.

Ensuring Co-ordination—Committees, reports, 'staff' appointments, a common doctrine.

'Standards' for Planning and Control—Budgetary and higher control systems. Presenting information; progress reports, statistics, charts, management ratios.

Research—The management audit.

CASE STUDY IN THE COURSE

Public Relations—Trade Associations, Trade Unions, Government Departments, Local Authorities, Technical and Professional Associations, Social Services.

The Human Element—Building and maintaining the team spirit; leadership and morale. Selection and training of managers. Promotion and succession.

NB Special attention must be drawn to the importance of interpreting and conducting the syllabus with reference to small firms as well as large.

The Teacher's Syllabus

On the basis of this he prepared his own version of the syllabus for the course:

MANAGEMENT PRACTICE

Purpose The course should attempt to integrate the various specialised subjects previously studied and to show how they affect management decisions. The primary aims would be:
1 To acquaint students with top management outlook.
2 To give them a realistic impression of director-level policy making and atmosphere.
3 To equip them with the mental approach needed to deal with management problems effectively.
4 To provide them with specific skills for communicating their ideas convincingly.

Method The value of this course rests on its ability to re-create the real management situation with all of its personality problems and complicating factors not provided for in the usual theoretical treatment of the subject.
1 Case studies will be the basis of the course. They will be selected to include as wide a range of policy problems as possible and to show how decisions are made at board level. They will be chosen also to illustrate the various subject headings in the syllabus.
2 The course will also include instruction and practical exercises in writing business reports, preparing verbal reports and other methods of selling suggested improvements to

CASE STUDY APPROACH TO MANAGEMENT EDUCATION

higher management. In so far as possible, efforts will be made to have the students act as a committee or board, when reports are being presented.

3 Short lectures will be used to convey new factual information and these will be followed by group discussions to consider how this information can be usefully applied.
4 Students will be encouraged to acquire most of the new facts in the course from their directed reading outside class.
5 Students will be required to prepare case studies, describing problems connected with their jobs, and to write critical reports, making recommendations for introducing improvements.

Case Discussion

During the first meetings, the teacher introduced limited objective cases, reading through them sentence by sentence with the class, picking out facts which might play a part in the analysis of the case. For example, from the following paragraph in a case about the dismissal of a foreman:

'The assistant foreman of the manufacturing department had worked there for twenty years and was a very close personal friend of the foreman. As a reward for his long service and in recognition of the unlikelihood of further promotion, the company granted him the privileges of a foreman, and still allowed him to earn overtime pay'

the class extracted these facts:

1 Assistant foreman twenty years service with company
  (part of long service clique?)
2 Close personal friend of the foreman
  (might this affect later dismissal problem?)
3 Unlikelihood of further promotion
  (not good enough? or no promotion policy?)
4 Privileges of a foreman, can earn overtime
  (possible jealousy and status problems?)

When the class had become accustomed to the case study

method he devoted one class to a discussion of the *Morgan By-Products Limited* case (see below). He read the case through and then had one of the students read out Mike Sweeney's version of the costing consultancy. The teacher retained the questions and kept them on hand in addition to his own notes analysing the case. He also kept in reserve some additional information on Nelson in case the discussion lagged and needed some additional data as a stimulant.

After the case discussion, he reviewed the purposes and advantages of the case study approach, placing cards on his magnetic blackboard to illustrate the points. Under the heading Educational Aims were listed Technical Knowledge, Critical-Constructive Approach, Ability to See the Problem, Ability to Collect the Facts, Ability to Analyse Them, Ability to Take Action, Ability to Check the Results. He next asked the class to tell him the elements of the real life management situation. As they provided him with the answers, he posted on his magnetic blackboard previously prepared cards bearing the headings: Group Discussion, Incomplete Data, Lack of Time, Interdependence, Personality Factor. He was then able to prove how closely the case study method resembled the real life conditions of the students' own jobs.

Report Writing

Later in the course when he was conducting a class on report writing, he again made use of this case.

MORGAN BY-PRODUCTS LIMITED[1]

Consultants and the Costing System

This company was originally set up in 1914 by a medium size oil processing firm to sell its paraffin and other by-products.

[1] Prepared by the Case Study Writers' Circle and reproduced by kind permission of the publishers, Newman Neame Ltd.

Ten years later the parent organisation decided to take full advantage of this cheap raw material supply and produce its own furniture polish and wood dyes.

A manager and twelve employees began manufacturing and packing these products in a small two storey eighteenth century factory on the outskirts of a large midlands industrial city. The process for making the polishes was quite simple. The waxes were melted, mixed in the proper proportions with solvent or spirit, poured and packed. Except for the synthetic wax all other raw materials had to be imported. Bottles and tins were purchased from local suppliers.

By 1930 the staff had doubled and the company was employing four travellers. The line of products was gradually simplified so that by the late thirties the wood dyes had been dropped in favour of various forms of wax polishes (paste and liquid emulsions). To deal with the increased demand, the premises and labour force had to be expanded.

World War II curtailed any further development. Approximately half of the space was devoted to the manufacture of decontamination tablets. Production of polishes was of course regulated by raw material quotas.

New Personnel

Although Morgan's had shown moderate profits with great consistency, the parent company was not satisfied with the production methods employed. Seven years ago they appointed a new managing director, Frank Williams with what might be termed a watching brief. The board of the parent company considered him to be a practical and dynamic man. He studied the situation carefully and recommended that a first class production man be co-opted from the company to reorganise the factory. George Nelson, one of the most promising junior production executives, was chosen to fill the post of works manager at Morgan's.

He was a soft spoken man with an easy going and genial disposition. This, together with his technical competence, soon won the respect and loyalty of the foremen and workers. Previously almost all the operations had been performed by hand. For example, the molten wax was poured from jugs into the tins; boxes were hand wrapped and wired; bottles were capped manually; and there was no mechanical materials handling equipment.

Post-war Reforms

Nelson made sweeping and fundamental changes. He purchased new machinery for filling, bottling and wiring. He rationalised production flow, so that it proceeded from floor to floor in logical sequence. He installed three production belts for the filling, setting and packaging of the paste wax (more than fifty per cent of the total output). He replaced the obsolete and inefficient coal burners with an oil heating system.

He also reorganised internal and external transport. Shipment by rail, which had proved very uneconomic, was supplanted where possible by lorries and drivers. Internal handling was considerably improved by the introduction of stillage trucks.

Coupled with the easing of supplies, these improvements led to a 350 per cent increase in production within four years of Nelson's appointment. Further expansion was impossible without additional space, and so applications for the necessary building licences to erect a new factory were submitted.

At this time there were about 150 employees in addition to 48 travellers, seven bulk salesmen and the company's executives. The 84 workers in the factory consisted of 60 girls, who handled filling and packing, and 24 men, who were responsible for direct manufacture, maintenance, receiving and shipping. All labour was drawn from the immediate area.

The chain of command was quite simple. George Nelson, the works manager, was responsible to the managing director. Directly under Nelson was the production manager, a forceful and colourful personality called Mike Sweeney.

Pressure from the Parent Company

Like Morgan's itself, the parent company had also undergone an extensive re-organisation soon after the end of the war, with the assistance of management consultants, two of whom had been appointed to the board of directors.

CASE STUDY APPROACH TO MANAGEMENT EDUCATION

Despite the impressive increase in output achieved by Morgan's, the parent company was not satisfied with the costing system in use. The two new directors in particular exerted pressure to induce Mr Williams to call in consultants. Instead of acceding to this suggestion, he resigned. He explained his objections to this interference at an extraordinary board meeting of his own board and refused to consider a compromise course. At the next session of the management committee he merely said that he 'wanted to retire while he was still young enough to enjoy life'.

The parent company sent one of their executives as a temporary managing director, while they decided on Williams' permanent successor. Messrs Bridewell and Keane, two management consultants, were called in and began their preliminary survey just four days after Williams had left. This gave rise to a variety of rumours about the real reasons for his departure.

Mr Keane called on the directors and the various department heads, beginning with the administrative executives and ending with Nelson and Sweeney. During the first weeks of the investigation, Keane's senior colleague, Bridewell, was elected to the Morgan board. No formal announcement of this appointment was made and rumours began to circulate again.

In his interviews with the directors, Mr Keane's main object was to fill in the background of the company's development. He learned that before Frank Williams arrived on the scene in 1945, Morgan's had been a one man show. Williams' predecessor had been managing director for thirty-one years and—as one director put it—'ran the company from the Royal Enclosure at Ascot'. When Williams assumed control, the board of directors was a 'paper' body, which consisted of the chairman of the parent company (who rarely attended meetings), the managing director, the company secretary and the chief accountant. The last two were elderly women, who had been rewarded for their long service with directorships.

Mr Keane also decided to find out as much as he could about the organisation within the company and the balance of power. He soon discovered that the only other organised unit apart from the board was the management committee. This proved to be a pet topic of George Nelson, who described its origins, development and functions to him in great detail.

Management Committee

Nelson told Keane that Frank Williams had noticed on his first visit to Morgan's that there was no real co-ordination at the executive level. He had therefore decided to follow the pattern of the parent company and set up a management committee to get the necessary backing for his decisions. At that time its members had included Frank Williams, Nelson, and the company secretary, the chief accountant, the sales manager, the purchasing agent and the advertising manager. The committee had met every two weeks at first, with Williams as chairman. Williams used to call on the members in turn to get views on special problems, such as the production target for the autumn sales drive, the purchase of machinery, or the introduction of a new product.

'It used to be quite a useful body until the end of 1948,' Nelson said. 'Then the new board was formed.' The parent company had reached the conclusion that the old board was not carrying out its responsibilities as it should. The retirement of the two elderly women had therefore been used as the occasion for bringing in more active outside directors, a solicitor and a chartered accountant. The board began to meet monthly instead of every six months and discussed many important matters which previously had been left in the hands of the management committee. 'It was then that the real trouble started,' Nelson continued. 'You couldn't get a damn thing done.'

The management committee began to meet less regularly and Frank Williams was often absent from the meetings. On these occasions, the members took turns as chairman. It was customary to discuss departmental problems as the last item on the agenda. Friction and antagonisms which had been simmering for a long time would either burst out into open argument or take the form of a very defensive silence. Every person felt on his guard and refused to discuss his own departmental problems frankly, for fear that someone would make unfair use of the information. The tension was particularly acute between sales and accounting and accounting and production for personality reasons. The accountant was disliked for what the sales manager described as his 'holier than thou' attitude and for unnecessarily interfering with other departments. Friction had also developed between sales and production because of a dispute over the purchase of a new lorry. The power of the management committee rapidly declined, especially after the board imposed a £100 limit to the expenditures which the committee could authorise. It was not long before they were devoting their meetings to discussing such questions as whether the errand boy should wear overalls or whether they should get new tyres for the trade bicycle. As far as Nelson was concerned, he was fed up with the whole committee.

With Mike Sweeney's help Mr Keane familiarised himself with the operations in the factory. From what he had seen, Keane decided that the fulcrum of power rested with the managing director and the works manager.

Changes Suggested

After spending two months in the factory Keane suggested several major changes in the material control and stores procedure. Both Nelson and Sweeney rejected the proposals as impractical. Keane also worked out standard times for the filling belts. On the basis of his statistics, he recommended that the labour force on this operation should be reduced. He also designed various forms for planning and recording production. These were printed and distributed to the factory departments concerned. Once again the works manager and his assistant felt that the suggestions were unrealistic and failed to co-operate fully, thus sabotaging the proposals quite effectively over a period of four months.

Bridewell and Keane decided that special steps would have to be taken to overcome this opposition. As soon as the new managing director was appointed, they decided to act. They called a special meeting to explain their plans and proposals to the management committee. They felt that the response was unsatisfactory.

Shortly afterwards, Nelson and the temporary managing director were recalled to the parent company. At the same time, a new managing director, who had worked his way up through

CASE STUDY IN THE COURSE

the sales department, was appointed. Keane submitted a report to Morgan's board, incorporating the recommendations resulting from his six months' research. He called on the board to implement his suggestions. Unofficially, through Bridewell, he urged the board to fire Sweeney, the acting works manager since Nelson's recall.

The Managing Director's Problems

The new managing director found this a very difficult problem. Although he and his fellow directors disapproved of the offhand, informal and undignified atmosphere which Sweeney fostered in the factory, his record was remarkably good. He had come to the factory in 1946 as a chemist from one of the two older universities. Nelson thought he had sufficient organisational ability and popularity with the workers to justify putting him in charge of all production. Sweeney also seemed to be dependable and very conscientious, although violent in his dislikes and prejudices, one of which was directed at the sales department.

MIKE SWEENEY'S VERSION OF THE COSTING CONSULTANCY

Williams was a first rate managing director. He knew his job. Four days after Frank Williams left, this Keane chap started work. What a smooth oily . . . . . . he was. He came around and told us in the nicest way possible the benefits of good costing and how he was going to introduce it. He was right about the old system, if you can call it a system. It was by guess and by God, but it worked. Frank Williams seemed to pick a figure out of the air, but he knew the trade inside out and had a jolly shrewd idea of costs. Then Keane got down to details. We taught him the trade for weeks at five guineas an hour. What a pompous . . . . he was, though. The first thing that caught his eye was materials control. All of our raw materials were stored in one place and each bloke responsible for manufacturing one of our products would come along and draw from it according to his requirements. Admittedly it was far from perfect, but losses were small. One morning he arrived and said, 'This is the system I suggest. What are your reactions?' I knew it wouldn't work and that if it did, it would hold up production; and I told him so. He wanted to instal a screen partition so that each manufacturing section would have its own material. There simply was no room for such a partition and George Nelson agreed with me. He also wanted to have signed requisitions before any material was issued. Now that's all right if you have plenty of men, but I only had three; one for the lorry, one for unloading and the other for storing. We couldn't possibly stop unloading all the time to issue material. Keane then says that we should be able to draw two or three weeks' stock at a time, but he doesn't know our sales department. Why, we're lucky if we know what we're going to do over the next three days. We talked him out of the screen partition but he insisted on our trying the requisition system. That didn't work either and I refused to hire any additional men just to work his .... system, when what we really needed was more new equipment for production purposes. And it was his friend on the board who was saying 'no' to every request we put in, and no one else could challenge him, since he was the only one on the board who understood anything about production.

The second bee in his bonnet was standard times. He measured the belts which we use for filling the wax paste tins. He then measured the tins and speed of the belts. One day he comes up to me and says 'What's your standard daily target?' I explained the unpredictable and intangible factors which affect our production, like the weather, badly fitting lids, group moods, etc. I told him we get between 22,500 and 25,000 average every day so that I set 23,500 and use that as a control figure. 'Sweeney,' he says, giving me that professional piercing look, 'you're losing 4,000 tins a day and, what's more, you are wasting eight girls on the line.'

George Nelson and I put our foot down and told him it was all baloney. They had moved from rule of thumb to the other extreme of mathematical theory, and, furthermore, they didn't bother to consult us about these things. Then they went and had all those forms printed without any experimental period. The only reason I still use any of them is because I hate to see all that money wasted. Speaking of forms, Keane designed one

CASE STUDY IN THE COURSE

for me that took no less than an hour to fill out. And what did I have then? — a list to tell me the things I had to do for the day.

It all came to a head about six months after they first started. They called a special meeting in the canteen to present their whole scheme to the management committee, junior executives and foremen. They couldn't have picked a worse place or time if they had tried. It was just before lunch and there was a terrific din of plates, carrot chopping and fruity language that drifted up over the partitions. Then a third consultant with a thick Oxford accent stands up and starts talking in a whisper. No one can hear anything until he starts mentioning the sales normal figure, which is the key to the whole costing system. Then up jumps the sales manager, shouting 'That's not what we agreed,' and they then proceed to have a bitter argument. When that is finished, the talk continues, but the bloke spoke so quietly that we were unable to hear nine-tenths of what he said.

If there had been any doubts about the stupidity of the plan, they were dispelled by that meeting. It was really just too complex. Derek — he's one of our foremen — was supposed to pour in wax to a 10,000th of a pound and they had everything else figured out to seven places; I suppose because that was the number of places on the calculating machine in the office. It was so complex I never tried to understand it.

Since the teacher was planning to use the case as a basis for the preparation of written reports, he did not distribute the following questions, which had previously been considered in the course of class discussions.

ANALYSIS OF THE SITUATION

1 In the light of Mike Sweeney's description of the costing system in use at Morgan's, do you feel that the parent company was justified in insisting that corrective action be taken?
2 What are your views on the way in which they induced their subsidiary, Morgan's, to take steps to improve the costing system?

CASE STUDY APPROACH TO MANAGEMENT EDUCATION

3 Do you think that the parent company dealt with Williams' resignation satisfactorily? If not, why not?
4 What do you think of the parent company's decision to send one of their executives as a temporary managing director, while they decided on Williams' permanent successor?
5 What were the implications of the manner and timing of the introduction of the two consultants, Bridewell and Keane, into Morgan's?
6 Do you think that the circulation of rumours following Williams' resignation and Bridewell's election to the Morgan board were a cause for concern?
7 What do you think of the way in which Mr Keane handled the initial stages of his investigation?
8 What factors in the early history of the company shed light on the present situation?
9 What do you think of Nelson's account of the rise and fall of the management committee?
10 How do you account for the changes in the status and functions of the management committee?
11 What functions could the management committee usefully perform as compared with the board?
12 What do you think of Nelson's and Sweeney's attitude towards Keane and what factors in the situation seem to you to account for their behaviour?
13 How do you assess Sweeney and the part he has played in the situation?
14 What are your views on the steps taken by Bridewell and Keane to gain acceptance of their recommendations, after the new managing director had been appointed?
15 Do you think that the behaviour of the consultants might have served to reduce the inter-departmental friction at Morgan's?
16 How would you summarise the main problems at Morgan's?

ACTION

17 If you were the new managing director, what would you do about Bridewell's and Keane's recommendations?

CASE STUDY IN THE COURSE

About the friction among the departments?
About relations with the parent company?

18 What steps, if any, would you take to reorganise the management structure?
19 If you were Sweeney, what action would you take, if any, about your position after Nelson was recalled? How would you have set about the job that Bridewell and Keane were employed to do?
20 As an outside consultant, what recommendations would you make about the management committee?
21 In Frank Williams' position, how would you have dealt with the suggestion of the parent company board that consultants should be called in to study the costing system?
22 What action, if any, should have been taken to fill the gap caused by Nelson's recall?

GENERAL IMPLICATIONS

23 Judging from this case, what problems are likely to arise in the relations between a parent company and its subsidiary?
24 Judging from this case, what problems are attached to the position of a consultant in a firm?
25 What lesson can be learned from the experience at Morgan's about the value of an effective information system?
26 What problems of the composition and functions of a board of directors are illustrated by this case?
27 What are the advantages and disadvantages of an organised management unit between the board of directors and the line and staff executives?

The wording of the homework assignment was as follows:

Write a report to the board of directors of the parent company, submitting your recommendations for action on those problems, which you, as managing director of Morgan By-Products Ltd, feel they can help to solve.

The two reports which follow are typical of the results produced. The teacher's comments and an explanation of the criteria he used are also given to show the way in which he assessed the work.

CASE STUDY APPROACH TO MANAGEMENT EDUCATION

One Student's Report (A)

MORGAN BY-PRODUCTS LTD

Part I—Immediate problems
Part II—Future organisation

PART I

(a) Introduction
(b) Present position
(c) Summary of recommendations
(d) Analysis of recommendations
    1 Keane's report
    2 Appointment of works manager
    3 Mr Sweeney
    4 Messrs Bridewell & Keane

PART II

(a) Introduction
(b) Recommendations
(c) Reasons for recommendations
(d) General conclusions

(Teacher's comments: Although a title page and table of contents might be useful for introducing a lengthy report, here it is not only out of place but might tend to discourage a busy executive from reading it. Furthermore, it is not clear what the report is about or to whom it is directed. As you will recall from class discussions, the problem can be solved by using a simple form of address: To: [the recipient] Re: [the subject of the report].)

PART I

(a) *Introduction*

The Morgan Company has been subjected to a great deal of internal strife in the last few months, resulting in a lowering of the morale throughout the works and a deterioration in the relationship between the board of directors and senior staff. The events which have been responsible for this, directly and

CASE STUDY IN THE COURSE

indirectly, can be summarised as follows:
1 The decision to investigate the costing system
2 The resignation of Frank Williams
3 The introduction of Messrs Bridewell and Keane immediately after Frank Williams had resigned
4 The failure of the Morgan Board to give any reason to the staff for Frank Williams' resignation, with the result that rumours were rife, particularly when Messrs Bridewell and Keane arrived on the scene
5 The presentation of Keane's report to the management committee when it was unanimously opposed
6 The transfer of George Nelson without any explanation, which gave rise to further rumours
7 The appointment of Mr Bridewell as a director

(Teacher's comments: What we described in class as the 'Summary of the Problem' and what you have called 'Introduction' should impress on the reader the urgency and importance of solving existing problems. By doing so, it should also serve to stimulate interest in the resumé of the recommendations which follow immediately. You have touched on the main problem — internal strife and its effect on morale, but you have obscured the issue by bringing in a detailed summary of the events leading to the present position. All of this material and the points listed under 1b could have been dealt with much more effectively by devoting a separate section to the description of the background and nature of the present problems, in effect, an elaboration of the 'Summary of the Problem'. This would logically follow the 'Summary of Recommendations'. Thus the order would be: Address, Summary of Problems, Summary of Recommendations, Conclusion. There is no hard and fast rule about this, but it is commonsense to prepare a report in such a way that the recipient can grasp the essentials by reading only the first two pages, especially if as in this case, the reader is the busy board chairman of the parent company.)

(b) *Present Position*

1 A new works manager must be appointed to replace George Nelson

CASE STUDY APPROACH TO MANAGEMENT EDUCATION

2 Keane has now submitted his report and Bridewell is pressing for some action to be taken
3 Action must be taken to restore the high morale that existed prior to the resignation of Frank Williams
4 The future of M. Sweeney, production manager and acting works manager, must be decided. Bridewell is asking for his dismissal mainly at the instigation of Keane.

Whether these matters may appear to be domestic ones to be dealt with by the Morgan board, they arise out of decisions and actions taken by the parent board and it is for that reason that I seek your approval of the following recommendations:

(Teacher's comment: In analysing the background and present situation, you have not organised your material well. You should have presented the facts in chronological sequence or classified them according to the various possible headings: Information, Personnel, etc. If you felt that the parent board was ill-informed, which it appeared to be, then the former would have been preferable.)

(c) *Summary of Recommendations*

1 *Keane's report*
   That this report be held over until the new factory is built, it being left to the board's discretion to incorporate such proposals as they see fit, when planning the new layout.
2 *The appointment of works manager*
   That George Nelson be returned to Morgan's as works manager with a seat on the board
3 *Mike Sweeney*
   That Mike Sweeney be confirmed in his appointment as production manager
4 *Messrs Bridewell and Keane*
   That we dispense with Mr Keane's services immediately and that Mr Bridewell be asked to resign.

(Teacher's comments: You may be weakening your hand by asking for support on recommendations which are a domestic responsibility of Morgan's. Furthermore, it might have been more effective to have dealt with the Part II re-organisation proposals here, since they affect the chairman and the parent

CASE STUDY IN THE COURSE

company more directly. It is also worth noting that you have made a mistake in section 3. Sweeney has always officially been production manager.)

(d) *Analysis of Recommendations*

1 *Keane's report*

There is no doubt that the existing cost system is a hit or miss affair and a more efficient system should have been installed some time ago when Frank Williams first started to expand the company. However, the company has shown good results with great consistency for a number of years which to a great degree justifies the present system.

Nevertheless Bridewell and Keane were introduced to survey the costing system and no mention is made of any other investigation to be carried out. Bridewell was appointed to the board and thereafter Keane carried out the survey.

From information I have gathered he appears to be a tactless individual who has succeeded in antagonising the whole of the management committee and in particular Nelson and Sweeney. The latter is a man of violent likes and dislikes and he has made no attempt to hide his opinion of Keane.

Keane's report includes recommendations which are outside his terms of reference in that he has made certain proposals concerning production matters. In addition he proposes that certain structural alterations are made which would encroach on the already limited production space and his system is quite unnecessary under the present conditions. I am certain that when the new factory is built we shall be able to incorporate many of his suggestions, and in that respect I consider it is money well spent.

Quite apart from the practical aspects of the report, I have given a great deal of consideration to the psychological aspect and I am convinced that it would be bad policy to implement it at this juncture. There is a tremendous amount of opposition to it, which was apparent when the report was presented to the management committee, and I am certain that if it is put forward now it will fail through lack of cooperation on the part of the staff. In addition it will arouse animosity to the board and, coupled with events of the last few months, give the impression that Bridewell is the boss.

I appreciate that rejection of this report will have repercussions on the parent board in that it amounts to a vote of no confidence in the consultants, but I must repeat that to accept Keane's report at the moment, good or bad, can only have a harmful effect on the board's relations with the management and employees in general.

2 *The appointment of a works manager*
The great strides that have been made in the past in improving production can be mainly attributed to George Nelson. We are now contemplating further expansion and I am certain that there is no better choice than Nelson. I give reasons for his appointment as a director in Part II.

3 *Mike Sweeney*
Sweeney is a man of violent likes and dislikes but he is also a first class organiser, very capable and very popular with all employees, so much so that labour turnover even among unskilled females is less than ten per cent. He has his faults but these I am sure can be eradicated by tactful handling and he can be made an even more valuable member of the team. He is in a strong position at the moment in that he has no understudy and his dismissal would mean the appointment of an outside man.

In the event of George Nelson not being available to return to Morgan's, this would mean the loss to the company of all the experience gained in the last few years.

I do not intend to allow such circumstances to arise in the future as it is my intention to arrange a training scheme so that we can promote from our own ranks.

4 *Bridewell and Keane*
In the case of Keane, there is no argument for his retention. He has completed his allotted task and I can see no further use for his services.

In the case of Bridewell the situation is more difficult. I have no personal objection to him, but the circumstances of his appointment and his association with Keane will mean that the staff will always be suspicious of him, and he is not likely to gain their confidence.

CASE STUDY IN THE COURSE

(*Teacher's comments:* You have argued convincingly about all your recommendations with the exception of the very last, The parent company board were responsible for the introduction of the consultants and probably had Bridewell placed on the Morgan board. Therefore the suggestion that he be asked to resign must be supported by much more evidence than has been produced here.)

PART II

(a) *Introduction*

I wish to make certain recommendations in this part of my report concerning the future organisation of the company. In this respect I would ask you to bear in mind the circumstances described in Part I, and the events which have led up to them.

(b) *Recommendations*

1 That the board of Morgan's be strengthened by giving George Nelson a post on the board.
2 That I am appointed to the board of the parent company so that Morgan's can be brought into closer touch with you.
3 That a vice chairman be appointed.

(c) *Reasons for recommendations*

1 With the departure of Bridewell there will be no member of the board with first class knowledge of production problems. The other directors are excellent men in their own spheres but when production problems have to be discussed they can make no great contribution.

In order to strengthen the contact between management and board, I propose to appoint myself chairman of the management committee. This committee has in the past had no link with the board and has acted more as a discussion group. I intend to empower the committee to pass resolutions for consideration by the board so that they can take a more effective part in the affairs of the company.

CASE STUDY APPROACH TO MANAGEMENT EDUCATION

2 My appointment as a director of the parent company should enable us to avoid the mistakes of the past few months which can undoubtedly be attributed to the fact that decisions were made in respect of Morgan's by the parent company, without that body being fully aware of all the circumstances. Had the board been kept fully aware of Morgan's activities, there is no doubt that they would never have agreed to the introduction of Bridewell and Keane.

3 I appreciate that the many calls upon your time make it extremely difficult for you to attend as many of Morgan's board meetings as you would like, and I therefore suggest that a vice chairman be appointed to deputise for you. I assure you that I will give whoever you appoint my wholehearted support.

(Teacher's comments: The Part II recommendations seem somewhat brash and tactless to me. For example, you might have suggested your election to the parent company board indirectly, perhaps by pointing out as you have done in *Reasons for Recommendations, 3* that since the chairman was too busy to attend Morgan board meetings, it might be helpful to have someone from Morgan's on the parent company board. As it is, you have given the impression that you are 'on the make' and that you think the chairman is not as efficient as he might be. This impression is heightened by the inaccurate reference to the management committee, which in its early days played an important role in policy-making and counted Frank Williams, the managing director then, as one of its regular members.)

(d) *General conclusions*

If the recommendations in the first part of this report are approved immediate action can be taken to restore morale to its previous high level.

The implementation of the recommendations in Part II will ensure that we do not make the same mistakes in the future and at the same time will enable Morgan's to go ahead and expand, knowing that they are no longer considered a 'poor relation' but a partner in your organisation.

CASE STUDY IN THE COURSE

GRADING SHEET
Score 83
Rank in Class 2

EFFECTIVENESS (60)   50
Despite the detailed criticisms in the report, as a whole it is well thought out and convincing—a good piece of work. In view of a certain tactlessness in its approach however, the report might conceivably miss its mark.

PRESENTATION (20)   15
Although the structure of the report departs from the form discussed in class, the reasons for your diversion are clear and must be judged in terms of their effectiveness in putting over your case. If there is legitimate doubt on that point there is no doubt about the beginning of the report which is weak.

STYLE (20)   18
Your style is clear and readable. Sentences are well constructed and you have varied your style to fit the needs of the different sections of the report.

Another Student's Report (B)

REPORT FROM THE MANAGING DIRECTOR OF MORGAN BY-PRODUCTS LTD TO THE BOARD OF DIRECTORS OF THE PARENT COMPANY

I am grateful to the board of directors to have this opportunity to put forward my views and to make certain recommendations on the condition of Morgan By-Products Ltd.

Background to Present Situation

Since 1945, when your board made what has since proved to be a very wise decision, that is to change the methods of production in the Morgan Company, there have been many fundamental changes leading to greater efficiency and higher productivity. My predecessor, Mr Williams, supported by Mr Nelson as works manager, was responsible for these production im-

CASE STUDY APPROACH TO MANAGEMENT EDUCATION

provements. As a result the production increased by about 350 per cent. However, the growth on the production side was not altogether matched by a growth in the rest of the organisation. For example, the costing methods used at Morgan's depended to a very great extent on the sagacity of one member of the staff. This, as well as other matters, were well known to your board, and you decided to call in management consultants to advise on these questions, following a method which had proved very successful within your own company.

Problems confronting Morgan By-Products Ltd

1 The decision to introduce management consultants into the Morgan Company were not well received by the management. It led to Mr Williams' resigning.
2 This event was closely followed by the introduction of Messrs Keane and Bridewell, management consultants, into the Morgan works—occurring only four days after the resignation of Mr Williams. The matter was not clearly explained in the works and rumours began to circulate.
3 The previous morale position of the factory was at once affected, the happy family atmosphere was lost.
4 Resistance to the management consultants existed at Morgan's right from the start, not least amongst some of the higher executives. The appointment of Mr Bridewell to the board of directors did not help in this direction especially as, once again, the appointment was not explained. The rumour-mongering now grew—as did the resistance.
5 These problems existed quite apart from any recommendations the consultant might make or any valuable opinions they might give.

Messrs Bridewell and Keane did make some very fundamental recommendations as a result of their detailed investigation in the Morgan company.

Their recommendations concerned major changes in (i) material control, (ii) stores procedure, (iii) after they had arrived at standard times for filling belt operations they recommended that the labour force should be reduced on this operation, (iv) they designed and distributed forms for planning and recording production.

CASE STUDY IN THE COURSE

These changes affect the works manager and the production manager—who were from the start biased against the consultants. Their attitude throughout was somewhat obstructionist, and they were positive in their disapproval and rejection of the consultants' recommendations, feeling that the proposals were impractical and could not be made to work satisfactorily in the Morgan works.

6 As the situation stands today, the works manager has been withdrawn, Mr Nelson was in fact recalled to your factory. The production manager, Mr Sweeney, has been acting works manager since Nelson's recall.

Mr Sweeney has a very informal and undignified manner in the works and he does hold violent prejudices against people. But in our present situation Mr Sweeney is something of a key figure, he has a very thorough knowledge of his job. But I have been urged to dismiss him by the consultants.

7 A permit has been applied for by the Morgan Company for a new factory. Further expansion of the works cannot go ahead until we get larger premises.

It can be seen that there are many troubles at Morgan By-Products Ltd. A major upheaval has taken place over the last few months. I have been appointed at a critical time but I have the advantage of having been within the organisation during this period.

Recommendations

1 In a small company like Morgan's it is essential, if things are to run smoothly, to have a good morale. Co-operation amongst all grades of employees is essential for harmonious working. This situation must be restored in the immediate future.

Two active steps can be taken to help in this direction. (i) To restore the feeling that the management is no longer in a state of flux. This will be done by settling the production side —time will do the rest. (ii) Some information must be spread concerning the happenings of the last few months; the rumours spreading around since Mr Williams' resignation must be stopped; and the real state of affairs must be made known.

2 The internal structure of the company could be strengthened

by making a few changes. I would like to see the management committee reconstituted, and performing a new function. It can achieve the co-ordination which is necessary between the various departments. In itself this will lead to the departmental heads having a wider view than merely their own department which will enable them to see their way to greater integration.

```
                       Managing director
                              |
                     Management committee
    ┌─────────────────────────┼─────────────────────────┐
Works manager            Chief accountant            Secretary
    ├─────────────────────────┬─────────────────────────┐
Production             Purchasing agent            Sales manager
 manager                      |                          |
                            Stores                 Advertising agent
```

3 Our primary aim is to achieve the ends desired by the parent company, and to do this the production side must be investigated.

Consultants have made very thorough investigations on these problems—and have put forward several proposals. These have been rejected by some members of the staff. I feel however that the problems with which they dealt are very real ones and must be dealt with. If Mr Sweeney cannot see his way to accepting them, or alternatively suggest other proposals which are equal or superior, then he must leave the company. However, at the present time the company needs his knowledge of the production techniques and I shall firstly endeavour to secure his co-operation. But I believe in the principle that nobody is irreplaceable and if it does not prove possible to do this then he must be asked to go. A new works manager must be obtained as soon as possible—possibly a man with experience in a works already using good costing methods, etc.

GRADING SHEET
Score 50
Rank in Class 12

CASE STUDY IN THE COURSE

EFFECTIVENESS (60) 27

This is a very disappointing report and far below the usual standard of your work. In fact, considering the material included and the recommendations put forward, one can only conclude that the report should never have been submitted to the chairman of the parent company. You are asking for permission to carry out policies well within your jurisdiction as Morgan's managing director. However, the proposals themselves are ill-considered, contradictory and inconclusive. You say in one breath that Sweeney is something of a key figure and in the next breath that you will sack him if he does not behave because you 'believe in the principle that nobody is irreplaceable'. You say you want the management committee reconstituted and performing a new function but you do not indicate what it is. You also make some suggestions for altering the internal structure, without explaining or justifying such extraordinary measures as making the sales manager responsible to the works manager.

The report is full of vague statements such as: 'the production side must be investigated.' 'Consultants have made very thorough investigations on these problems.'

PRESENTATION (20) 11

There is no title to the report, no brief statement of the urgency of the problem or summary of the recommendations. In fact the report reflects very little constructive thought and logical planning.

STYLE (20) 12

The style is discursive and rambling. Frequently the sentences and paragraphs do not seem to follow on logically. It is difficult to read and the choice of words is careless and slipshod.

In order to give the class some indication of the criteria he had used in assessing their reports and the standards against which they were measured, the teacher read out the best report and his comments on it, having first secured the author's permission to do so. He then asked members of the group to consider his comments on their work in the light of what they had just heard. This enabled him to avoid writing detailed comments on the majority of reports, to give them some indication of the quality which they were expected to attain, and to provide them with an opportunity for a follow up discussion on the techniques of report writing.

Role playing and speaking

After a lecture and discussion on the verbal report, this same case problem was used for an experiment in role playing and speaking. The class undertook to act as the board of directors of Morgan's parent company with members taking the part of the board chairman and Morgan's managing director in turn. The object was for Morgan's managing director to try to get the parent company's board to accept his recommendations for a reorganisation in the relations between the two companies. The procedure was simple. The person taking the part of Morgan's managing director had fifteen minutes to present his case to the board. At the end of the period he and his successor left the room. The board then prepared a five minute critique of the performance before the next presentation began.

Three of these critiques, commenting on the most successful performance, the most disappointing and one representative of the average, will indicate the methods used for measuring the effectiveness of the exercise.

Critique on Speaker A

1 The speaker showed an intimate knowledge of the subject although she had too many notes with her, which distracted the board.
2 Her manner was sincere and convincing and she used her feminine charm to the best advantage.
3 She spoke audibly and distinctly.
4 Her introduction was very effective and put the problem in perspective.
5 She displayed tact in the choice of the simile comparing the

CASE STUDY IN THE COURSE

Morgan Company's problem to the growing years of an adolescent. She was also wise to avoid a direct attack on the consultants.

6 Her emphasis on the lack of information and the effect of this policy on morale was commendable.
7 She did not allow herself enough time for the final summary.
8 She did not tie up the report by asking for any specific action but made a moving plea for re-establishing morale through closer co-ordination.

DECISION: The board would have accepted her proposals.

Critique on Speaker B

1 The speaker did not seem to know the facts and kept searching for relevant notes, which resulted in long pauses, embarrassing to the board.
2 His manner was uncertain and on some points patently insincere. He showed no real interest in what he was doing.
3 His voice was inaudible and indistinct, and he spoke too slowly.
4 He was also too informal in his approach, treating the board with ill-concealed indifference.
5 His introduction, which consisted of a long apology for his own faults and errors, struck the wrong initial note and made the board feel antagonistic towards him.
6 He failed to give a detailed logical picture of the situation but rambled on about the problems and the unpleasant atmosphere in the company.
7 He made his recommendations but gave no evidence in support of them. Even these points were presented without emphasis.
8 Some of his criticisms of the parent company board in his very inadequate summing up were tactless to say the least.

DECISION: The board would sack the managing director.

Critique on Speaker C

1 The speaker knew his facts but seemed to be slightly overwhelmed with too much information.
2 His manner was confident and sincere.
3 He spoke clearly and effectively.

4 Although he had captured the interest and attention of the board during his introduction, he soon lost it because he was long winded.
5 His initial tactful remarks about the ability of the parent board were offset by his intemperate criticism of them and the consultants in the latter part of his report.
6 He failed to emphasise his points and wasted considerable time by bringing in one or two red herrings.
7 Too much of his report dealt with Sweeney and not the broader, more important issues.
8 He did not seem to have a very clear idea about his recommendations and ended up by suggesting that no action be taken until the new factory was built.

DECISION: The board would take no action, since it had the impression that the situation was not very serious.

Assignments

The final stage of the group's training in the case study approach to Management Practice consisted of a series of assignments, which required students to write case studies and management reports about their own firms. Since it was too much work to expect students to complete in their own time, the teacher set aside two class periods for the project.

In this example, the teacher used various kinds of case study to achieve the fourfold purpose of the course. Although he taught other cases during the year, he devoted this amount of time to the *Morgan* case because it dealt with board level problems and conveyed something of the top management outlook and atmosphere. Furthermore, he felt that it would help students to develop the mental approach required for dealing with similar high level problems. In all, he spent eight sessions out of twenty-nine laying the foundations of his course and then built on them a superstructure of further factual information.

Another experiment, which has been carried out with great success at Birmingham Technical College, not only

CASE STUDY IN THE COURSE

presents 'live' case study problems but enlists the active aid of practising managers. A company director or a top manager is invited to attend an evening class and to act as a one-man Brains Trust for an hour and a half. During this period he describes informally a problem he has encountered in his work and the group discusses it, asking him questions and exchanging views about it with other members of the group. This session requires no advance preparation on the part of the visitor and takes so little time that the busy executive finds it both convenient and agreeable to take part.

This experiment represents a significant advance towards the closer relationship between education and industry, which serves the valuable twofold purpose of showing top executives the value of management education and at the same time of injecting an air of practical reality into the educational process.

PART III
MEASURING THE RESULTS OF MANAGEMENT EDUCATION

INTRODUCTION

A QUARTER of a century ago Dr Bowie pointed out that the functions of a management educational institution embraced more than just 'stocking the student with facts or even with ideas that are simply given him to absorb'. He felt that it should 'introduce the student to a world where he will be required to do his own thinking. It should strive to develop an analytical ability to break a problem down into its causal relations and reach conclusions on a logical basis.' Furthermore he recognised that an educational institute could only develop talent, not create it. Therefore he insisted on the importance of selection, for as he saw so clearly 'the final task of the school is to fit the young man to assume responsibility and to handle industrial situations wisely and well.'

Few if any thinking people would disagree with these criteria for assessing the effectiveness of management education, but in fact are these the standards of measurement which form the basis of the present examination system?

This is a question of fundamental importance, for it is the examination as much as the syllabus which shapes the curriculum and determines where the emphasis will be placed and how the time available for instruction will be allotted.

The final section of this book attempts to study this basic question against the background of the same practical assumptions as those which Dr Bowie set forth twenty-five years ago. The results of the study are not intended to imply criticism, but merely to shed light on a fundamental problem which may have been obscured by the acceptance of respectable academic tradition at a time when a completely fresh appraisal is needed.

CHAPTER ELEVEN

RECEPTION AND ASSIMILATION

THE ultimate test of an individual's management ability is performance on the job. However, this test has done less to influence the form of management education than the examinations which are set at the end of a training course, either in an individual company or in the many technical colleges operating the joint British Institute of Management—Ministry of Education Management Studies Scheme.

Students and trainees are primarily concerned to make a success in their courses and if the criterion for success is a high mark in the final examination, then the quality of that examination will largely determine the value of the course. In new training programmes, where examinations are borrowed from outside sources and used as models, they can affect the form and objects of the course and often perpetuate the approach they embody, however unsuitable it may be. Therefore, it is of the utmost importance to examine critically the existing state of affairs and decide if there is any need for a change in emphasis or direction. The problem, not simple in itself, is greatly complicated by other considerations, such as the time available to examiners and assessors, the validity of measurements used, the application of consistent standards. The frightening spectacle of the millions of true and false tests used in America, which are marked by automatic machines, shows to what extremes the time saving mentality can lead in the search for solutions to these problems. It also emphasises the need for a careful and thorough re-evaluation of the present situation.

The Academic Tradition

Although there has been a trend towards more practical

problems in management examinations in the last few years, the abstract question, deriving as it does from the great British academic tradition, still holds sway. Those who favour abstract questions argue persuasively that with classes scattered all over the country and teachers of widely different qualities having to do their best with students from widely differing backgrounds, a degree of abstraction in the questions is inevitable in order to achieve any even roughly uniform standards of measurement. Surely this line of reasoning implies that the form of questions is dictated more by the convenience of the examiners and their desire for a simple and standard grading formula than by the real objects of the examinations, namely to test the skill of the student in a management situation. Admittedly, the ability to answer a practical question well does not necessarily prove that the student would be as effective in the real life situation. However, the understanding of what is the correct solution to a specific problem requires only one step to be translated into action. The understanding of the correct abstract principle, on the other hand, does not guarantee that the student will even be able to apply it to a situation, much less evolve a practical solution.

One teacher, particularly interested in finding the most effective type of question to test management ability, collected 200 of what he called 'abstract questions' which had been used in various management examinations over the past five years. The following are typical examples.

1 State the functional divisions of management and discuss how each may affect the industrial activities of a manufacturing concern.
2 Explain what is meant by 'general policy' and 'sectional policies' and critically examine their inter-relationships.
3 There are certain stages in the development of a product from the invention to distribution. Describe these and the factors which should be considered before policy is decided upon.

RECEPTION AND ASSIMILATION

4 Describe in detail the types of relationships which are found in various forms of organisations.
5 Discuss in some detail the idea of extending the leader's personality by the use of subordinates in a 'staff' relationship.
6 What are the elements of the process of management? Write short notes about each of them.
7 What groups of qualifications are required for the effective discharge of executive responsibilities at any level?
8 Write an essay on the delegation of authority and responsibility.
9 List the basic principles of organisation. Define their meaning and inter-relationship.
10 Describe the characteristics of a good interviewer and the essentials of a good employment interview.

On one occasion he chose No 7—What groups of qualifications are required for the effective discharge of executive responsibilities at any level?—and asked each member of a management class to write the answer on a card. These he collected and compiled in a master list, which included:

Experience
Tact
Justice
Ability to delegate
Personality
Self confidence
Willingness to admit mistakes
Enterprise
Capacity for getting relevant facts
Decisiveness
Drive
Leadership (natural leadership)
Broad mindedness
Integrity
Thoroughness
Industriousness
Understanding of human relationships
Ability to express himself
Nous
Humility
Honesty
Vision
Humanity
Character
Physical fitness
Approachability
Test of education
Responsibility
Willingness to accept responsibility

MEASURING RESULTS OF MANAGEMENT EDUCATION

Technical knowledge
Organising ability
Dignity
Tenacity
Courage
Clear thinking
Forcefulness
Analytical approach
Intelligence
Adaptability
Ability
Knowledge of own
  organisation
Foresight

The teacher then selected the four qualities which had been listed most frequently: Integrity, *Nous,* Leadership and Personality. There were four syndicates in the class composed of eight members each. The teacher asked members of each syndicate to prepare a definition of one of the four qualities. They were then read aloud. There were eight different definitions of integrity, *nous* and personality respectively, and only one duplication among the definitions of leadership.

From this experiment alone, he claimed that it was clear that abstract questions were worse than useless, unless the terms were first defined in detail and were generously illustrated by examples.

Validity of the System

Another teacher in a technical college decided to analyse the results of a final examination in order to help to clarify his thoughts on the validity of the examination system. He chose papers which had been set for Management Practice, the final subject in the five year course leading to a Diploma in Management Studies. Students were allowed three hours to complete the examination and were given a choice of six of the following questions:

1 Good management practice rests primarily upon accumulated experience, sound judgment and inherent ability, and cannot be secured by the application of a body of well thought out principles and well designed methods. Discuss this statement.

RECEPTION AND ASSIMILATION

2 How can the managerial policy and the organisational structure of a company be framed to meet the following needs of labour:
 (a) economic security
 (b) physical security
 (c) satisfaction and advancement
 (d) representation?

3 State the main sources from which the working capital of a company is derived. Discuss the importance of reserves in financial management. Indicate the most adequate method of obtaining capital for development purposes in the case of an engineering concern, the present capital of which consists of
 (a) £350,000 of Ordinary shares, on which a dividend amounting to from eight per cent to ten per cent was paid during the last five years, and
 (b) £150,000 non-cumulative six per cent Preference shares. There are no debentures or mortgage.

4 Define the meaning of the term 'common doctrine'. Discuss its significance under different managerial systems.

5 What contribution to the success of joint consultation in industry must be made by:
 (a) board of directors;
 (b) executive and supervisory management;
 (c) the trade union organisation on factory level.

6 Outline the scope of activities of the board of directors and indicate its relationship to various levels of higher management:
 (a) managing director;
 (b) directors with executive departmental responsibilities;
 (c) directors without executive responsibilities.

7 Describe the main types of *entrepreneur* which can be met in British industry and indicate their abilities and disabilities for carrying out the functions of higher management.

8 Describe the composition of a business budget, either of a manufacturing or of a distributive concern. State the main essential of a successful budget system. Describe the stages through which the preparation of a budget must pass and indicate the part played by:

(a) supervisory management;
(b) executive management;
(c) higher management;
(d) the board of directors as a body.

9 Discuss the place of financial control in management practice. Give the reasons why management at different levels must be balance sheet minded. Indicate the connection between financial control and the organisational structure of the firm.

10 Define the meaning of planning as a function of management activity. Draw a distinction between planning and control. Describe the main tools at the disposal of the management for carrying out its planning and controlling functions.

Questions 2 and 6 were chosen by twelve out of thirteen students, while numbers 5 and 7 were next most popular with ten and nine answers respectively. It was clear from the similarity in the framework of the answers to these questions that the subjects had been thoroughly covered, either in class or in a textbook, and hence had seemed familiar when they appeared in the examination. In the question about the types of personalities encountered among managing directors in business, for example, the headings showed a likeness which could be explained only in this way:

Types	Number of times mentioned (out of a possible 9)
Head of an originally one-man concern	9
Head of family concern	9
Prestige director	9
Financier	8
Trained administrator	8
Interlocking directors	7
Ex-employee	7
Ex-technician	6
Specialist or professional director	5

RECEPTION AND ASSIMILATION

The teacher then examined the marking of the thirteen papers. Questions numbers 3, 9 and 10, the questions which required the most technical and practical knowledge, were least popular. Final marks ranged from 85.7 to 52.5. Three of the papers were 80 or above; four were in the 70s; three in the 60s and three in the 50s. He next consulted the official regulations to confirm that to qualify for the award of an Intermediate Certificate or a Diploma, 'a candidate must have:
(a) made not less than sixty per cent of the possible attendances for each subject in each year of the course;
(b) obtained in each subject and in each year of the course not less than forty per cent of the possible marks for homework, course work and in examinations;
(c) obtained not less than fifty per cent of the total of the possible marks in each assessed subject. (The possible marks in the examinations in these subjects shall constitute seventy per cent of this total and homework and course work thirty per cent.)

Comparing Students' Answers

It was clear to him, therefore, that all the students had passed, assuming they had fulfilled the other conditions. To get some indication of the standards and criteria applied in the assessment of the papers, he selected an answer with one of the highest marks and an answer with one of the lowest marks to the following two questions (4 and 8 above):
(i) Define the meaning of the term 'common doctrine'. Discuss its significance under different managerial systems. (ii) Describe the composition of a business budget, either of a manufacturing or of a distributive concern. State the main essential of a successful budget system. Describe the stages through which the preparation of a budget must pass and indicate the part played by:
(a) supervisory management;
(b) executive management;
(c) higher management;
(d) the board of directors as a body.

MEASURING RESULTS OF MANAGEMENT EDUCATION

These were the two answers to the 'common doctrine' question:

Paper A (QUESTION 4)

Common Doctrine

Common doctrine is a body of information as to the purpose and policies of the organisation, together with a definition of relative authorities and responsibilities, and of function. In other words, it is a picture of what the organisation is trying to do, how it is trying to do it, and which particular persons in the organisation will be held accountable for performing which particular duties.

The three managerial systems are:
1 The line organisation. This system is dominated by, in fact based upon, the scale chain and span of control. The chain of authority and responsibility is clearly defined. Each executive is responsible for all the functions of his department, eg buying, selling, etc, and has a specified number of supervisors under his control. He is responsible for the work of those supervisors and they are responsible only to him. The span of control, ie the number of men any one man may have directly under him, is clearly defined. The number becomes less at the top of the chain, ie as responsibility increases. The system maintains unity of command, but leaves no room for specialisation. Indoctrination is not particularly important here, since a man need only know to whom he is responsible and for whom he is responsible, and have a clear definition of his own duties.
2 Functional. Here the line still exists as far as the main function of the organisation of the firm is concerned, but those duties which apply to all departments, eg purchasing, are delegated to one functional department. This system is based on division of labour and specialisation, but it is essential that all duties should be allocated and that there should be no gaps in that allocation nor any overlapping, and that all the work within one functional department should be homogeneous. Unity of command is difficult and any changes in

RECEPTION AND ASSIMILATION

the system, eg the splitting of the work of one department into two (separating methods study from rating), involves a completely new set of relationships. Indoctrination is absolutely essential in the functional organisation, since definition of the duties of all departments must be known to everyone for efficient working.

3 Line and staff. Here the line operates rigidly, so that unity of command is retained. But specialist advice is made available by the appointment of 'staff' in a purely advisory capacity. Here indoctrination is important but not essential. It certainly assists the staff element in overcoming prejudice and resistance which it may meet from the line.

Paper B (QUESTION 4)

Common Doctrine and Structure

The common doctrine of a firm is that range of policies, aims, purposes, that are passed right down from the top to the bottom of the enterprise and are the basic principles, or *raison d'etre* of the company. That *policy* that the day to day policy of the Company tries to live up to.

There are three main types of organisation of management that are recognised today, and they are firstly:

1 *The line system:*

The line runs through the firm from superior to supervised, in a direct and complete chain, no link can be missed, *all* must understand and know their position, rank and responsibility and range of authority, *that* is, authority to the one below them and responsibility to the one above them.

The authority starts and ends, and also does the responsibility from the top of the tree, the very head of the organisation, it runs down to the lowest of the low without losing any of its power.

An order, directive or policy instruction is sent down through all members of the chain and must not 'skip' or miss any, no short cuts are allowed. Time is wasted here.

Information of the greatest importance must pass back up

MEASURING RESULTS OF MANAGEMENT EDUCATION

the chain again, no 'overstepping the mark'—no rush of important advice, at its end, it may be too late at the head's desk and an upset in being already.

Discipline is very strict. Harsh 'carpeting' for people who side step a link or two of the chain.

The 'span of control' limits responsibility of each link only, maybe five or six links, it depends on the amount of decision allowed to the operatives or supervisors concerned.

Overhaul is not needed at all for years in this type of system.

2 *Functional system:*

All processes and skills, operations have been investigated and grouped into one shop or department as near a homogeneous arrangement as possible is made.

Supervisors and heads are responsible solely for that type of work, specialisation is sought after, by the division of labour principle.

But overhaul is necessary here to make sure that no overlaps or gaps are allowed to appear, this must be done quite often and regularly.

Decisions are functionalised, co-ordination requirements are tremendous to hold a firm in one solid group.

Policies are translated for the departments and functions concerned and operations concerned.

There is not the strict discipline of the line system here.

F. W. Taylor, 1850-1920 approx., was the most set on strict functionalisation, with the idea of 'functional foremen'—who had only one responsibility for one type of function—'speed boss', 'gang boss', 'speed and feed boss' and the like.

In the functional system the foreman and supervisor is responsible for all hiring and firing, rates of pay, speeds of machines in his shop.

3 *The line and staff system:*

This is by far the most efficient and easily worked structure possible. For it combines the benefits of the line system with the strict discipline entailed, straight down the main line of authority and orders, policy and directives—with the functional, advisory system of the pure *functional organisation.*

The span of control and division of labour and specialisation result come into the picture.

RECEPTION AND ASSIMILATION

By limiting the numbers of persons, a supervisor can be responsible for efficiency.

While with a staff system that is made up of experts and advisors, who are not endowed with order authority, but merely give information and advice at their specialised field of operations.

Of course, antagonisms *may* arise between the line men and staff side, but this is not always the case.

One Teacher's Analysis

On the 'common doctrine' question, paper A, the teacher noted, had been marked 95 and paper B 60. Both had passed. Neither answer indicated any first hand experience with a common doctrine as it might apply to a real life organisation. For example, to someone from industry who had never heard of the term before, it would not be clear from the paper whether the common doctrine was an unwritten body of information gradually accumulated through experience like the British Constitution or a written doctrine like the American Constitution prepared by a member of a committee drawn from top management. Other questions might also occur to the untutored executive from industry, the teacher felt. Does every company have some kind of common doctrine, either recognised as such or not? How essential is it? At what stage should it be consciously conceived as a policy statement? Is it set forth in any greater detail in most organisations than the preliminary statement of objects in the articles of association?

However, in terms of the question and the two answers, it was indisputable that A was fuller, more understandable, better expressed and superior to B.

The teacher next considered the possible reaction to the answers of a managing director in search of an assistant to concentrate on organisational problems. In reading through the section on the line organisation in the better paper, the teacher felt the practical executive might make the following comments:

'This system is dominated by, in fact based upon, the scale chain and span of control'

(The writer knows the jargon, but surely in every organisation there is some span of control?)

'The chain of authority and responsibility is clearly defined'

(What precisely is meant by the 'chain of authority and responsibility'? Should this be quite separate from the organisation chart? Who should prepare it? And what is meant by 'clearly defined'? The aim of every business is to have its organisation clearly defined regardless of the managerial system in use, but the problem is *how* to do it.)

'Each executive is responsible for all the functions of his department, eg buying, selling, etc, and has a specified number of supervisors under his control.'

(What department in a business would be responsible for 'buying and selling', assuming that buying refers to purchasing and the supply of raw materials? The writer does not seem to have much practical grasp of a real life company. It is not quite clear what 'supervisors' means in this context.)

'He is responsible for the work of those supervisors and they are responsible only to him. The span of control, ie the number of men any one man may have directly under him, is clearly defined. The number becomes less at the top of the chain, ie as responsibility increases.'

(At least three examples come to mind where the last statement does not apply. It may be a desirable aim in some businesses but should not be presented as an immutable law. 'Clearly defined' is here again. By whom, and how?)

'The system maintains unity of command but leaves no room for specialisation.'

(Any system if it is functioning successfully, ie meeting its production targets and making profits, tries to maintain unity

RECEPTION AND ASSIMILATION

of command, and even if the works manager is doing the personnel, planning and other staff functions, he is still first and foremost a works manager.)

'Indoctrination is not particularly important here, since a man need only know to whom he is responsible and for whom he is responsible and have a clear definition of his own duties.'

(If by 'indoctrination' the writer means keeping all the departments informed of what is going on, then the statement is patent nonsense. No one who has ever been inside a functioning business could believe that letting the right hand know what the left hand is doing is 'not particularly important'. Furthermore, could the writer cite one example or type of business which could operate without any functional departments?)

Reverting to the treatment of the same material in B, the teacher felt that the writer had been given the same information in the course as writer A, and could visualise the 'tree' and 'chain', but lacked the ability to express this concept as clearly in writing. It was also apparent that writer B was not clear in his mind about the basic differences between line and functional organisations, thereby justifying the differential in the marking.

After pondering the evidence for some time the teacher came to the following conclusions:

First, he felt that the type of question was designed to test the student's ability to express thoughts clearly and logically in writing, his capacity for conceptual thinking, and his memory of textbook or lecture material.

Secondly, he decided that the criteria for marking were determined by the examination policy and the aims implicit in it. From the evidence it appeared that the assessors marked against a 100 per cent model, which included all the possible factual points and that the greatest value was placed on clarity and logic of expression.

Further Answers

The teacher next turned his attention to two representative

MEASURING RESULTS OF MANAGEMENT EDUCATION

answers to question number 8, on the composition of a business budget.

Paper C (QUESTION 8)

A business budget is general policy resolved into financial terms. It is a task of management at all levels and its composition necessitates decisions of the most important kind.

The business budget of a manufacturing concern will be built up from several budgets relating to particular aspects of the company's business. The first and basic budget is that produced by sales. This is a forecast of market condtions in relation to the company's products and often errs on the optimistic side. It is the job of market research to prune this budget in the light of objective research and the result is then passed to production. Production has to take into account the needs of sales, the stock position at the moment and the stock position which it is considered should be in existence at the end of the period. Production then plans to manufacture goods at as even a rate as possible over the period, bearing in mind deliveries and stock. The materials budget is then calculated, based on the requirements of production and this is passed to purchasing for them to prepare their forecast, bearing in mind terms of contract, quantities necessary for manufacture at given times, and seasonal availability (if this applies) of materials. So the overall budget is built up until it includes sales, production, materials, labour, purchasing, equipment, finance and expenses.

A successful budget system therefore implies that there shall be a great awareness on the part of higher management of the need to forecast, to supply policies on which budgets can be built. It needs an efficient costing and accounting system in order to ensure good calculations, proper functional definition, and a department, preferably under one of the most important executives, whose job it is to see that the budget is followed and to investigate deviations. Supervisory management has then a clearly defined standard to which it can work and within which it has scope for initiative. Executive management has a policy to which it can refer when problems arise. Higher management

RECEPTION AND ASSIMILATION

has forewarning of, eg, the financial requirements of the coming period and can plan accordingly. The board as a body has a policy submitted to it, which it approves and which acts as a yardstick against which to measure executive action and achievement during the period covered by the budget.

Paper D (QUESTION 8)

Manufacturing Concern

The composition of a budget is as follows:
A. *The sales budget.* This is based on how much the company can sell of its products in what areas and at what time, and at which price. This budget leads to the
B. *Production budget,* which uses the figures supplied by the sales budget to decide how the factory can meet the requirements set by the sales budget, ie
(a) the flow of goods to meet the forecast sales in such a way that production can be balanced, and that
(b) stocks of the product can be maintained at all distributive points.
The production budget is split further into,
(a) the labour budget which is an estimate of the amount of labour that is required to carry out the production targets set. It will also state the cost of that labour. (This is invaluable to higher management, for if labour cost is a high proportion of the total cost, it will aid them in the fixing of prices.)
(b) stocks of the product can be maintained at all distributive times required, in order that production requirements are met. Must also take into account,
    (i) the buying of economic lots;
    (ii) the state of the market.

Financial Budget

The capital outlay necessary to purchase new equipment or the overhaul of old equipment so that targets can be met.

The main essentials of a successful budget system are:
(a) the proper definitions of authority and responsibility;

(b) the traditional practice of the board of directors forecasting and formulating sound policies and plans;
(c) the existence of a small but necessary department to administer the budget;
(d) the keeping of accurate and intelligent accountancy practices to ensure that all information required is supplied.

The board of directors
Responsible for the broad plan of the budget on a company level—they are not responsible for the detailed breaking down of it into departments.

Higher management:
The setting of the budget tasks and breaking it down to departmental levels.

Executive management:
Seeing that the tasks set by the budgets are met by their departments and to see where methods have to be changed in order to meet these tasks.

Supervisory management:
The budget sets a plan by which they work, within the limits of which he can use his discretion to the best advantage.

The Teacher's Comments

Paper C, which got a mark of 85 per cent, was clearly and concisely written. It showed a grasp of the concepts of the budgetary contract, and it repeated the information previously absorbed from textbook reading and lectures. However, the teacher felt that it contained statements and assumptions which would have given the writer's employer considerable qualms about giving him greater managerial authority. For example, the student blithely stated 'It is the job of market research to prune this budget in the light of objective research'. He then added later in his answer 'It needs an efficient costing and accounting system in order to ensure good calculations, proper functional definition, and a department, preferably under one of the most important executives, whose job it is to see that the budget is followed and to investigate deviations'.

RECEPTION AND ASSIMILATION

How much would it cost to carry out market research on a sufficient scale to provide the information required? How-large would a company have to be before it could afford a separate department devoted to budgetary control? The teacher felt that the student was out of touch with the realities of pounds shillings and pence.

In examining paper D the teacher decided that the student had reproduced much of the material from lectures and reading, but had failed on the other two counts mentioned earlier, viz, ability to write clearly and capacity for conceptual thinking.

Alternative Methods of Examination

If the logic of this analysis is accepted, two fundamental problems immediately arise. What other qualities should examinations test apart from the three mentioned above and, secondly, what technique can be devised to test them adequately?

If it can be assumed that the object is to train people for management jobs in industry and commerce, then there are a number of other essential qualities and skills required.

1 Capacity for realising the importance of the human factor in most business situations, and the skill to deal with it
2 Ability to apply theoretical knowledge to practical ends
3 Critical ability needed to recognise a technical and/or human relations problem, get the facts, decide on a solution and implement it
4 Ability to express oneself verbally with the same logic, clarity and persuasiveness as in writing

As we have seen from the previous chapter, one teacher found that the case study method enabled him to develop and measure these additional skills as well as those tested by the present examination system.

A number of other attempts have also been made to test these qualities and skills. The following three questions, for example, are typical of several final examination papers which have been set recently.

1 Submit your proposals (with reasons), for the functions, staff and budget of a personnel department, given the following circumstances. 'It is a firm manufacturing electric wall plugs, located in a town of 5,000 population, twenty miles outside London. There are 355 employees, divided as follows: 240 productive workers (80 per cent girls, aged 17-22), 75 office and overhead staff, 20 travellers and the remainder departmental heads and directors. Labour is drawn from the town and surrounding countryside. There is a new British Electricity Authority power station being built nearby and it will open soon.'

This question assumes that the student knows the tool information, viz, the various functions of a personnel department. It tests the student's ability to apply the knowledge to a concrete situation. It also requires him to exercise his judgment and critical faculty, because he must consider policy, staff, and functions in relation to costs and in terms of one particular firm with its special requirements. The question will also measure the individual's understanding of the human factor by the extent to which he realises the implications of the white collar job appeal of the new power station in terms of the recruitment problem.

2 Draw an organisation chart of the company (or a department in it) where you are now employed, giving a brief job description of the key positions. Make a critical appraisal of the chart and job descriptions.

Here the student must relate his classwork to his job in order to answer the question. In the course of his appraisal he will reveal how much he understands of the way in which the personalities of the individuals concerned affect the organisation chart and job descriptions.

3 Describe in detail two wage incentive plans you have read

RECEPTION AND ASSIMILATION

about or seen in operation. Explain their merits and limitations.

The answer to this question tests the student's understanding of wage incentive schemes, also their underlying principles and the problems arising from them, far more extensively than an abstract question. There would be no harm in either this or the previous question, if the student were given the opportunity to collect the factual details before the examination. It is in fact the process of getting the facts and analysing them which is the object of the question.

Less Conventional Examinations

These examples are in keeping with the traditional form of examination. There have also been some less conventional attempts to solve the examination problem. At the conclusion of a series of special lectures on management to the member of a third year Management Studies class, the following final examination was set. Students were allowed three hours:

PART I (90 minutes)

Drawing on your personal experience and any reference material you may have with you, describe in detail one of the following functions performed by the firm in which you happen to be employed: executive administration, personnel management, finances and cost accounting, production organisation and control, sales and marketing.

Model your description on the various case studies used during the course. (NOTE: if your particular position does not fall in any of the above categories, choose what you want to discuss in Part II and write your case study accordingly.)

PART II (90 minutes)

Write a business report addressed to the board of directors of your company, based on the information included in Part I. Present the major problem or problems and then make specific recommendations for their solution, following the form suggested in class. The report should be written from the standpoint of a management consultant.

MEASURING RESULTS OF MANAGEMENT EDUCATION

(*Note:* Part I will be graded on the accuracy, completeness and readability of the description. Part II will be scored on the degree of success achieved in persuading a sceptical board of directors to adopt your recommendations, purely on the strength of your presentation, and on the basis of the information provided in the case study and report.)

The teacher prepared disguised versions of three of the papers and for the next group gave the following assignment, as an exercise to prepare them in studying for their own final examination:

Enclosed are three case studies and management reports compiled and written by students. The material was drawn from their own jobs and the companies that employed them.

The object in each case was to prepare a case study describing the general background of the company and details of some specific problem. On the basis of the information thus provided, a management report had to be written, making specific recommendations for corrective action.

1 Read the enclosed cases and report carefully
2 Rate them in order of effectiveness
3 Be prepared to discuss the reasons for your rating in class

Although this last approach to the problem of the final examination could be introduced into the Management Studies scheme only with the greatest of difficulty, it could be used to advantage on residential courses attended by students from different industrial backgrounds. In a company training course, such a test is generally inadvisable, since the students are too close to the situation and may be emotionally involved.

The adoption of the more searching type of examination question is only the first step in the process. However, it is a step as open to management teachers as to their training colleagues in industry and commerce. The teacher can improve the standard of examinations by setting more practical and realistic questions. This course of corrective action is already open to the teacher under the Management Studies scheme. It is up to him to take advantage of this opportunity and not to assume that the complete responsibility rests with the central authorities. Having changed the nature of the examination the teacher must be prepared to reassess his instructional methods and to find those best suited for the new task.

Self Evaluation for the Teacher

In a course for management several years ago, the teachers were asked to write down what they considered the most important single problem confronting them. The questions were then collected in a hat. As they were drawn out, one question kept recurring in various forms. The gist of it was 'How can a teacher measure his own effectiveness?'

The two leaders of this specialist course had their own answer to the problem and at the end of the course circulated the following questionnaire.

Confidential

Do not sign your name
POST MORTEM
1 Tick the lectures attended
2 What did you think of the course?
3 Which lecture did you like best? Give reasons
4 Which lecture did you like least? Give reasons
5 What was the most worthwhile feature of the course? The least valuable?
6 What is your opinion of the questioning technique and class discussion method of teaching used during the course?
7 Give your frank valuation of the visual aids used on the course
8 What suggestions do you have for changes or improvements on the course?
9 Note any other criticisms and comments on the back

In this case where the teachers were being judged by teachers with the same professional standards, they received some extremely helpful information but usually the post mortem is of very limited use. With most courses it would indicate only whether the students liked the teacher or, alternatively, thought his efforts were futile.

In the final analysis the teacher's effectiveness can be measured only in terms of the student's performance on his job, where the responsibility for recognition and reward lies with management. However, the teacher and training officer can, within the scope of their individual courses and their educational programmes as a whole, evaluate their own effectiveness with reasonable accuracy.

In order to do so the teacher must first attempt to assess the stage of development which a student has reached when he begins the course. He must also have as exact an appreciation as possible of the individual's abilities and latent capacities. Only if this is done at the very beginning of the course is it possible to measure the progress which the student makes in relation to the objects of the course, the work of the other students, and, most important, in terms of his own potential development. If progress is satisfactory on each score the teacher can feel that he has accomplished the first and most important part of his task.

There is a second function, however, without which much of the point and purpose of the first is vitiated. No teacher should feel that he has discharged his full responsibility until he has, personally or through his department head, established contact with the student's superiors and informed them not only of the latter's progress but of his potential attainments.

Finally, the end of the course should not mark the end of the contact between student and teacher, for the ability to continue to stimulate the student's interest in expanding his knowledge and developing his mental prowess is perhaps the most profound measure of the teacher's effectiveness. Naturally this is very much easier for the training officer in a firm than it is for the teacher at a technical college.

RECEPTION AND ASSIMILATION

Challenge and Mission

If teachers will adopt this policy as their creed, management education will begin to have much more direct relevance to industry and commerce, because it will be performing a useful and practical job, the value of which can readily be recognised by the businessman. This understanding and mutual respect may gradually lead to the closer co-operation between industry and commerce on the one hand and the educational bodies on the other which is a pre-requisite if certificates, diplomas and eventually degrees in management studies are to have any real significance.

Meanwhile, until that essential partnership is established, and even afterwards, the ultimate test of an individual's management ability will continue to be performance on the job. We can therefore conclude that the management student must be judged both by his factual knowledge and even more so by his ability to interpret and apply it to the real life situation. Above all, the student should be able to deal with his fellows; so the degree of his understanding of psychological problems must play an important part in assessing his attainments. Finally, because no individual can be isolated from the group with which he is studying or working, he must be judged in relation to his colleagues and preferably by them.

Just as the market place makes its values felt in business in terms of salaries and working conditions, so the academic yardstick must inevitably give way to the more realistic measure of practical value if management education is to survive and perform the essential function which Britain so desperately needs.

In 1897 a course was offered at the London School of Economics which was directed towards the provision of 'a system of higher education which stands in the same relation to the life and calling of the manufacturer, the merchants and other men of business as the medical schools of the Universities to that of the doctor—a system, that is, which provides a scientific training in the structure and organisation of modern industry and commerce, and the general causes and criteria of prosperity'.[1]

More than half a century later, Sir Hugh Beaver was able to say 'We require then at a modest computation something between 50,000 and 75,000 new entrants each year to management positions of whom at least 1,000 are to be fit and available for the highest level of management. At present we can hardly claim that there is a recognised education or training outside their own companies for more than a few hundreds a year of all classes and a few dozens of the top management class. That cannot be allowed to continue'.[2]

Here is the challenge for management teachers and training officers; and here too is their mission.

---

[1] p. 14, Prof. R. S. Edwards, *Administrative Studies in the Universities, The Three Banks Review*, September 1952.
[2] p. 17, Sir Hugh Beaver, *Training for Management, The Summing Up*, Financial Times, October 1952.

APPENDIX A

SOURCES OF VISUAL AIDS

LISTED below are some of the many organisations which supply visual aids (films, filmstrips, wall charts or photographs) and/or information about them. In most cases films are lent free of charge. They range from scientific or technical subjects to those which deal with industrial training and human relations problems.

British Association for Commercial and Industrial Education
    Management House, 8 Hill Street, London W1
Central Film Library
    Government Building, Bromyard Avenue, Acton W3
Central Film Library of Wales
    42 Park Place, Cardiff
Central Office of Information (London and SE Region)
    64 Victoria Street, London SW1
Current Affairs Limited
    174 Brompton Road, London SW3
FOA (formerly MSA)
    5 Grosvenor Square, London W1
Educational Foundation for Visual Aids
    33 Queen Anne Street, London W1
Gaumont British Instructional
    Aintree Road, Perivale, Greenford, Middlesex
National Film Board of Canada
    Colquhoun House, Broadwick Street, London W1
Scottish Central Film Library
    16-17 Woodside Terrace, Charing Cross, Glasgow C3
The Scientific Film Association
    164 Shaftesbury Avenue, London WC2
United States Information Service
    American Embassy, Grosvenor Square, London W1

APPENDIX B

IN 1951 the Anglo-American Productivity Team studying management education visited the Harvard Graduate School of Business Administration. In a letter to the Dean, the leader of the Team, Lt Col L. F. Urwick, wrote:

'I had never realised before that the "case method" was so much more than a methodology of teaching. I had always imagined that much of your astounding success in winning and holding the enthusiasm of practical business men was due to a combination of favourable factors—American enthusiasm for education as such, the general prestige of business as a career, so much more pronounced than in the older countries, your association with Harvard, for even in the U.S. social and academic status are not without influence, your care in recruiting a faculty with knowledge of practical affairs and in keeping that knowledge bright.

'But it seems to me now, after this week's experience, that while all these things have, no doubt, contributed to your pre-eminence, you are attempting something far more fundamental.

'Ortega y Gasset in his *Mission of the University* attributes much of the confusion of our time to a failure by universities all over the world to fulfil their historic role. Caught in the net of modern specialisation they have lost sight of the fact that their primary purpose is to transmit culture, to equip succeeding generations with a system of ideas which will enable them to live "at the height of their times".

'Faced by the ramifications and complexity of modern knowledge they have allowed their real objective to become occluded by the enthusiasm of academic minds for their particular byeways. The vastness of the intellectual heritage

APPENDIX B

is, to be sure, a difficulty. But it is a difficulty which they have not faced. They have run away from it into the ivory towers of the innumerable specialisations which attract the scholarly enthusiasm of their professors. Instead of squaring up to the essential pedagogic problem of how, in a few short years, to introduce adolescent minds to the continents of learning, they have chosen to ignore the fact that they are *teaching* institutions. They have attempted to deal with the difficulty by ignoring it.

'The Business School is the first place I have ever encountered which is not doing this. You may say that you are merely preparing men to be good business leaders. But by trying to do this in a totally new way, by ignoring conventional categories of learning and the established academic traditions, you are, it seems to me, doing much more. By putting your teaching mission *first,* you are breaking through the barriers which have increasingly over the last century tended to divide learning from life.... In other words, by being strictly and simply vocational, you are in fact showing institutions of learning how to escape from that exile from the practical, from the main stream of contemporary life, to which they have condemned themselves.

'That is one part of it. Further this entirely original attack on the problem of how to develop leaders seems to me to be, in part at least, an answer to the criticism of our old friend Elton Mayo that "in the social sciences the equivalent of the clinic or even the laboratory is still to seek". True, when you "hospitalise" your young men, you present them only with synthetic cases, not with living patients. But this is an enormous step forward, and the care and consistency with which the new method is applied may, I feel, lead to some apparently miraculous developments in a not very distant future.

'It would be impertinent to pretend that in a few short days of intermittent inspection we have penetrated your

APPENDIX B

secret.... But I think the whole team will return to England thoroughly convinced of three things:

'1. That the "case method" as practised at the Business School is something far more fundamental and revolutionary than anyone on our side of the water has yet imagined. It is not merely supplementing normal academic methods with a little colouring matter of illustrative cases. It is a completely different approach to the whole problem of training people for positions of administrative responsibility. Its principal feature is not that it uses cases, but that it has abandoned traditional methods of teaching altogether for a process which turns the student into his own instructor.

'2. That all the evidence we have been able to collect in so short a period shows that it works. It attracts the enthusiastic support of business men. It is building a great highway bridge across the chasm which academic specialisation has driven between learning and life.

'3. It behoves all who are interested in education in Great Britain to examine what you are doing far more carefully than we have been able to do in this brief time. It is of vital importance to the future of western civilisation that every industrialised country should learn to understand it.'

INDEX

"Accounting", 115
Allen, Walter, 152
Annual assessment form, 24, 27
Application form, 148, 149
Audit: environmental, 4-6
   personal, 6-8

Balchin, Nigel, 152
Beaver, Sir Hugh, 270
Biographical forms, 23-28, 49
Birmingham Technical College, 242
Blackboard: magnetic, 67, 68, 217
   use of, 23, 33, 47, 50, 61, 63-66, 71, 192, 193, 208
Bowie, J. A., 3, 114, 246

Cambridge, 8
Case Study:
   categories of;
      Brief Illustrations, 117, 118, 153
      Descriptive, 152, 153
      Dramatic Statement, 120, 121, 154
      Human Relations, 125-135, 174, 177, 181
      Limited Objective, 121-124, 132, 133, 154, 216
      Success Story, 118-120, 154
      Technical, 135-140
   leader, 158, 188, 190, 194-203, 216, 217, 225
      task of the, 204-213
   method, 10, 22, 29, 76, 78, 81, 83, 100, 101, 106, 114-116, 124, 133, 183, 194-196, 209, 210, 215-217, 242, 263

Case Study method (*cont.*),
   advantages of, 114, 115, 155-157, 159, 160, 217
   definition of, 117, 118, 121
   disadvantages of, 115, 157, 158
   uses of, 153, 154, 217
   sessions;
      analysis of, 195-198, 200-203
      conduct of, 183-195, 199, 200
      preparations for, 188-194
   Writers' Circle, 100, 125, 141, 183, 217
   writing of a, 161-182
      rules for, 181, 182
Chance of a Life Time, The, 72
Changing Culture of a Factory, 152
Class list, advance, 9, 16, 17, 23, 199
   analysis of, 10, 17-23
Classroom, 10, 46-48, 61, 66, 78
Clewes, Winston, 152
Commerce, 9, 263, 266, 269
Committees, 106, 109-111
"Communications", 37, 65, 73
"Control", 39, 49, 115
Course Library, 34
Current Affairs, Bureau of, 77

Dead Man Over All, 152
"Development", 39, 49
Diagrams, 61, 68-70, 73
Discussion groups, 76-79, 85, 86, 92-94, 115, 124, 159, 210, 216
   directed, 74, 78-84, 86-88, 92, 93, 97, 190, 195
   non-directed, 79, 81, 88-94

xxiii

Index

"Distribution", 39, 49

Economics, 6, 11
Education for Business Manageagement, 3
Education, Ministry of, 5, 39, 247
Examinations, 35-37, 39, 42, 44, 246-249, 266
  alternative methods of, 263-267
  validity of, 250-263
Executive development schemes, 8
Executive Suite, 152

Films, 71-73
Filmstrips, 71, 72, 100, 101, 123
Follett, Mary Parker, 157

General Electric Co., 72
Glacier Metal Co., 152
Grading sheet, 235, 238
  outside assignment, 24
Gramophone, use of, 72, 73
Group discussion, (see 'Discussion groups')

Harvard Graduate School of Business Administration, 154, 158, 209
Hawley, Cameron, 152
Homework, 5, 33-37, 227
"Human Factor in Industry", 37
Human Problems at Work, 100

Incentive schemes, 119
Industrial: Relations, 37
  Welfare Society, 100, 123
Industry, 3, 4, 7-11, 15, 30, 95, 101, 115, 154, 243, 257, 263, 269
  Human Factor in, 37
  training officers in, 15, 23, 29,

Industry, training officers in (*cont.*), 30 (see also 'Training officer')
Inner Man Steps Out, The, 72
Interviewing, 85, 97-99, 124, 141-147, 149-151

Jaques, Elliott, 152
"Job Relations", 30
Joint Consultation over Thirty Years: a Case Study, 152

King, S.D.M., 152

Labour, Ministry of, 87
Lecture method, 7, 32, 33, 42, 54-73, 76, 78, 117, 153, 154, 216
Lesson plan, 4
Line production, 119
London Docks: a Framework for Study, 152
London School of Economics, 269
Lynton, R. P., 152

Maier, N. R. F., 100
Management: British Institute of, 39, 247
  Diploma in, 250, 253
  Intermediate Certificate of, 5, 253
  Nature of, 39, 43, 49, 161
  Practice, 214, 215, 242
  Studies, joint Ministry of Education-British Institute of Management, course on, 39, 247, 266, 267
  and Supervision, 37
  teacher: environmental audit of the, 4, 5, 9, 10
  motives of the, 6-8

Index

Management teacher (*cont.*)
  personal audit of the, 5-8, 48
  problems of the, 4, 8, 16, 17, 22, 23, 45, 46, 203, 267
  qualities of the, 6, 7, 10 12-14, 30, 46, 53, 78, 86, 87, 203
  task of the, 3, 4, 7, 11, 12, 15, 31, 33, 48, 49, 79, 116, 153, 268-270 (see also 'Case study leader', 'Training officer' and 'Technical college teacher')
Manchester University, Faculty of Technology of, 3
Massachusetts Institute of Technology, 155
Mayo, Professor Elton, 118
Men at Work, 152
Mock trials, 95
"Modern Developments", 49
Motion study, 71 (see also 'Time and motion study')

"Nature of Management", 39, 43, 49, 161
Note-taking, 7, 24, 48, 51, 52

Organisation, 39, 49, 115
  chart, 171, 172

Personnel, 40, 49
  Administration, 32
  department, 16, 56, 58, 60, 61, 110
  records, 102-105
Principles of Human Relations, 100
"Production", 39, 49
Progress reports, 16, 24, 26
Project work, 36, 76, 107, 152

Psychology, 11, 30, 115
  tests, 60
"Purchasing", 39, 49, 115

Reading lists, 7, 33, 34, 36, 45, 51, 52, 152, 153, 216
Record keeping, 23-31
Refresher training courses, 8
Renold, Sir Charles, 152
Report writing, 217, 225, 227-240
Rimmer, Norman C., 154
Role playing, 78, 81, 95-111, 124, 133, 240-242

Schell, Professor Erwin, 155
Scott, Jerome F., 152
Seating plan, 199, 200, 201
Selection methods, 56-60, 79, 80
Sociology, 11
"Statistics", 115
Students: biography of, 16, 23-29, 49
  types of, 11, 12, 15-23, 28-31, 33-37
Sundry creditors, 152
Supervisory Management Notebook, 38
Syllabus, 15-17, 39, 40, 44, 49, 154
  case studies in the, 214, 215, 242
  interpreting the, 37-39, 42-44
  planning the, 31-33, 37, 42

Tape recorder, 61, 72, 84-86
Tawney, Professor, 92
Taylor, F. W., 157
Technical College, 8, 29, 54, 161, 214, 247
  teacher, 5, 6, 13, 15-17, 23, 29, 49-52, 84, 214, 250, 268
Tennessee Valley project, 72

xxv

Index

Three Studies in Management, 152
Time and motion study, 50, 71, 72, 119
Training: officer, 5-7, 10, 15, 16, 23, 29-31, 45, 46, 50, 55, 56, 58-62, 80, 91, 106, 110, 161
task of the, 88, 89, 91, 92, 115, 116, 153, 268-270
records, 16
Within Industry, 15, 16, 30, 81, 86, 87, 129

Universities, 6-9, 114, 115
Visual Aids, 4, 6, 9, 10, 49, 57-59, 66, 68, 71-73, 194, 208
use of, 33, 50, 62, 63
Western Electric Co., 118
Workers' Educational Association lectures, 7
"Work Study", 50, 71, 115